The Truth in Both Extremes

The Truth in Both Extremes

Paradox in Biblical Revelation

ROBERT S. RAYBURN

WIPF & STOCK · Eugene, Oregon

THE TRUTH IN BOTH EXTREMES
Paradox in Biblical Revelation

Wipf & Stock
An Imprint of Wipf and Stock Publishers
199 W. 8th Ave., Suite 3
Eugene, OR 97401

www.wipfandstock.com

PAPERBACK ISBN: 978-1-6667-3207-8
HARDCOVER ISBN: 978-1-6667-2535-3
EBOOK ISBN: 978-1-6667-2536-0

To Florence

. . . tu supergressa es universas

Contents

Preface

IF BOOK TITLES WERE nowadays what they were in the seventeenth and eighteenth centuries, this book might have been entitled *The Simplicity of Holy Scripture, or Learning to Dwell with Equal Pleasure on Two Seemingly Opposite Truths*. That language, as indeed that of the actual title of this book, is taken from the never-enough-praised Charles Simeon, whose brilliant observations about biblical revelation should have produced book-length demonstrations and applications long before this. It was Simeon who put me on to the facts, obvious as they are, that the Bible is chock-full of seeming inconsistencies, if not contradictions, and is unembarrassed by the fact, and that coming to terms with this feature of biblical revelation is fundamental to a faithful and useful interpretation and application of the teaching of the Word of God.

I have been a preacher of the Bible for nearly half a century and, like many preachers, have thought a great deal about both the substance and the craft of the sermon. The argument that follows is one fruit of that thinking and so, I very much hope, the subject of this book will be of immediate interest and relevance to preachers. They, of all men, must appreciate *how* the Bible teaches us what is true if they are effectively to teach that truth to others. So, while this is not a book about preaching, it is a book for preachers and is intended to help them come to grips with the challenge every thoughtful preacher must face repeatedly as he seeks to impress upon the hearts and minds of his congregation the truth as it is found in the Word of God. What is to be done when one impressive emphasis in the biblical text seems difficult to harmonize with other teaching, equally emphatic, found elsewhere in the Bible? How are they to relate the one truth to the other? In sermon after sermon should they even make the attempt?

But this book is not for preachers only. I have sought to demonstrate that the pedagogy of Holy Scripture, however unique, however unfamiliar, is, after all, only what thoughtful readers of the Bible will have encountered times without number. They may have had no vocabulary with which to describe the phenomenon, but they will have no difficulty recognizing it. They may never have been taught *to expect* this in their reading of the Bible; they may never have been told what to do when confronting such "contradictions," but they are certainly familiar with the problem. The complex of competing and seemingly inconsistent emphases one finds in the Bible has been the source of unending disagreement, confusion, and doubt. Christians read the Bible seeking both understanding and the voice of God in their souls. And it is those serious readers who have long struggled to know what to think when they find statements in Holy Scripture difficult to reconcile with teaching found elsewhere in the same Bible.

As often as I have preached or lectured on the implications of this distinctive biblical pedagogy, I have found not just their pastors but the people themselves not only nodding their heads in recognition of the age-old problem but heaving a sigh of relief both to learn that they are not alone in the struggle to make sense of biblical paradoxes and to learn what they are supposed to do when confronted with them. They are comforted to learn that they are free to believe everything and to lose nothing and that they are not obliged somehow to resolve the tension created by the Bible's seemingly discordant assertions. Indeed, it seems immediately right to them that, as Charles Simeon put it, they are to learn to dwell with equal pleasure on statements that appear to be opposed to one another. Both God and reality are far greater than our capacity to comprehend them. The best way for us to grasp the truth that sets us free, the Bible's way to ensure that we are confronted with the truth in all its liberating power, is for God to give it to us in its discrete pieces—the pieces we can comprehend, if the whole lies beyond us, and the pieces, so explicit and so categorical, we cannot so easily ignore.

If the argument that follows serves, for both preachers and people, to add to the sizzle, the profundity, both the mystery and the clarity, and the emotive power of biblical revelation, it will have served its purpose and I will be most grateful.

Acknowledgments

THIS IS A BOOK that has been years in the making and, whether they realized it at the time, the congregation of Faith Presbyterian Church, Tacoma, Washington, has witnessed its conception in the sermons to which they gave their concentrated attention through those many years. No preacher has been inspired by or profited from his congregation more than I have mine. This book is a testament to their morning and evening faithfulness to the pulpit it was my honor and privilege to fill for more than forty years. Upon my retirement in May 2019, the officers of the congregation gifted me with a year-long sabbatical during which the book was written. I owe them a great debt. Many others have made more specific contributions. Professors C. John (Jack) Collins, Robert Letham, and Richard B. Gaffin, Jr. were both generous with their time and interest and immensely helpful. No one should conclude from my expression of gratitude to these superb scholars that they would accept all my conclusions or would express in the same way even those arguments with which they may be in substantial agreement. But I know how much better the book is for their advice and counsel. My longtime friend and much-admired colleague in the ministry of the Word, the Rev. Ian Hamilton, encouraged me in this work from beginning to end and added his own thoughtful critique. I have long felt, and for the best of reasons, that if Ian approved of an argument, I must be on the right track! Dr. Robert Case was very helpful once the manuscript was largely complete and required a publisher. My son, Dr. Robert G. Rayburn II, and my son-in-law, Dr. Joshua Moon, were in on the project from its beginning, years before pen was put to paper, and served as my sounding boards as the argument took shape. I have much to be thankful for in the iron the Lord supplied me by which to sharpen the more modest measure of the same element I may have possessed myself. My wife, Florence, was my primary proofreader and crept through the entire manuscript three times. I am grateful for her contribution, but for much more important reasons the book is dedicated to her!

1

Paradox in Holy Scripture

The truth is not in the middle, and not in one extreme, but in both extremes.

—CHARLES SIMEON

THIS IS A BOOK about how to read the Bible. I want especially to help you appreciate a remarkable feature of Holy Scripture, a mark of its genius and an important reason for its enthralling power. And by doing so I hope to help you account for one of the most significant challenges the Word of God poses to those who seek to understand its teaching. People disagree, sometimes seriously, about what the Bible actually teaches. We know that. Even people who revere Holy Scripture, who sincerely desire to understand it correctly, and who both confess and appreciate the divine authority of the Bible do not understand its teaching in the same way. To be sure, much of what we are taught in the Bible all Christians understand in much the same way. This is especially true of its historical narrative, but it is also true of the majority of its imperatives, from "Believe in the Lord Jesus Christ" to "Love one another." But the Bible's exposition of that narrative—its theology, if you will—and its explanation of those imperatives—its ethics—are something else altogether. In regard to that, as we know all too well and as every thoughtful Christian must regret, there has always been and remains today substantial disagreement. Indeed, there exist entire parties or traditions in Christendom that are isolated from one another in some large part due to those disagreements. I am going to

1

argue that one reason, if not the principal reason, for such disagreement is to be found in the Bible's characteristic way of communicating its truth.

When I was a young pastor I learned from several wise and experienced ministers the importance of reading the entire Bible right through again and again. Through the years I have noticed how often the men whose understanding of the Bible and skill in teaching and preaching it I came most to admire, both past and present, are men who made a habit of the comprehensive and systematic reading of the entire Bible. Representative of the English and Scottish Puritans, important mentors of my Christian life, I will mention William Gouge, who read fifteen chapters of the Bible every day. T. C. Hammond, the twentieth-century Anglican who conducted a wonderfully fruitful ministry as a teacher, preacher, and writer, read the Bible through every three months. A. W. Pink, fiercely independent in his ecclesiology, in the twenty-four years following his conversion read through the Bible more than fifty times. But many more, such as the late influential London preachers Martyn Lloyd-Jones and John Stott, made a habit of reading the Bible through at least once a year. They thought that familiarity with the whole of Holy Scripture was essential to a right understanding of any part of the Bible; that to understand the Bible aright and to have it exercise its proper influence upon one's heart and life one needed to absorb it—all of it—and hold its teaching, as it were, in permanent solution in the mind. Charles Spurgeon, the great London preacher of Victorian England, famously said of John Bunyan that he had absorbed the Scripture in just this way: "Why, this man is a living Bible! Prick him anywhere; and you will find that his blood is Bibline, the very essence of the Bible flows from him."[1] These men wanted *everything the Bible taught* to be weighing on their minds and hearts all the time.

Convinced by their example, for the past thirty-eight years I have made it my practice to read the Bible through each year and, I believe, that practice has made a real difference in the way I understand the Word of God. What is more, I have preached the Bible for more than forty years and a great deal of my preaching—different sermons morning and evening every Lord's Day—has been the consecutive exposition of books of the Bible paragraph by paragraph. In this way I have preached through almost all of the Bible and much of it twice. This intimate engagement with Holy Scripture over many years and, especially, this constant exposure to

1. Spurgeon, *Autobiography*, 2:159.

the entire Bible have wonderfully served to increase my love for the Word of God, taught me to appreciate its literary genius, convinced me that it contains the same message from beginning to end, have piqued my fascination with the uniqueness of the extraordinary gift God has given us in his Word, and have only further strengthened my conviction that the Bible, this magnificent library of canonical literature, is nothing less than the oracles of God. But they have also confirmed for me an observation that has been made by others regarding *how* the Bible teaches us the truth about God, about ourselves, and the way of faith and salvation.

I have found this insight into the Bible's pedagogy, its way of teaching, expressed occasionally in the sermons or books of Christian preachers and theologians. But, in my experience, more often than not such references to this feature of the biblical form of communication have the nature of *obiter dicta*, passing comments or observations. I have come to believe this characteristic of the Bible's pedagogy deserves a much more careful and thorough demonstration and the implications of it need to be identified in a more explicit and comprehensive way. Its ramifications are too significant for it not to be a major principle of the interpretation of Holy Scripture self-consciously held and intentionally applied. But I have never found it worked out in a thoroughgoing fashion in any work of biblical hermeneutics or homiletics, that is, in books about how to interpret the Bible or books about how to preach it. And in my reading I have yet to find the evidence that most preachers and most biblical interpreters and theologians as a rule regard this insight into the biblical pedagogy as fundamental to their way of understanding the Word of God.

The Thesis: Truth in Its Polarities

I am speaking of the Bible's characteristic way of presenting truth *in its polarities*. By polarity I mean the characteristic of a system that exhibits opposing or contrasting principles or tendencies. The Bible not only constantly makes assertions that on their face seem virtually the contradiction of one another, but then seems studiously to avoid any effort to reconcile or harmonize them. It never, or almost never, makes any attempt to resolve the tension created by seemingly antithetical assertions, assertions sometimes found in the writing of the same biblical author, sometimes in the same book, sometimes even on the same page.

Examples abound of every kind. We have, famously, in consecutive verses in Proverbs:

> Answer not a fool according to his folly, lest you be like him yourself.
>
> Answer a fool according to his folly, lest he be wise in his own eyes. (26:4–5).

In 1 Samuel we read, over the course of a single chapter, these statements from the mouth of the Lord himself or from the mouth of Samuel on the Lord's behalf:

> I regret that I have made Saul king, for he has turned back from following me and has not performed my commandments. (1 Sam 15:10–11)
>
> The Lord has torn the kingdom of Israel from you this day and has given it to a neighbor of yours, who is better than you. And also the Glory of Israel will not lie or have regret, for he is not a man, that he should have regret. (vv. 28–29)
>
> And the Lord regretted that he had made Saul king over Israel. (v. 35)

But in speaking of the biblical penchant for polarities I do not mean to refer only to discordant or seemingly contradictory declarations made in the same immediate context. Throughout the Bible, in one place then in another, we are taught to believe something that seems, at least to us, impossible or certainly very difficult to harmonize or reconcile with something we are taught elsewhere. In some places, for example, God is said to be or shown to be in absolute control of events and outcomes in this world, down to the very thoughts of our heart and the hairs of our head. It is the teaching of Holy Scripture that God does what pleases him in heaven and on earth and that no one can shorten his hand. Everything happens in this world according to the counsel of his omnipotent will. Statements to this effect and illustrations of his sovereign rule are found everywhere in the Bible.

However, we also find in Holy Scripture that at many other times and in other circumstances the Almighty appears to stand helpless to effect his will before the intransigent rebellion of mankind or of his people. He is said to be frustrated, to grieve, even to be brokenhearted over man's unbelief and disobedience (Gen 6:6; Isa 1:14; Jer 23:7; Ezek 6:8–9).

Moreover, the way both these descriptions of God are presented in the Bible—simply, frequently, artlessly, and emphatically—renders it impossible for an honest reader to treat one or the other assertion, one or the other description, as simply an artifice or affectation, a way of speaking we are obviously intended to take less seriously, as if the biblical author were winking at us as he wrote. If this were the only case in which we encounter such a "contradiction," it would be a problem. But the fact is we encounter them at every turn.

The Wisdom of Charles Simeon

My first encounter with an explicit recognition that this penchant for polarity is a phenomenon of biblical revelation, and so of the importance of reckoning with its consequences, was in reading Charles Simeon, the great Cambridge preacher of the late eighteenth and early nineteenth centuries. It is no accident that it was a great preacher who took careful notice of the Bible's characteristic pedagogy. It is thoughtful preachers, after all, working over paragraphs of Holy Scripture, one after another, week after week and year after year, who are most likely to notice the polarities, to notice the lack of qualification or harmonization, and so to feel the constant tension polarities create. What is more, as pastors of the Lord's people, they must face the difficult existential questions provoked by such polarities when brought to them by their confused or brokenhearted parishioners. Nothing has so sharpened my own sense of the tension created by the Bible's assertion of seemingly contrary facts or of the importance of acknowledging it than conversations with earnest Christians struggling to know what to think. It is thoughtful preachers of the Word of God who, expounding text after text to their congregations, must Lord's Day after Lord's Day answer the question of whether the powerful emphasis of this text should be allowed to stand undiminished or, instead, be qualified by the introduction of another biblical emphasis from some other text. Simeon's immense influence was no doubt a result of his sterling character, but it was also due to the power of his preaching. That power, I have come to believe, derived in some large part from the approach he took to the biblical text, an approach firmly grounded in his recognition that it is polarities that we encounter in Holy Scripture, not a nicely systematized unity of truth. I was subsequently to learn that Simeon's observation on the nature of biblical revelation had been influential in the thinking of others whose teaching or preaching I had come to admire.[2]

Simeon was a man who had crept through the Bible, was extraordinarily familiar with it, and so a man whose observations carry impressive authority. He took so seriously the Bible's characteristic method of revealing the truth in its polarities that he made that method of revelation vital to his theory and practice of preaching the Word of God. What is more, Simeon was one of the first to realize the importance of teaching other men how to preach more effectively. In the preface to the first volume of his celebrated *Horae Homileticae*, his twenty-one volumes of notes on the biblical text for the use of preachers, Simeon described an approach to preaching the Bible that self-consciously acknowledged its characteristic polarities. Speaking of himself in the third person, Simeon laid out a plan for the preacher based on the fact that the Bible typically asserts without qualification certain facts that are, on their face, difficult to harmonize with other facts asserted elsewhere.

> He has no desire to be wise above what is written, nor any conceit that he can teach the Apostles to speak with more propriety and correctness than they have spoken. It may be asked perhaps, how do you reconcile these doctrines, which you believe to be of equal authority and equal importance? But what right has any man to impose this task on the preachers of God's word? God has not required it of them; nor is the truth or falsehood of any doctrine to be determined absolutely by this criterion.[3]

> While too many set these passages at variance, and espouse the one in opposition to the other, he dwells with equal pleasure on them both; and thinks it, on the whole, better to state these apparently opposite truths in the plain and unsophisticated manner of the Scriptures, than to enter into scholastic subtleties, that have been invented for the upholding of human systems. He is aware, that they who are warm advocates for this or that system of religion, will be ready to condemn him as inconsistent: but,

---

2. "Charles Simeon of Cambridge remains something of a guru to me, since he warned, 'Beware of the systematizers of religion!' Instead he affirmed his submission to everything Scripture teaches, including the antinomies which cannot be neatly systematized or reconciled to one another. . . . As Simeon constantly said, the truth lies neither at one extreme, nor at the opposite extreme, nor in a confused admixture of both extremes', but at both extremes, even if we cannot reconcile them." John Stott, cited in Dudley-Smith, *John Stott*, 2:428.

3. Simeon, *Horae Homileticae*, 1:loc. 259–66 of 36288.

if he speak in exact conformity with the Scriptures, he shall rest
the vindication of his conduct simply on the authority and example of the Inspired Writers.[4]

On other occasions Simeon would again emphasize these same convictions regarding the interpretation and preaching of the Bible.

I love the simplicity of the Scriptures; and I wish to receive and
inculcate every truth precisely in the way, and to the extent, that
it is set forth in the inspired volume. Were this the habit of all
divines, there would soon be an end of most of the controversies
that have agitated and divided the Church of Christ.[5]

My endeavor is to bring out of Scripture what is there, and not
to thrust in what I think might be there. I have a great jealousy
on this head; never to speak more or less than I believe to be the
mind of the Spirit in the passage I am expounding.[6]

In a letter to a friend in 1825 Simeon wrote, ". . . to you I can say in
words what these thirty years I have proclaimed in deeds, that the truth is
not in the middle, and not in one extreme, but in both extremes."[7] What
Simeon was referring to is precisely this fact: that the Bible concentrates
almost exclusively on the polarities of any continuum of truth, what he
calls the "extremes." In his view it was the preacher's task to proclaim the
message in the text before him, not to weaken, still less to undo that message by qualifying it with a message found in some other text, especially
with another message that is virtually, if only seemingly, the reverse of
what is found in the text being preached.

According to Simeon, *one must embrace both poles of any biblical
continuum of truth in order to have embraced the truth.* And the Bible's
way of forcing those polarities upon us is to teach us without qualification each pole, one here, one there. One typically—not always, but typically—finds only one pole in any particular passage, even in some cases
only one pole in large tracts of biblical material. In this way the reader of
the Bible is schooled in the truth of God with all of its simplicity and all
of its power. That was Charles Simeon's conviction: the Bible ought to be
preached in the way in which the Bible *reads*: one emphasis here, another
there, with each getting its day! According to Simeon the preacher should

---

4. Simeon, *Horae Homileticae*, 1:loc. 259.

5. Cited in Moule, *Charles Simeon*, 77.

6. Simeon in a letter to his publisher, cited in Stott, *Between Two Worlds*, 129.

7. Moule, *Charles Simeon*, 77.

preach one "extreme" at a time in the same way that the Bible *reveals* one "extreme" at a time. Since this is the way God chose to reveal his truth, this is the way the preacher should proclaim and teach it. Otherwise, the truth, or more typically one truth or the other, dies in our hearts either from constant qualification or, just as often, from simply being ignored in favor of the truth at the opposite end of that continuum.

Any reader of the Bible has encountered this distinctive pedagogy repeatedly, whether or not it has occurred to him or her that it is characteristic of the Bible's way of teaching its theology, its ethics, and the experience of the life of faith. In one place an absolute sovereignty of divine grace; in another every person's responsibility for his or her own salvation and the salvation of others. In one place an immutable divine will; in another God changing his mind (2 Sam 24:16; Ezek 16:42; Hos 9:15). In one place God desiring the salvation of everyone; in another choosing to save some and reject others. In one place God promising lavish blessing for those who prove themselves faithful to him; in another faithful saints crying out to God in confusion for want of that blessing. In one place through union with Jesus Christ we have been delivered from the power of sin; in another we remain, even as Christians, its groveling slaves. In one place an exemplar of the life of faith is found bemoaning his many and serious sins and crying out to God for mercy; in another that same godly man confidently proclaims not only that he had kept the ways of the Lord and was blameless before him and kept himself from guilt, but that the Lord had rewarded him according to his righteousness and the cleanness of his hands (2 Sam 22:21–25). In one place we are told that the Lord Christ is coming soon; in another place we are taught to prepare for a long wait. In one place we are warned that the punishment of hell is a lake of fire prepared for the devil and his angels, where the worm does not die and the fire does not go out; in another we read that some in hell will receive a light beating (Luke 12:47–48). In one place we are commanded to tell the truth even when it hurts; in another we find the godly telling lies with God's active encouragement or approval. In one place we are told to bend every effort to preserve the unity of the church; in another to exert equal effort to preserve the fidelity of the church. In one place we are taught to seek first the kingdom of God and his righteousness and leave the provision of food, clothing, and shelter to our faithful Heavenly Father. In other words, we are to exhibit a cheerful unconcern about income, possessions, and worldly security. But in another place we are sternly warned that a person who does not provide for his or her family—which, one would think, absolutely requires attention to income, possessions, and security—is worse than an infidel.

But what we do *not* find in the Bible is any explanation as to how we are to believe both or do both at one and the same time. Indeed, the Bible almost never even acknowledges the tension created by these seemingly discordant assertions or commandments. Who can deny that Christians have found it all too easy to wrap themselves around one pole at the expense of the other, confidently to assert one biblical truth while virtually ignoring the other, to practice one obligation while almost entirely forgetting the other! It is not a simple matter to believe truths that seem opposed to one another or to meet obligations that seem to be the reverse of one another! Who can deny that many of our disagreements and much of our disunity originate here?

Is it not here, in this penchant for revealing the truth in its polarities, that we find an explanation for the fact that the Bible so regularly surprises us, even confuses us, with its statements or form of words? We do not expect to read this or that in Holy Scripture because we are sure that Scripture, given what we have read in its pages, would not say such a thing. We do not expect to hear that God "incited David" to commit a sinful act (2 Sam 24:1; cf. 1 Sam 18:10–11), all the more when we read in the other version of the same episode that it was the devil who incited David (1 Chr 21:1). But this troubles us primarily because we are taught elsewhere in the Bible that God tempts no one to sin (Jas 1:13). We do not expect Paul, in laying the foundation for his exposition of justification by faith, to say that God "will render to each one according to his works" or that "it is not the hearers of the law who are righteous before God, but the doers of the law who will be justified" (Rom 2:6, 13).[8] Still less do

---

8. Many commentators seek to resolve the paradox by taking those remarks concerning the Lord's judgment of our works as expressing not Paul's own view but the view of those advancing a legalistic theory of justification. In other words, Paul's statement that "[God] will render to each one according to his works" (Rom 2:6) is employed only hypothetically, for the purposes of argument, to represent the viewpoint he is about to disprove. The problem with this interpretation is twofold. First, as a matter of fact, Paul asserts God's final judgment of our lives according to our works—that is, the totality of our behavior: thought, word, and deed—frequently in his writing, as we will have occasion later to demonstrate. In other words, Rom 2:6, 13 are typical specimens of the apostle's exhortation to faith and godliness. Paul can hardly be taken to be stating a falsehood in Romans 2 when he enthusiastically commends the same assertion as the truth throughout his letters as fundamental to a Christian understanding of salvation. Ridderbos, *Paul*, 178–81; Gathercole, *Where Is Boasting?*, 126–35. What is more, the Lord says the same thing (Matt 12:37). The second objection is

we expect the great champion of justification by faith alone to speak of anyone being *worthy* of salvation, as the apostle does—worthy of death certainly (Rom 1:32), but worthy of salvation (2 Thess 1:5)? And the Lord Jesus spoke in the same way (Matt 10:13; Luke 20:35; cf. Ezek 14:14, 20). John jars us still further when in Rev 3:4 he speaks of those who will walk with the Lord in white "for they are worthy" and then uses the same word in the next chapter to say that the Lord God Almighty is *worthy* to receive glory, and honor, and power. Would any evangelical nowadays speak in such a way of a sinner saved by grace: that a Christian may be said to be worthy of salvation because of his or her obedience to and service for God? What evangelical with *sola gratia* in his or her bones would say, as David did, "Vindicate me, O Lord, for I have walked in my integrity, and I have trusted in the Lord without wavering" (Ps 26:1; 2 Sam 22:21–25), all the more when in the previous psalm David pled with the Lord not to remember the sins of his youth (Ps 25:7)? Paul said something similar: "I have fought the good fight, I have finished the race, I have kept the faith. Henceforth there is laid up for me the crown of righteousness, which the Lord, the righteous judge, will *award* to me on that Day. . . ."[9] This is the same Paul who with great discouragement admitted his continuing captivity to sin in Rom 7:14–25. That statement in 2 Tim 4:7–8 has been taken by some commentators as proof that Paul could not have written 2 Timothy, since the champion of justification by faith would never have said such a thing![10] "Make yourselves a new heart and a new spirit!" in Ezek 18:31 grates on our ears precisely because the Bible teaches us, even in Ezekiel, and one would have thought unmistakably, that God alone can transform a heart of stone into a heart of flesh. I could multiply such examples at great length. But why do such statements jolt us as they do?

that such apparent inconsistency, such an unlikely juxtaposition, is characteristic of Paul's argument, all the more in Romans. Again, as we shall see, the sense of tension created by Rom 2:6–16 in the context of Paul's impassioned defense of justification by faith and not by works is hardly different from that created by his juxtaposition of our liberation from the power of sin and continued slavery to it in Romans 6 and 7, or the suspension of salvation upon the exercise of an absolute sovereign divine will but then, at the same time, upon the responsible acts of the human will in chapters 9 and 10.

9. The form of words Paul employs is drawn from contemporary edicts of commendation in which honor and recognition are bestowed on someone by a king. The problem felt by many is precisely that they find it difficult to believe that in such a situation Paul would have spoken only of his successes and not of his weakness and drawn attention to *his* faithfulness rather than to God's. Dibelius and Conzelmann, *Pastoral Epistles*, 121.

10. Dibelius and Conzelmann, *Pastoral Epistles*, 121.

Why have commentators and preachers searched for other ways to read such statements except for the fact that we find them at odds with what we take to be the Bible's own teaching elsewhere? The polarities make for tension and often for nearly unbearable tension. We are inclined to remove or relax tension, not to preserve it, still less to highlight or emphasize it!

Dialectics, Antinomies, and Paradoxes

For want of more helpful and illuminating terminology I have come to describe this phenomenon as the Bible's *dialectical pedagogy*. *Dialectic* is a term with a long history in philosophy and theology and has been used in quite different ways. But one of its approved definitions is *the juxtaposition of or setting side by side apparently conflicting ideas.*[11] This, without question, is what we find everywhere in the Bible. In some historical instances of the use of the term *dialectic* the juxtaposition of the conflicting ideas is intended to lead to a resolution, an integration or harmony of truth; either a golden mean between the two truths or a new synthesis of them. Either the truth is thought to be found in the coalescence or fusion of the two ideas or principles, or the conflict between them will cause a new idea or principle to appear. But not so in the Bible. There the poles remain distinct and unmixed and the tension between them remains unrelaxed and unresolved. No solution is sought or proposed. Discordant truths are maintained and preserved in their entirety in the Bible's description of reality.

A term that has been employed to describe these seemingly contradictory assertions is *antinomy*, a word that can mean either an actual or an apparent contradiction between equally valid conclusions or assertions. J. I. Packer, for example, used the term to describe the relationship between the sovereignty of God and the responsibility of man in his early masterpiece *Evangelism and the Sovereignty of God*.[12] He characterized the

11. Thiselton, *Concise Encyclopedia*, 66. As to its use in the history of philosophy, Thiselton writes, "Dialectic denotes a largely exploratory rather than demonstrative use of logical processes, especially those that involve contradiction, opposition or paradox, to take us beyond an initial assumption or opinion."

12. Packer, *Evangelism*, 18–19. "More recently, Gabriel Fackre has noted the tendency in Christian history for believers to shy away from what he calls the 'antinomies all over scripture and Christian teaching, paradigmatically in the doctrine of the incarnation.' The reason, claims Fackre, is that 'the assertion of mutually exclusive

relationship between those two biblical teachings—salvation as the gift of God to the helpless and salvation as the blessing God bestows on those and only those who choose to confess Jesus Christ as Lord and Savior—as an antinomy, an apparent contradiction. God holds man responsible for making a choice that we are taught he is incapable of making apart from God's gracious working in his heart. To believe one or the other is not difficult. We have no difficulty believing that we are free to choose and responsible for the choices we make. Similarly, we have no difficulty believing that salvation is God's gift to the helpless and his achievement from beginning to end. But believing both *at the same time* is another matter. The history of Christian theology has proved that believing both at the same time is more than many Christians have been willing to do!

Or we might describe the Bible's practice of asserting seemingly antithetical ideas with the term *paradox*. Again, the word *paradox* is used in different ways, but it has regularly been used to describe the relationship of statements or principles that are both true but appear to contradict or undermine one another.[13] I am going to argue that the Bible is throughout artlessly paradoxical; that is, it asserts simply, innocently, and unaffectedly, without explanation or evident self-consciousness, two truths, each perfectly understandable by itself but seemingly the contradiction of the other. The late Vernon Grounds, in a fine article published more than half a century ago, reminds us that paradox, as a feature of biblical revelation, is ubiquitous. We encounter it in many more places than the Bible's teaching of the causes of salvation.

> In Christianity, as I see it, paradox is not a concession; it is an indispensable category, a sheer necessity—a logical necessity!—if our faith is to be unswervingly biblical.[14]

propositions—humanity and deity in one person—never satisfies human reason, which is always interested in relaxing the tension in one direction or the other.'" Noll, *Jesus Christ*, 48.

13. "Paradox" is often used by Christian writers in a softer, less precise way, though not untrue to its historic usage, to describe biblical assertions that taken together are less apparent contradictions than simply surprising or complex in their relationship. Thomas Oden uses "paradox" regularly in this weaker sense, as when he considers love as "a confluence of two seemingly paradoxical impulses: the hunger for the desired object and the desire to do good for the beloved" or in the biblical teaching that servanthood and equality belong together. *Living God*, 119; *Word of Life*, 65. The same imprecision is typical of J. P. Michel's *Surprised by Paradox*, 16. For example, that God can be both loving and severe is not a paradox in the stricter sense of the term.

14. Grounds, "Postulate of Paradox," 5.

And with a nod to Charles Simeon he concludes,

> Let us do as Simeon does. Let us emphatically assert "apparently opposite truths," remembering as a sort of criterion that very likely we are being loyal to the Bible as long as we feel upon our minds the tug of logical tension. Let us as evangelicals unhesitatingly postulate paradox.[15]

And Dr. Packer, in speaking of the seeming contradiction between divine foreordination and human freedom and accountability, goes on to say, "The antinomy which we face now is only one of a number that the Bible contains."[16] Indeed, Packer goes further to say that "All doctrines terminate in mystery; for they deal with the works of God."[17]

The Truth Is One and Perfectly Consistent

Now, in regard to Holy Scripture, we must use all such terms—*polarity*, *dialectic*, *antinomy*, and *paradox*—in a guarded and carefully circumscribed way. *There are no contradictions in the teaching of Holy Scripture* since the truth cannot contradict itself. However, that is not at all the same thing as saying that there cannot be *apparent* or *seeming* contradictions. The limitations of the human mind being what they are, it is hardly difficult to believe that we may be unable to grasp the harmony of truth known to the infinite mind of God. Herman Bavinck, one of the finest of Christian theologians, emphasized the importance of this recognition.

> When because of [Christian theology's] weakness or limitations it is faced with the choice of simply letting the truths of faith stand alongside one another or, in the interest of maintaining the systematic form, of failing to do justice to one of them, dogmatics must absolutely opt for the former and resist the desire

---

15. Grounds, "Postulate of Paradox," 20.

16. Packer, *Evangelism*, 24. Louis Berkhof says a similar thing. After noting what he calls the "two seemingly contradictory lines of thought in Scripture respecting the time of the second coming of Christ"—he is referring to those statements that tell us that the Lord is coming soon and those that teach us to expect a long wait —he writes: "At this point it is well to bear in mind that the Bible often speaks paradoxically by asserting two things that are seemingly contradictory, that is, by saying yes and no in answer to the same question. Yet in view of the veracity of God and of Jesus Christ, we shall have to proceed on the assumption that there can be no real contradiction in his revelation nor in the promises he has given us." *Second Coming of Christ*, 19–20.

17. Cited in Ryken, *J. I. Packer*, 238. Cf. Packer's "What Did the Cross Achieve," 8.

for a well-integrated system. On the other hand, one must maintain the position that such a dilemma can occur only as a result
of the limitations of our insight, for, if the knowledge of God has
been revealed by himself in his Word, it cannot contain contradictory elements. . . . God's thoughts cannot be opposed to one
another and thus necessarily form an organic unity.[18]

Modern physics has furnished us with illustration after illustration
of reality's penchant for presenting us with truths very difficult, if not impossible, to reconcile to one another. A well-known example is the nature
of light. Is it a wave or is it a particle? It betrays characteristics of each.
Sir William Bragg, an English physicist, once wrote with tongue in cheek,

On Mondays, Wednesdays, and Fridays we teach the wave theory and on Tuesdays, Thursdays and Saturdays the corpuscular
theory.[19]

In the interpretation of the Bible it is too often, alas, not so much a
matter of the same preacher or the same theologian repeating at different times the different assertions of the Bible, so much as it is each one
concentrating on the set of assertions he prefers and ignoring the other.

But physics has also taught us that our struggles to comprehend are
due to the limitations of the human mind to grasp reality in its immensity and profound complexity. Take, for example, the experience we all
have had when reading and thinking about the vastness of space. It is
remarkable—certainly a testimony to the power of human intellect—that
astronomers can now calculate the distance between objects in the universe, between galaxies and between the stars they contain. We are now
familiar with the fact that the distance between one object in the heavens and another is computed to be so many millions of light-years. But
while an astronomer can calculate the distance and we can understand
the figures used to measure that distance, none of us comprehends the
distances themselves. Our powers are insufficient to grasp spaces so vast,
to see the distances for what they are or to appreciate their true scope.[20]

18. Bavinck, *Reformed Dogmatics*, 1:44.

19. "Electrons and Ether Waves," cited in Gaither, *Physically Speaking*, 209. I thank
Michael Pfefferle for drawing my attention to Bragg's remark.

20. Paul Davies, the English physicist admits that "Of course, physicists, like every-
body else, carry around mental models of atoms, light waves, the expanding universe,
electrons, and so on, but the images are often widely inaccurate or misleading. In fact,
it may be logically impossible for anyone to be able to accurately visualize certain
physical systems, such as atoms, because they contain features that simply do not

So it is with reality as a whole and so it is supremely with the truth about God and his ways. What we know, the truth we have been taught in the Word of God, is wonderful beyond the power of words to describe. To know such things is life itself; it is the truth that sets us free. But we are mere creatures. What we know is very little; what we do not know is vast beyond our capacity to measure. To suppose that we could understand or hold in mind all that is known to the infinite and eternal God is preposterous. And the more we think about who and what God is and what he has done and is doing, what he knows and how he exercises his sovereign will, the more obvious it should become to us that the limitations of our mind impose strict limits upon our grasp of reality.

Paradox but Not Confusion

We must also be careful to say that the Bible's penchant for paradox or its dialectical pedagogy does not mean that its teaching is, for that reason, unclear, as if these apparent contradictions leave us in a muddle, unable to understand for sure what the Bible is saying. Some have argued that it is impossible to believe what we cannot understand or to understand two truths we cannot harmonize. But there are many things that we know to be true that we do not and cannot understand. How our minds move our muscles remains a deep mystery: how a mere thought activates their motion even without the conscious exercise of our will. But we do not doubt that our minds exercise that power. There is a great difference between what we are incapable of understanding and what is in its very nature incomprehensible, as if God could not understand what we cannot.[21] There

---

exist in the world of our experience." *God and the New Physics*, 18, cited in Macleod, *Person of Christ*, 68. "In the case of quantum phenomena, it is logically impossible to state in classical terms what the empirical situation reveals, so one must choose to introduce complementarity as the most reasonable option, which involves a logical contradiction. This does not mean that classical logic has been abandoned; it means that the observer, in keeping with the concept of contradiction, is using the opposition to (1) declare the limits of the classical concept of reason, and (2) declare that there are two radically distinct fields of inquiry which cannot be harmonized or unified in actuality—and therefore must not be speculatively unified either." Loder and Neidhardt, *Knight's Move*, 142. Mathematics likewise furnishes us with various paradoxes, a number of which concern infinite numbers and sets, and which mathematicians agree cannot be resolved in the nature of the case. Bradley and Howell, *Mathematics*, 54. I am grateful to Dr. Chris Cyr, Assistant Professor of Mathematics, Covenant College, for directing my attention to such paradoxes now identified by mathematicians.

21. Crawford, *Mysteries of Christianity*, 3–6. "Although knowledge is attainable in

are a great many things we know but only very partially understand. As a child may find mysterious what an adult easily understands, so we may find incomprehensible what is perfectly plain to God.

The clarity or perspicuity of the Bible's teaching is one of its outstanding features. The Bible was written to be understood! Accordingly, in the Word of God we find the truth taught simply, variously, repeatedly, and relentlessly. It is taught both positively and negatively, both asserted and illustrated, and it is applied to faith and life in first this way and then in that. *The fact that its teaching is so clear is precisely why it is so obvious to us that two of its teachings seem to be the virtual contradiction of one another.* We feel the tension precisely because we understand so well what the Bible is actually saying. The teaching of God's Word is remarkably intelligible, all the more remarkable for a library of literature as old as it is and originally written in languages that no one has spoken for ages. But, clear as each biblical teaching may be, the interrelation between biblical truths is another matter.

Some Helpful Examples

E. A. Dowey, in his study of the theology of John Calvin, makes this observation.

> Calvin . . . was completely convinced of a high degree of clarity and comprehensibility of individual themes of the Bible, but he was also utterly submissive before divine mystery as to create a theology containing many logical inconsistencies rather than a rationally coherent whole. While Calvin as an exegete was a virtuoso at harmonizing surface inconsistencies in Scripture, he never conceived of his theological task as an effort to harmonize the deeper paradoxes of Scripture or to explain what he regarded as its central mysteries. Clarity of individual themes,

---

theology, this is not true of comprehension. There is substantial difference between 'being acquainted with' 'knowing,' and 'comprehending.' True, these words are often used interchangeably. But there are demonstrable differences among them. . . . Disclosed to us in revelation is 'the mystery of our religion': the mystery of God's grace [1 Tim. 3:16]. We see it; it comes out to meet us as a reality in history and in our own life. But we do not fathom it. In that sense Christian theology always has to do with mysteries that it knows and marvels at but does not comprehend and fathom." Bavinck, *Reformed Dogmatics*, 1:619.

incomprehensibility of their interrelations—this is a hallmark of
Calvin's theology.[22]

Dowey continues: Holy Scripture teaches one thing and then it teaches
another. But "the orderly scheme is marred by elements of both Scripture
and experience."

> . . . Calvin is too vigorous an exegete, too honest an observer,
> and too little a lover of logical symmetry to maintain the pattern
> unblemished.[23]

There is mystery, incomprehensibility that attaches to biblical revelation that must be respected fully as much as its clarity. I would prefer the
phrase "*apparent* logical inconsistencies," but Dowey's characterization of
Calvin's theology, in my opinion, is not only accurate as an account of the
reformer's thought but works equally well as a description of the Bible's
teaching taken as a whole. Each doctrine or teaching, what Dowey calls
an "individual theme," is clear and convincing; but how we are to believe
one such teaching and, at the same time, believe with equal firmness the
truth that lies at the other end of that continuum of truth is the difficulty
we encounter repeatedly as we read Holy Scripture.

The Bible leaves us in no doubt that there is but one God. It also
unmistakably asserts that God is Father, Son, and Holy Spirit, persons

22. Dowey, *Knowledge of God*, 39–40. Dowey quotes Hermann Bauke to the effect
that Calvin is a "dialectician rather than a systematic thinker, or at best a dialectical
systematizer." His theology is a *complexio oppositorum*. That is, the elements of his
theology stand side by side and are bound together dialectically. *Knowledge of God*,
38. Typical examples of Calvin's acceptance of paradox, though only rarely using the
term, would be his acknowledgment of the fact that God sometimes sovereignly grants
the inward illumination of the Spirit to the unworthy and undeserving and then, on
account of their unworthiness, he forsakes them [*Institutes of the Christian Religion*,
III, xxiv, 8], or his assertion that "the will of God is the cause of all things that hap-
pen in the world; and yet God is not the author of evil. . . . Whatever things are done
wrongly and unjustly by man, these very things are the right and just works of God.
This may seem paradoxical [esse paradoxum videtur]. . . ." "In a wonderful and ineffable way, what was done contrary to His will was yet not done without His will. . . .
To this opinion [of Augustine] I subscribe: in sinning, they did what God did not will
in order that God through their evil will might do what He willed. If anyone object
that this is beyond comprehension, I confess it. But what wonder if the immense and
incomprehensible majesty of God exceed the limits of our intellect? I am so far from
undertaking the explanation of this sublime, hidden secret . . . that those who seek to
know more than God has revealed are crazy." *Concerning the Eternal Predestination of
God*, X, 7; VIII, 5, 123, 169.

23. Dowey, *Knowledge of God*, 39.

who are distinct from one another and who relate to and converse with one another. What it does not do is explain how we are to believe both the unity and the triple personality of God at one and the same time. Indeed, though the question was and is obvious and inevitable, though the Bible's assertions were bound to provoke not only intellectual conundrums but real crises of conscience, the Bible hardly acknowledges the difficulty we have in simultaneously asserting both truths about God. And the unity and triple personality of God is but one of a host of such continua of truth, each described only in terms of the poles that lie at either end. Comfort is *never* found in some middle ground, regardless of how often Christian thinkers have sought to find it there. As Simeon put it, the truth is not found in the middle and not in one extreme, but in both extremes. David was hardly denying that he knew true things about God and God's ways when he confessed that his knowledge took him only so far: "Such knowledge is too wonderful for me; it is high; I cannot attain it" (Ps 139:6). He was confessing the *limitations* of his understanding; perhaps even that what he *knew* about God only threw into sharper focus how much *he did not know*.

This dialectical pedagogy is so universal in the Bible that once I realized it I came to expect it, and was rarely, if ever, disappointed. Simone Weil, the Marxist Jewess philosopher who became a Christian later in her life, once jotted a note to herself.

> Method of investigation—as soon as one has arrived at any position, try to find in what sense the contrary is true.

As often as I have thought to do that in regard to the teaching of the Bible, I have been able to answer her challenge. This was Weil's way of seeking not a synthesis of or a golden mean between truths but rather an equilibrium of truths.[24] And is that not what we find in the Bible: an equilibrium of truths? I have found her method to be very useful in my reading and preaching of the Bible. I have come to think, for example, that not only is it not surprising; it is almost predictable that we find Paul's weary and melancholy confession of his still great sinfulness, as an experienced Christian and as an apostle of Jesus Christ, cheek to jowl with his teaching that in union with Christ the power of sin has been broken in our hearts and we have been liberated to live a new and holy life. Why have so many found it impossible to believe that Paul in Rom 7:14–25 could be describing his life *as a mature Christian*? It is because he

24 Leslie Fieldler's introduction to Weil, *Waiting for God*, 31.

has just spoken of the liberation of the Christian from the power of sin in Romans 6![25] The Bible's dialectical pedagogy being what it is, such jarring juxtapositions are more the rule than the exception. Such antinomies litter the pages of Holy Scripture.

25. Having already made mention of this text twice, I should acknowledge that I have always been unimpressed with efforts to take Paul speaking in these verses in some other guise than as a long-serving apostle of the Lord Jesus Christ, much nearer the end of his Christian life than its beginning. Not only do I judge conclusive the exegetical demonstration that Paul is speaking of his mournful experience as an earnest Christian, but the undeniable fact is that what he describes in his own case is the universal experience of the godly. But there is this further argument: the fact that it represents a jarring juxtaposition with Paul's argument in Romans 6 actually *favors* this interpretation. Dunn, *Romans 1–8*, 411–12. Cf. Packer, *Keep in Step*, 263–70; Cranfield, *Commentary on Romans*, 1:344–47; Dryden, "Revisiting Romans 7," 129–51.

2

The Origin and Nature of Biblical Paradox

"Tensions," the balancing of opposing truths that prompt one to extend understanding to embrace both, do not trouble me. Paradoxes mirror the messiness of life and are the grist for profitable theological reflection. The Semites have a saying with which I tend to agree: "You do not have truth until you have paradox."

—BRUCE WALTKE

A Liberating Recognition

I AM NOT OVERSTATING the case when I say it was an epoch in my life when I realized that the presentation of truth in its polarities *is* the biblical pedagogy. It liberated me to believe *everything* that I found in Holy Scripture and to believe it *without qualification*. Most Christians have been taught and, with whatever degree of intention or comprehension, have embraced a *system* of biblical doctrine. Each major theological tradition has such a system, whether Roman Catholic, Orthodox, or Protestant. And each major tradition is further subdivided into various theological subsystems of interpretation. Within the Protestant world, for example, we find, among others, Reformed, Lutheran, Arminian, and Pentecostal traditions. They certainly overlap substantially, but each is defined by a particular set of interpretations of the teaching of the Bible. I was myself taught such a system and embrace such a system today. System-making, in my view, is inevitable and, for a variety of reasons, renders important service to the church. Systems organize biblical teaching in a way that makes it easier to learn and remember. They inevitably lay proper stress on certain important teachings of the Word of God, often different doctrines from system to system. Systems of biblical interpretation draw their followers into communities of the like-minded and produce unity. They also shape preaching and make it easier for Christians to grasp what they are being taught from the pulpit. I am not arguing against theological systems or systematic theology. Surely some are better than others, but we will inevitably organize the biblical data in our minds. But we must also respect the limitations of man-made systems of theology and ethics.

The weakness of theological systems is that they are all, *without exception*, beset with problems that originate in the Bible's own form of words. Systems being man-made as they are, some biblical statements are invariably easier to integrate into the system than others. This is some proof, if proof were needed, that the Bible's teaching is not the simple and easily comprehended unity that system builders often seem to suggest it is. God being infinite as he is, his ways being far above us as they are, the Bible confronts us with the mysterious and ineffable at every turn. Without thinking about what we are saying, we guilelessly refer to our system's "problem texts," as if any statement of Holy Scripture should ever be a problem for us. This is all the more the case when the statements made in such problem texts ordinarily are, in and of themselves, quite simple, straightforward, and easy to understand. Every system has its problem texts, texts that do not fit neatly into that particular organization and statement of biblical truth. A system's authorities have typically devoted a great deal of time and intellectual effort to explain their problem texts in a way consistent with their system. But, in my experience, such explanations are the weakest and least impressive part of any theological system. Such texts, after all, are precisely the reason other systems of theology exist! Such explanations or rationalizations typically appeal only to those already convinced or willing to be and strike everyone else as special pleading.

Too often the proposed solutions to a system's problem texts appear to outsiders as little more than an effort to avoid the obvious. In such cases, so it appears to the devotees of a different system, biblical texts are taken to mean what it is difficult to imagine *any* original reader of the

Bible would have thought them to mean. On the other hand, the texts that lie in the foundation of our system we understand in the natural sense of their words. We take such statements to mean what any unprejudiced reader would think they mean. The texts that are difficult to harmonize with our system we take to mean something no one, at first reading, would take them to mean; as Charles Simeon put it, our "whole endeavor is to make the text speak a different language from that which it appeared to do."[1] I will supply examples of this in later chapters. For now my simple point is that the problem posed for anyone seeking to create a fully coherent or consistent system of theology from the biblical data is precisely that the Bible consistently presents us with paradoxes, with truths very difficult to harmonize with one another or reconcile to one another. John Newton put this challenge in a more homely way.

> An attachment to a rigid system is dangerous. Luther once turned out the Epistle of St. James, because it disturbed his system. I shall preach, perhaps very usefully upon two opposite texts, while kept apart; but, if I attempt nicely to reconcile them, it is ten to one if I do not begin to bungle.[2]

Once again, systems have important uses and, in any case, I doubt anyone can escape their use. But the nature of the Bible's pedagogy, dialectical as it is, requires us to acknowledge that the more consistent and well integrated any theological system is, the more furiously it seeks to incorporate its problem texts into a harmony of truth, the less likely it is successfully to have accommodated *everything* that the Bible teaches. Systems in this way often render certain biblical teaching virtually invisible or render ourselves blind to it. But systems don't have to do this.

The advocates of other systems must judge to what extent their system is faithful to biblical polarities and how well it accommodates the discordant assertions found in Holy Scripture. I can speak only to my own case. In my experience as a Calvinist I have found that the best Calvinists, following Calvin himself, Simeon, and many others, cheerfully acknowledge the limits of their capacity to harmonize the biblical polarities and accept a significant measure of tension and of mystery because of the impossibility of reducing the biblical "extremes" to a consistent unity of truth. There is a certain type of Calvinist, however, of whom this is not true. I will have occasion later to draw attention to their efforts to

1. "Preface," *Horae Homileticae*, 1:loc. 381 of 36288.
2. Newton, *Works*, 1:102.

harmonize the system, invariably by ignoring or minimizing one polarity in favor of the other.

The better any theological system, the more it will acknowledge paradox, refuse to force harmony upon truths the Bible leaves in dialectical tension with one another, and the more it will make a point of acknowledging the limits of our understanding. Similarly, the better the system, the more cheerfully it will admit that Holy Scripture does not systematize its teaching and characteristically leaves us holding together truths that would otherwise fly apart, truths we must preserve in tension lest we weaken, if we do not silence, the Bible's voice in one respect or the other. Geerhardus Vos, the founder of modern Reformed biblical theology, put it more bluntly: "You may never force your system upon the Bible."[3] We have all done this, of course; but in doing so we fail to respect the way the Bible teaches us its truth.

The Virtue of Paradox: Reflection

Troublesome as this biblical pedagogy has proved to be, it is not difficult to appreciate the virtues, even the power of this dialectical approach. In the first place, it provokes reflection. Holy Scripture compels reflection at every turn. It is written in a way that seems clearly designed to make us think, consider, wonder, and ponder. The Bible is truth to turn over in the mind, upon which to meditate. We all tend to think superficially about things, even the most precious and important things. But by posing antinomies the Bible forces us to go deeper. Professor Bruce Waltke put it this way.

> "Tensions," the balancing of opposing truths that prompt one to extend understanding to embrace both, do not trouble me. Paradoxes mirror the messiness of life and are the grist for profitable theological reflection The Semites have a saying with which I tend to agree: "You do not have truth until you have paradox."[4]

Indeed, might it not be said that the history of Christian theology, with its hard thinking, with the impressive intellectual labor that was necessary to produce its precise definitions and complex arguments, is to a great extent the direct fruit of the Bible's dialectical pedagogy? It made

3. Cited in Olinger, *Geerhardus Vos*, 278–79.
4. Waltke, "Interaction with Peter Enns," 115.

it necessary to find a way to represent the teaching of Holy Scripture that is faithful to *everything* it says. No easy task, as the last two millennia of Christian theological reflection have proved beyond doubt! This was, for example, the challenge that had to be overcome in the church's early wrestling with the identity of the person of Jesus Christ and her eventual settlement on a formula that respected the polarities of the revelation of his person in Holy Scripture. We will address that challenge later. And so it is with both Christian ethics and Christian experience. We are told that there is no condemnation for the man who is in Christ Jesus, but Jesus also taught *his disciples* that if they do not forgive the sins that others commit against them their own sins will not be forgiven. We are also taught in Holy Scripture that we must continue to confess our sins that they may be forgiven. But take note: Scripture does not itself teach us how to incorporate these various assertions concerning the forgiveness of sin into a simple harmony of truth. In such cases we will not find Holy Scripture parsing the distinctions for us. We must do that for ourselves. God gave us our intellectual powers and has given us a book that requires us to put them to use. Every one of the biblical dialectics that we encounter, page after page, requires contemplation, careful and thoughtful discrimination, and patient and submissive reflection on the whole counsel of God.

The Virtue of Paradox: Humility

By this dialectical way of communicating its truth Holy Scripture also humbles us. The human mind has remarkable powers, but its powers are hardly unlimited. There is a great deal we do not and cannot understand. Our intellect can take us only so far. God himself, his relation to the world that he has made, and his manner of working: these are only some of the things that we are simply incapable of comprehending in anything more than the most rudimentary way. We may understand what the words mean—and that is by no means unimportant—but we may understand little more than that. By forcing us to face paradox again and again, the Bible confronts us with our creaturely limitations and reminds us that reality is far greater than our grasp of it. And if, as Augustine thought, humility was the first, second, and third necessity of believing life, all that humbles us by teaching us our place as mere creatures is of the utmost importance.[5]

The same might be said of the importance of humility for the work of preachers and theologians! A besetting sin of ministers is to give the impression that they know more than they do. Alexander Moody Stuart was one of the greatest in a galaxy of great preachers in mid-nineteenth-century Scotland. He tells us that when he was a seminary student one of the church's elders warned him against what he found to be a chronic defect in the preachers and preaching he had long listened to.

> "You ministers should have more of the infinite in your sermons." Showing me two family portraits by eminent painters, he said, "That is by an artist; this by a genius. In the one you have the whole before you but nothing beyond; in the other the lines run off into infinity. You will never reach the people by teaching us as if you knew it all, and giving us our lesson as if we were children. If you wish to move us, you must make us feel that you see more than you are able to express, and that you think and know that there is an infinite height and depth beyond what you can see. But you go to the brim of the great ocean, you dip your tumbler into it, and set it down before us, and you tell us 'That's the Ocean.'"[6]

The apostle Paul never spoke truer words than these:

> Oh, the depth of the riches and wisdom and knowledge of God! How unsearchable are his judgments and how inscrutable his ways. For who has known the mind of the Lord, or who has been his counselor? (Rom 11:33–34)

If the great apostle to the Gentiles, with all that he had learned of God and salvation, with all the breathtaking things he had himself seen and done, had to confess how little he really comprehended the divine life and work, how much more must we! To indulge the conceit that we can explain God and his ways is to suppose that God must be like ourselves. To confess the depths of our ignorance is to acknowledge and revere his majesty and glory!

<hr>

5. Augustine, letter 118.22, 116–17. In speaking of the way that God appointed for the gaining of the truth, "That first way . . . is humility, the second way is humility, and the third way is humility. . . ."

6. Moody Stuart, *Alexander Moody Stuart*, 273.

The Virtue of Paradox: Submission

This method of teaching—the polarities without the resolution of tension—also serves to force the truth upon our minds even, perhaps especially, when that truth is unwelcome to us. Every honest reader of the Bible knows that he or she is more inclined to believe certain things than others. We prefer certain biblical teachings to others. The Bible's dialectical method serves to hunt out our prejudices and disinclinations and forces us to face them. It will not let us get away with the one-sidedness to which we are invariably and relentlessly tempted. One Anglican bishop put it this way.

> At starting, each of us, according to his disposition, is conscious of liking some books of Scripture better than others. This, however, should lead us to recognize that, in some way, we specially need the teaching that is less attractive to us. We should set ourselves to study what we less like, till that, too, has had its proper effect in moulding our conscience and shaping our character.[7]

Why would anyone like the teaching of some books of the Bible better than others? Precisely because certain biblical teachings are virtually the reverse of others. We prefer one pole to the other. I know this is true of myself. I am a Calvinist and I remember very well the first time I read this, again from Charles Simeon, himself a Calvinist.

> Of this he is sure, that there is not a decided Calvinist or Arminian in the world who equally approves of the whole of Scripture . . . who, if he had been in the company of St. Paul whilst he was writing his epistles, would not have recommended him to alter one or other of his expressions.
>
> But the author would not wish one of them altered; he finds as much satisfaction in one class of passages as in another; and employs the one, he believes, as freely as the other.[8]

When I first read that, I thought immediately of several statements of the apostle Paul that, had I been looking over his shoulder as he wrote, I might have suggested he alter in some way! Of course it is true that we take to one biblical teaching more easily than to another. We find some statements confusing and largely ignore them, not because we don't know what the words mean, but because we find them difficult to reconcile

7. Charles Gore, cited in Whyte, *Biblical Characters*, 231.
8. "Preface," *Horae Homileticae*, 1:loc. 427–33 of 36288.

with what we otherwise expect the Bible to say or, if truth be told, with what we want the Bible to say. Again, I know that about myself. On the other hand, surely it is right, the Bible being the very Word of God, that we should not want any biblical statement to be altered to suit our sense of fitness or consistency. Let God be true and every man a liar (Rom 3:4)! Simeon was on to something regarding the danger that systems of theological interpretation pose; how they can deafen us to what the Bible actually says.

When captivated by the grace of God and reveling in the full and free forgiveness of our sins, or when, as happens to us all sooner or later, we have come to take that forgiveness too much for granted, or when disappointed and discouraged with ourselves and our failures, we can—and I suppose we all do sometimes—find unwelcome the Bible's emphasis on the necessity of obedience and its promise that there will be a reckoning of our lives according to that obedience. But a faithful Christian life obviously requires a commitment both to God's free grace and the Lord Christ's annihilation of our sins, on the one hand, and, on the other, to God's law as the inflexible rule of our daily living, a rule by which our lives will be measured whether we like it or not. The Bible will not allow us to pit the grace of God against our obligation to obey and serve, for it asserts the one as clearly, as relentlessly, even as bluntly as it asserts the other. Indeed, the Bible sometimes asserts both realities in terms so stark as to almost seem calculated to offend. To prevent us from ignoring the whole counsel of God, all the truth, the parts we like and the parts we like less, God has given each truth its day. Every biblical doctrine is taught without qualification and with all the bark on precisely so that we will be forced to reckon with it, no matter how much we might wish not to. Is this not why Calvinists instinctively understand that they are responsible for the choices they make and why Arminians understand that they cannot thank themselves for their salvation? However they seek to address the tension created by both assertions, the Bible's relentless insistence on these "contraries" has fixed both convictions in the Christian heart and mind.

It is a simple fact of the history of theology that we don't all prefer the same truths: Roman Catholics have their set, the Orthodox theirs, Calvinists theirs, Arminians theirs, and Pentecostals theirs. And among the adherents of those theological systems are those who disagree among themselves about which of other sets of biblical statements to prefer. But we need the texts at both ends of every biblical continuum of truth if we are to grasp the truth in its wholeness and in its life-giving power.

John Duncan, the remarkably fruitful missionary to Jews in Hungary and later professor of Hebrew in Edinburgh, a leading light of the nineteenth-century Scottish Free Church, was a man of uncommon theological and spiritual insight. He had a knack both for seeing things very clearly and putting them memorably. More important still, his friend and ministerial colleague, the previously mentioned Alexander Moody Stuart, said of John Duncan, "More than any man I ever knew, he trusted every word, reverenced every word, and loved every word in the book of God."[9] Duncan had this advice for preachers.

> Preach the antinomies of truth, and carry each out as far as it is possible to carry it. But don't attempt to reconcile them. These two lines [/ \] will meet if produced far enough. But if I try to make them meet, I give one or other of them a twist, and so reduce it from being a straight line. If the stones of an arch were to become animated and speak, the stones on the right hand would say, "Right-hand pressure is right pressure;" and the stones of the left hand would say, "left-hand pressure is right pressure;" but by pressing in opposite directions they keep up the keystone of the arch.[10]

In one set of texts Jesus of Nazareth is identifed as the Creator of heaven and earth, the Yahweh who delivered Israel from bondage in Egypt, the destroyer of her enemies, the one before whom men trembled in terror, and the omniscient Judge of the human race who on the Great Day will impose upon every human life an exact reckoning and dispense reward or punishment accordingly. In another set of texts the same Jesus is tired, frustrated, terrified, or heartbroken, weeping in sympathy for another's sorrow, gently consoling the fallen, frustrated at the unbelief of so many, and unable to tell without going over to look whether a fig tree is bearing fruit. Any thoughtful Christian knows only too well which description of Jesus dominates his or her mind. But we who believe the Bible to be the Word of God must also know that we do not know Jesus Christ *as he is* if he is not the Christ of both descriptions! He is our Savior *and* our King. He is our friend *and* our Judge. He both sympathizes with us in our trials *and* demands our obedience. He rewards *and* he punishes.

9. Cited in Brentnall, *Just a Talker*, xxxiv.
10. Moody Stuart, *Life of John Duncan*, 212.

He takes us by the hand *and* requires us to fall at his feet. It is the same Jesus upon whose breast John laid his head in the upper room and before whom the same John fell at his feet as though dead when given his vision of the glorified Christ on the Island of Patmos. But—and this is important to notice—rarely are those discordant descriptions of Jesus found in the same text; in the same author, to be sure, but not usually in the same text.

We have in Christ freedom from condemnation in Rom 8:1; we have the necessity of standing before the judgment seat of Christ to receive what is due us for what we have done, good *or bad*, in 2 Cor 5:10. Throughout the history of the church people have struggled to believe that both descriptions of the Lord's reckoning with our sin could possibly be true, in large part because the Bible never addresses the relation between them. It asserts both but it does not explain how both are, at one and the same time, dimensions of the same picture. Indeed, it never even acknowledges the problem that such seemingly incompatible or contradictory accounts of divine judgment could be expected to create. As a result most thoughtful Christians would admit that to one degree or another they have believed one of the Bible's assertions about the judgment of God more than the other, or at least have taken one more seriously than the other.

I suppose that most Christians believe that on the Great Day they will hear the Lord Christ tell them, "Well done, good and faithful servant" (Matt 25:21)! Certainly a great many preachers have given their congregations that impression. But would the Lord say those words to the man—a man who must represent a sizable number of God's elect—who is saved, but only as through fire, while his work is burned up (1 Cor 3:13–15)? Where does the Bible compare those two scenarios of the Last Judgment? How are we to reconcile them? But can anyone doubt that in the Christian mind the happier picture is widely preferred to the more sobering? Indeed, are there not multitudes of Christians, sincere believers, who have never once heard a sermon on the judgment of their lives according to their behavior or have never seriously reckoned with the possibility that on the Last Day, granted entrance into eternal life as they may be, the Lord will not commend them for the lives they lived and the work they did in his name?

In a similar way we have salvation as the sovereign gift of God in Romans 9 and human accountability for salvation, our own and others, in Romans 10. We are not free to take our pick; we must believe both and must live in the light of both. By themselves those texts speak to us with perfect clarity. We know what the words mean. Together, however, they baffle us in their asymmetry. Each teaching is perfectly straightforward, clear, and unmistakable, however mysterious the relation between them. Alexander Whyte, a hero of mine, in his own inimitable style described this as the preacher's great challenge.

> You have all heard of the difficulty the voyager had in steering between Scylla and Charybdis in the Latin adage. Well, the true preacher's difficulty is just like that. Indeed, it is beyond the wit of man, and it takes all the wit of God, aright to unite the doctrine of our utter inability with the companion doctrine of our strict responsibility; free grace with full reward; the cross of Christ once for all, with the saint's continual crucifixion; the Savior's blood with the sinner's; and atonement with attainment; in short, salvation without works with no salvation without works. Deft steersman as the devil is, he never yet took his ship clear through those Charybdic passages.[11]

But the contraries are there, and so plainly and emphatically that they cannot be ignored without a willful determination to refuse to submit to some of the Bible's teaching.

The Virtue of Paradox: Truth

Finally and ultimately, the dialectical pedagogy of Holy Scripture, accommodated as it is to the limitations of the human intellect, enables us to to know the truth *to the extent that we can know it.* The Bible asserts two truths, no matter that they strike us as contrary to or inconsistent with one another, because only in this way can we know the truth that sets us free. The harmony of those truths lies beyond us. It lies in the infinity of the divine mind. Truth must be broken into pieces small enough for us to grasp; the whole cannot be comprehended by mere creatures. The characteristic pedagogy of Holy Scripture—the presentation of truth in its polarities—presupposes that the effort to impose unity on such discordant assertions would either utterly confuse us or inevitably weaken one assertion or the other; truth would die the death of constant qualification. It is this purpose of paradox—the unqualified assertion of seeming contraries—that I will highlight in the following chapters. It is in this way, for example, that we learn all we can know of the nature of God, or of the

11. Whyte, *Bunyan Characters,* 145.

nature of the incarnation, or of the interplay between divine sovereignty and human freedom and accountability. There is much we do not and cannot know, but if we know the polarities, if we know each and know it well, we know what we can know and must know. We will also know that there is much that remains beyond us; that we do not know and will not know.[12]

Dialectic, Antinomy, and Paradox as a feature of Biblical Literature: Parataxis

There are several features of classical Hebrew rhetorical form that have been suggested as at least partial explanations for the polarities we find in the Bible. Some have argued that the dialectical character of biblical teaching reflects the classical Hebrew language itself, which both reflected and shaped, as all languages do, the patterns of thought and expression of those who spoke that language. As has been long observed, Hebrew is a paratactical language. *Parataxis*, an English word derived from a Greek verb meaning "to place side by side," is the setting of words, phrases, thoughts, or ideas side by side (literally a "side-by-side arrangement"). The celebrated *Oxford English Dictionary* defines *parataxis* as "the placing of propositions or clauses one after another, without indicating by connecting words the relation (of co-ordination or subordination) between them." In classical Hebrew, the Hebrew of the Bible, parataxis is immediately a feature of the individual sentence. As Robert Alter explains,

> Although there are certainly instances of significant syntactic subordination, the characteristic biblical syntax is additive, working with parallel clauses linked by "and"....[13]

That is, Hebrew is a language that favors simple sentences with few subordinate clauses. It is in this respect, to be sure only by degrees, different from Greek and Latin, and for that matter English, which are hypotactical languages, languages in which ideas or statements are placed more often, not side by side, but *under* one another, one subordinate to the other.[14] In

12. "The true wisdom of the theologian is to know that he or she does not know." McGinn, *Thomas Aquinas' Summa Theologiae*, 63.

13. Alter, *Genesis*, xvii.

14. Translations of the Hebrew Bible into hypotactical languages typically retain Hebrew parataxis in their effort to remain faithful to the text of the Bible. "Roughly speaking, it is true to say that in the Greek of the LXX there is no syntax, only parataxis.

those languages the main clause in a sentence is regularly linked by conjunctions or prepositions to other clauses that relate to, define, or qualify the main clause in various ways. In hypotactical languages sentences are characteristically more complicated and can include all manner of subordinate clauses. Such languages abound in qualifications: causal, conditional, circumstantial, relative, temporal, and so on. In a paratactical language the connections between thoughts and expressions are more often inferred, not explicit as they are in hypotactical languages. G. B. Caird, a scholar of acute insight into the peculiarities of biblical communication, observes,

> Anyone who habitually employs parataxis in expression will be sure to think paratactically as well. He will set two ideas side by side and allow the one to qualify the other without bothering to spell out in detail the relation between them.

> Paratactical thinking enabled the ancient Hebrew to set in close proximity two different, even apparently contradictory, senses of a word, without the discomfort felt by the modern reader.[15]

Robert Alter agrees. Parataxis, he says,

> is the essential literary vehicle of biblical narrative: it is the way the ancient Hebrew writers saw the world, linked events in it, artfully ordered it, and narrated it, and one gets a very different world if their syntax is jettisoned.[16]

These scholars suggest, in other words, that parataxis, the side-by-side arrangement of ideas, is not only a feature of the Hebrew sentence, but at least partially explains the penchant of the Bible for the juxtaposition of discordant assertions, whether in the immediate context or more remote, without regard to their interrelation. In other words, the same fundamental structures of thought and expression that explain the typical form of the Hebrew sentence—the side-by-side arrangement of assertions without explicit attention to their relation to one another—go some way toward explaining why in a single chapter we are told that God regretted that he had made Saul king and that God is not a man that he

The whole is one great scheme of clauses connected by *kaí*, and we have to trust to the sense to tell us which is to be so emphasized as to make it into the apodosis." Conybeare and Stock, *Grammar of Septuagint Greek*, 38.

15. Caird, *Language and Imagery of the Bible*, 117–19.

16. *Genesis*, xvii.

should regret; that there will be no poor among the people of God and that we will always have the poor among us; and that Moses spoke to God face to face and that no one can see God's face and live.

Dialectic, Antinomy, and Paradox as a Feature of Biblical Literature: Absoluteness

A second feature of Hebrew literary style that contributes to the Bible's characteristic polarities, its dialectical pedagogy, is its penchant for what Professor Caird calls "absoluteness," something he and others have argued is a "habitual cast of mind" among Semitic peoples. He means by the term "a tendency to think in extremes without qualification, in black and white without intervening shades of grey."[17] He cites the fascinating observation of T. E. Lawrence, the famous Lawrence of Arabia, who after living among the Arabs during the First World War was particularly impressed by this quality of their thought and speech.

> Semites had no half-tones in their register of vision. They were a people of primary colours, or rather of black and white.... They did not understand our metaphysical difficulties, our introspective questionings. They knew only truth and untruth, belief and unbelief, without our hesitating retinue of finer shades....
>
> Their thoughts were at ease only in extremes. They inhabited superlatives by choice. Sometimes inconsistents seemed to possess them at once in joint sway; but they never compromised: they pursued the logic of several incompatible opinions to absurd ends, without perceiving the incongruity....[18]

Professor Caird then goes on to say, "This description of the modern Arab could equally well have been written about the ancient Hebrew." He offers the example—an example every avid reader of the Bible will recollect—of the use of "love" and "hate."

> When the Hebrew uses these words, he may mean by them what we should mean, i.e. affection and detestation; but he may merely be using an absolute turn of phrase to express a preference. Where we should say "I prefer A to B", he says, "I love A and hate B". "Jacob loved Rachel more than Leah . . . the Lord

17. Caird, *Language and Imagery of the Bible*, 110.

18. Cited from *The Seven Pillars of Wisdom*, chapter 3, in Caird, *Language and Imagery of the Bible*, 110.

saw that Leah was hated" (Gen. 29:30–31). These two forms of expression are clearly interchangeable, and the use of both in successive verses is sure proof that the narrator could distinguish between hate (detest) and hate (love less); he was not a prisoner within his own hyperbole. The same idiom is found three times in the teaching of Jesus, and it is interesting to note that in one instance Luke has recorded a saying in the Semitic idiom which Matthew gives in a form better attuned to Gentile ears and sensibilities.

> If anyone comes to me and does not hate his father and mother, wife and children, brothers and sisters, even his own life, he cannot be my disciple (Luke 14:26).

> He who loves father or mother more than me is not worthy of me; he who loves son or daughter more than me is not worthy of me (Matt 10:37).

The point is clear enough. The statement is made in an absolute, even an exaggerated form, and the reader is expected to understand how to relate it to other things said or taught in the Bible, such as our obligation to love the members of our family. And so readers trained by the Bible to respect its manner of speaking take in stride a statement as absolute and unqualified as

> Whoever loves his life loses it, and whoever hates his life in this world will keep it for eternal life. (John 12:25)

That a host of biblical assertions are absolute, extreme, or unqualified in their statement can hardly be denied. Nor can it be denied that the Bible characteristically does not address the possible confusion when such statements seem to conflict with one another. It is this absolute, unqualified form of biblical statement that explains, for example, why John should say that the Christian does not "keep on sinning" (1 John 3:6) and does so in the same letter in which he also says, "If we say we have no sin, we deceive ourselves, and the truth is not in us." In a similar way, the history of both exegesis and theology proves easily enough the difficulty of reconciling Phil 1:6—"He who began a good work in you will bring it to completion at the day of Jesus Christ"—with Heb 6:3–6—"For it is impossible, in the case of those who have once been enlightened, who have tasted the heavenly gift, and have shared in the Holy Spirit, and have tasted the goodness of the word of God and the powers of the age to come, and then have fallen away, to restore them again to repentance. . . ."

Try as we will, and as we must, to understand the interrelationship between asssertions as absolute or as unqualified as these are, the incontestable fact is that the Bible itself makes no effort to harmonize or reconcile
such statements or resolve the dissonance between them. Such assertions
as these are made many times in the Bible—that the gifts and callings of
God are irrevocable *and* that some begin but do not finish—but nowhere
are we taught how to reconcile these statements to one another. Where, as
Professor Caird puts it, are "the intervening shades of grey?"

Dialectic, Antinomy, and Paradox as a Feature of Biblical Literature: Lack of Abstraction

A third feature of Hebrew style is its simplicity, concreteness, and lack
of abstraction or generalization. The Bible is the furthest thing from a
textbook of theology or philosophy. It does not present us with a system
of theological truth. It does not consolidate its various teachings or doctrines into categories or organize them in some logical outline such as we
find in manuals of theology or ethics. It requires of us that we attend to
the entirety of its teaching—"all Scripture is breathed out by God"—but
it does not itself explain the interrelations of its various teachings as a
systematic theology attempts to do. It does not usually even notice the
problems of seeming inconsistency that Christian thinkers have devoted
themselves to resolving through the ages since. In the same way, it does
not seek to provide philosophical justifications for or explanations of its
descriptions of reality. The raw material for such constructions may well,
at least to a certain extent, be found in the Bible, but the constructions
themselves are not. The deep reflections on epistemology—how we know
what we know—for example, so common in the Western philosophical
tradition, are absent from the Bible. So too is any reflection on the relationship between divine sovereignty and human freedom such as might
be found in any number of works of philosophy and theology.

A recent study by Professor Richard Muller is a case in point. In
his *Divine Will and Human Choice* Muller skillfully surveys the field
from Augustine to Francis Turretin, the Reformed theologian of the later
seventeenth century. No one should decry the hard thinking that was
invested by Christian theologians in seeking answers to questions posed
by the Bible's assertion of both destiny and contingency: God's absolute
sovereignty and man's freedom and accountability. The history of the

theological/philosophical debate is complex because the problem is ter-
ribly difficult and, in large part, simply defeats the effort to provide a
simple and plausible solution to the problem, at least a solution that does
not consist in the depreciation or reinterpretation of one of the biblical
polarities. But one has only to read Muller's sophisticated study to be impressed by how different such discussions are from the simple, straightforward, and emphatic assertions of both divine sovereignty and human
responsibility that we find in the Bible. There is in Holy Scripture nothing
of the technical terminology of the debate, nothing of the fine distinctions that have typically been drawn by theologians and philosophers,
and, supremely, nothing of the recognition that there is a problem here
requiring a solution or the assumption that a solution lies at hand. The
Bible simply leaves us in the tension created by these polarities regarding
the causation of the salvation of sinners. It does so even in Romans 9, as
we will observe later. It makes no effort to solve the problem, if problem
there be. It appeals to human beings to make the right choices, to avail
themselves of the day of salvation. It teaches them that they have no one
to blame but themselves if they do not. And it teaches that salvation is the
gift and the work of God from beginning to end and in all links of the
chain. And that is all that it ever does.

To be sure, explaining the dialectical character of biblical revelation
in terms of distinctive features of classical Hebrew as a language or of
the Hebrew or Semitic mind is controversial. Theories of the relationship
between Hebrew and Greek as biblical languages or between the Semitic
and the Greco-Roman ways of thinking have long been debated, with the
pendulum of scholarly opinion swinging back and forth. I am further
aware that the distinctions between both the languages and the patterns
of thought have sometimes been overdrawn and emphasized beyond
the evidence.[19] Nevertheless, while the Greek Bible is predictably less

---

19. We know better now than to say, as G. R. Driver said in reference to Hebrew
parataxis, "It will, therefore, be readily understood that philosophical reasoning and
sustained argument were beyond the grasp of the Hebrew intellect. . . ." Cited in
Caird, *Language and Imagery of the Bible*, 117. Similarly, A. T. Robertson argued that
"Parataxis is the rule in the speech of children, primitive men, unlettered men, and
also of Homer." *Grammar of the Greek New Testament*, 426. "Just because parataxis
happens to be a mark of colloquial speech in many languages, it does not follow that
it is a proof of naiveté when we find it in literary Hebrew. It is simply not true that
the Hebrew speaker was unable to express logical connections. What is true is that
Hebrew idiom prefers the paratactical style in which such connections are implicit and
taken for granted." Caird, *Language and Imagery of the Bible*, 118.

paratactical than the Hebrew Bible, apparently because it too was written almost entirely by men steeped in the Hebrew Scriptures, it also betrays the side-by-side assertions of ideas, absoluteness of statement, and a lack of generalization, abstraction, or theoretical analysis to a degree uncharacteristic of the Greek of the period.[20]

There is no need to argue for more than the obvious. I am no linguist and can supply no comprehensive anatomy of Hebrew and Greek rhetorical forms by which the two languages and their literary art may be compared. Some may disagree with Professor Caird that the ancient Hebrew "thought paratactically." Obviously, no one has access to their thoughts. Others may make more of the fact, which Professor Alter himself acknowledged, that classical Hebrew was also capable of syntatic qualification and subordination. Still others will point out that hyperbole and absoluteness of statement is hardly unique to biblical Hebrew. Fair enough. But what cannot be denied is that in the Bible we find, to an almost unique degree, the side-by-side arrangement of ideas and, accordingly, a penchant for making assertions, now here, now there, that seem to be inconsistent with one another and whose interrelationship is provided no explanation. What is more, many of those assertions are made in an absolute and unqualifed form, heightening the tension created by the seemingly conflicting ideas themselves. And, again, it is a simple fact that a lack of generalization or systematic analysis is likewise characteristic of the Bible to a degree highly unusual if not actually unique.

It is surely reasonable to conclude that these striking features of biblical communication originated *to some degree* in the linguistic milieu in which the Bible was written. What is more, it is a fact long observed that polarities litter the pages of the Greek Bible as well. Even the apostles, who also thought and wrote in Greek and could, therefore, write long, involved sentences with all manner of qualifying and clarifying subordinate clauses, still blithely set seemingly contradictory thoughts side by side without explanation, certainly without any obvious effort to help us understand how both could be true at one and the same time. It was the apostle Paul, after all, who taught, as part of his exposition of justification by faith, that it is the doers of the law who will be justified and that God will render to each one according to his works. It was Paul who, immediately after declaring that by union with Christ we are no longer slaves to sin, confessed his continuing bondage to it. And it was Paul who taught

20. According to Caird, the "relative frequency [of parataxis] in the New Testament is almost certainly due to Semitic influence." *Language and Imagery of the Bible*, 118.

us in the space of three verses both that we should bear one another's burdens and that each of us must bear his own load (Gal 6:2–4). It is surely reasonable to suppose that Paul and the others thought and wrote as they did because they were Jews who had learned their craft from the Scriptures themselves.

I am more interested in the fact of these striking characteristics of biblical communication than in their origin, but I find it easy to believe that Professor Caird has put his finger on at least part of their explanation. One may quibble over the extension of the parataxis of the Hebrew sentence to the broader canvas, as in Caird's suggestion that the ancient Hebrews thought "paratactically" or in Alter's suggestion that parataxis was "the way the ancient Hebrew writers saw the world," but what cannot be denied is that they repeatedly set seemingly discordant assertions side by side, often stated them in the most absolute terms, and virtually never discussed, much less explained their interrelationship. Readers of the Bible have been grappling with these facts ever since! These features of Hebrew style—the side-by-side arrangement of ideas, its preference for absoluteness in statement, and its lack of systematic analysis—go a long way toward accounting for the dialectical character of biblical revelation: the interaction between and the equilibrium of what Simeon called the "extremes" that lie at either end of any biblical continuum of truth.

It is significant that Christian writers after the apostolic age generally did not reproduce in their own work these same features of the Bible's rhetorical form or style. When the early church fathers—Greek or Latin thinkers, speakers, and writers as they were—encountered the biblical text, they sought, as we do today, to resolve its paradoxes in precisely that way the biblical writers did not. And when they could not, when they acknowledged that in this case or that biblical revelation confronts us with paradox, that very acknowledgement distinguished them from the biblical writers themselves, who characteristically left unnoticed the tension created by their discordant assertions. When, for example, Augustine, facing a biblical antinomy, urged his readers to choose both truths, confess both, and confirm both by the faith of piety,[21] he was not writing as the biblical writers themselves wrote. Holy Scripture forces polarities upon us, but it does not observe that the result is paradoxical.

The Bible might have been written differently, more like a systematic theology, but it was not. No doubt that the Bible reads as it does, that it

---

21. Augustine, *City of God*, V, 9–10, as translated in Bavinck, *Reformed Dogmatics*, 2:198.

scatters paradoxes in every direction, is at least in part the result of its being written when it was, in the languages that it was, and by the men who wrote it. *But what matters is that this is the form of divine revelation that has been given to us.* We must submit to it as to the Lord! In any case, presumably the virtues of this form of communication, not an inability on the part of the prophets and apostles to think or write in a different way, account for the fact that it is the Bible's literary form or rhetorical style.

Most Christian theology has been both developed and communicated in a different form than that found in the Bible. The side-by-side arrangement of assertions has been transformed into systematic expositions and explanations. This is as it should be. But the best of Christian theology has also respected revelation's original form. We will have occasion to notice many examples later. If Holy Scripture leaves us with an equilibrium of truths and does not teach us how to subject one truth to another or how to reconcile a seeming contradiction, we often must be satisfied to confess both truths with equal confidence, however little we may be able to penetrate their interrelationship. The best biblical exegesis and Christian theology have been careful to respect this limitation. Many of what Dowey called "surface inconsistencies" can be and have been explained. But his "deeper paradoxes," of which there are many, simply defy rationalization. The Bible's dialectical pedagogy requires us to respect the polarities as polarities, and if that leaves us with a mystery we cannot penetrate and with a confession we cannot explain, so be it. If that requires us to devote ourselves at one and the same time to two forms of obedience that may seem to be inconsistent with one another, that is nevertheless our duty. The acknowledgment of the Bible's fondness for antinomy, paradox, and mystery provides a check to our penchant for an illicit theological or ethical creativity. It works against our tendency to one-sidedness. It also produces, as history well demonstrates, a humble, thoughtful, careful, but confident Christian mind.

I'm going to argue that while some of the Bible's many seemingly incompatible or inconsistent assertions can be harmonized comparatively easily, as above in the case of the Bible's sometime use of "hate" and "love," many more of them, and the more important of them, cannot. The use of "hate" to mean "love less" is one thing; the assertion of both deity and humanity, each unchanged and unchanging in the one person Jesus Christ, is another thing altogether. So too is the Bible's impressive witness to God's desire that all be saved and its equally unmistakable teaching that only those he has appointed to eternal life will be saved. The appreciation of the way certain absolute terms may be faithfully rendered in a relative sense is hardly the same thing as having to confess at one and the same time that we have been born again by the imperishable seed of the Word, on the one hand, and, on the other, that some branches once in Christ the true vine have been, for their lack of fruit, cut off and thrown into the fire. In the one case there is a resolution; in the other we are left with an equilibrium of truths and with tension that is never relaxed or seeming contradictions that are never explained or resolved.

The vital point of these observations is that *the Almighty chose to communicate his truth and will to us in this way*. However much the Bible's mannner of expression may be typical of a language such as classical Hebrew,[22] it remains the fact that this was the manner of expression God himself chose to employ, the particular form of revelation he chose to give to the world. Indeed, as we said, given the limitations of the human intellect, the immensity and complexity of reality, and the ineffable nature of God and his ways, it is not difficult to believe that this *had to be* the way God revealed the truth to us: in its poles. To grasp the whole truth of the will and the works of the infinite God, fully to appreciate both the facts and all their interrelations, to understand how all of reality coheres in a single unity, and to grasp in some systematic way how competing obligations can be met at one and the same time require an infinite mind. The communication of truth in its polarities was and is divine accommodation to the limitations of the human intellect.

What follows is the demonstration of this phenomenon in the teaching of Holy Scripture and an examination of the importance of recognizing it in our reading of the Word of God. First to be considered will be the three greatest mysteries of the Christian faith—the Holy Trinity, the hypostatic union in the person of Jesus Christ, and divine sovereignty and human responsibility—the biblical revelation of at least the first two of which mysteries has been widely admitted to be paradoxical or dialectical, if not described in those terms. Then will follow a demonstration of how ubiquitous paradox or antinomy is in biblical revelation: in its teaching of the faith once and for all delivered to the saints, in its description of the experience of believing life in the world, and in its ethical instruction. A final chapter will summarize the results of the study and draw out briefly some of their implications for Christian faith and life, for preaching, and for Christian unity.

22. Prof. C. John (Jack) Collins, in a personal communication, informed me that Modern Hebrew has largely lost this characteristic.

3

The Holy Trinity

This self-revelation involves a yet greater self-concealment. There will be the manifestation of God in the voluntary condescension of his love: and there will be the necessary seclusion within the clouds of his unapproachable glory. When a finite being seeks to understand anything of the Infinite, it must always be so. There will be a fragment of truth which the student has made and is making his own, and the illimitable expanse beneath, above, and beyond him.

—E. H. BICKERSTETH

WE TURN NOW TO some principal biblical doctrines or teachings that demonstrate the dialectical or paradoxical nature of biblical revelation. We are not primarily interested in the doctrines themselves but in the way we find them taught in Holy Scripture. We begin then with the Holy Trinity. Here we find a perfect example of the biblical method of revelation: paratactical, with contraries laid side by side; absolute and unqualified in expression; and lacking abstraction, generalization, or theoretical analysis.

The Knowledge of God

It is a first principle of the gospel that salvation, the gift of eternal life, is nothing less than the knowledge of God, whom to know is life eternal

(John 17:3; 1 John 5:20). The promise of the gospel in its most concentrated form was, from the beginning, "I will be your God" (Gen 17:7), and it is this same promise that crowns its end (Rev 21:3). The fulfillment of human life is to be found in an I-Thou relationship with God himself!

> Thus says the Lord: "Let not the wise man boast in his wisdom, let not the mighty man boast in his might, let not the rich man boast in his riches, but let him who boasts boast in this, that he understands and knows me, that I am the Lord who practices steadfast love, justice, and righteousness in the earth." (Jer 9:23–24)

So it is hardly surprising to find in Holy Scripture a great deal of information about God: who he is, what he is like, and what he has done. Indeed, it may be said that the Bible is first and foremost the self-revelation of God. To be sure, God has revealed himself to us in the things he has made (Rom 1:19–20), but it is in his Word—which includes the record of his many appearances and communications to his prophets and his apostles and, supremely, the record of the incarnation, ministry, death, and resurrection of the Lord Jesus Christ—that we learn of God and learn how we can come to know him (Heb 1:1–4; Col 1:19). The bane of unbelief, as the Lord Jesus said, is precisely that the unbeliever *does not know* the Father, the Son, and the Holy Spirit (John 8:19; 14:16–17). Unbelievers may profess to know God, but their lives are proof that they do not (Titus 1:16; 1 John 2:4). The lives of believers, on the other hand, prove in various ways that they *know* God (1 John 2:3). In sum, saving faith *is* the knowledge of God in his three persons: the Father (John 17:3), the Son (Phil 3:10), and the Holy Spirit (John 14:17; 1 John 4:2). Saving faith is the knowledge of God in large part because knowledge of him is the foundation of our confidence that God will be true to his Word and keep the promises he has made (Heb 11:1, 6). That the living God, the Creator of heaven and earth, has revealed himself and may be known is thus the heart of the gospel.

> And we know that the Son of God has come and has given us understanding, so that we may know him who is true; and we are in him who is true, in his Son Jesus Christ. He is the true God and eternal life. (1 John 5:20)

But even here, at the outset of the Bible's revelation of God and in its declaration that God has made himself known, we encounter the typical biblical juxtaposition and assertion of contraries. The Bible is a manifesto of the living God, who wants all people to find him and to know him (Isa 55:6–7; Matt 11:28). But throughout it also acknowledges that God is beyond our knowing and past our finding out. In a typical parataxis, Yahweh tells Moses that he cannot not see God's face and live (Exod 33:20). Earlier in the same chapter, however, we learn that the Lord used to speak to Moses face to face, "as a man speaks to his friend" (33:11). The apostle Paul can exuberantly proclaim, "I know whom I have believed" (2 Tim 1:12), but also declare with equal confidence that God "dwells in unapproachable light, whom no one has ever seen or can see" (1 Tim 6:16). As full as the Bible is of the knowledge of God, both knowledge about God and the personal acquaintance of believers with God himself, it is equally full of the impenetrable mystery of God and the infinite distance that separates us from him. Throughout Holy Scripture we encounter this juxtaposition of a certain knowledge of God and our necessarily invincible ignorance of the same God.

> For thus says the One who is high and lifted up,
>   who inhabits eternity, whose name is Holy:
> "I dwell in the high and holy place,
>   and also with him who is of a
>   contrite and lowly spirit. . . ." (Isa 57:15)

This parataxis and this typically absolute form of statement does not trouble us because, as with the example of the Bible's use of "love" and "hate," we easily detect the relative contrast in the absolute form of words. It hardly surprises us that while we can know God, our knowledge of him is, in the nature of the case, severely limited. The Bible's revelation of God is partial, not complete. We are given knowledge of God, to be sure, but that knowledge is hardly exhaustive. But knowledge is not less real knowledge for its being incomplete.

The Holy Trinity: A Mystery

In the Bible the term *mystery* is sometimes used to describe a truth that had been hidden, or largely hidden, but is now revealed. The Gentile mission, for example, was such a mystery (Eph 3:6; Rom 16:25–26). That the gospel was to penetrate the entire world and make believers of every tongue, tribe, and nation was prophesied in the Scriptures of the ancient epoch, but the manner in which the kingdom of God was to expand throughout the world was not. Pentecost, what Herman Bavinck called, after the creation and the incarnation, "the third great work of God,"[1] was a development only dimly seen beforehand. That the Gentile nations were to be incorporated into the people of God *as Gentiles* came as a surprise, and accordingly caused significant confusion and consternation when the gospel began its course of conquest through the world. *The Holy Trinity is such a mystery.* That the living God, the Creator of heaven and earth, the one and only God, is Father, Son, and Holy Spirit has been the confession of the Christian church since the resurrection of the Lord Jesus Christ. It is, in fact, an important fact of biblical revelation that the knowledge of the triune life of God awaited the incarnation and, particularly, the once-for-all ratification of the incarnation in the resurrection of the Son of God. There surely were anticipations of the Trinitarian life of God in the ancient Scriptures,[2] but it is beyond dispute that the revelation of the three-person God awaited the incarnation.

So it was that, as the English theologian Leonard Hodgson observed, "Christianity began as a Trinitarian religion with a unitarian theology."[3]

> The Divine revelation had been given in the Divine action, in the life, death, resurrection, and ascension of Christ, in the coming of the Spirit and the adoption of Christians to share in the sonship of their Lord. What the church had to do was to grasp the significance of this revelation for the doctrine of God.[4]

In other words, the theology of the triune God—the unifying and systematic account of the Bible's teaching—would have to catch up to the religion, as indeed it did over the next several centuries.[5] Hodgson's point was that for a Gentile to become a Christian after Pentecost meant, in the nature of the case, the abandonment of polytheism. But, at the same time, Trinitarian formulas are scattered throughout the New Testament;

---

1. Bavinck, *Reformed Dogmatics*, 3:500.

2. Cf. Collins, *Genesis 1–4*, 59–61; Kelly, *Systematic Theology*, 1:456–71.

3. Hodgson, *Doctrine of the Trinity*, 103.

4. Hodgson, *Doctrine of the Trinity*, 98–99. He goes on to say, "Orthodoxy clung to the revelation even at the cost of apparent self-contradiction which was eased, but never completely resolved, by the adoption of an agreed terminology." Warfield makes a similar point. "The revelation itself was made not in word but in deed. It was made in the incarnation of God the Son, and the outpouring of God the Holy Spirit." "Biblical Doctrine of the Trinity," 33.

5. "Belief in the triune God, confessed on the basis of revelation, came first; the dogma of the Trinity established by the church came second." Genderen and Velema, *Concise Reformed Dogmatics*, 146.

baptism was performed in the name of the Father, the Son, and the Holy Spirit; the divine name and the attributes of deity were artlessly assigned to all three persons; and the interaction of the three persons in the economy of salvation was fundamental to the apostolic proclamation of the gospel. As Herman Bavinck observed, all the apostles "know and glory in the threefold divine cause of salvation."[6] Further, in the New Testament

> we now discover that the God of the covenant is and has to be a triune God, that is, that there is a threefold principle in operation in the work of salvation. Not merely a few isolated texts but the whole New Testament is Trinitarian in that sense.[7]

For that reason, from its inception and before a theology of the Holy Trinity had been created and perfected, Christian worship was uniformly Trinitarian. As the Roman governor Pliny the Younger famously reported to Emperor Trajan early in the second century, the Christians in Bithynia "on an appointed day they had been accustomed to meet before daybreak, and to recite a hymn antiphonally to Christ, as to a god. . . ."[8] Monotheistic Christian worshippers did that! But there is no theology of the Holy Trinity in the New Testament, no account or explanation of the three-person God. The church had to create such a theology from the materials found in the New Testament, materials that existed in a typically dialectical or paradoxical form, data that amounted to deeply discordant polarities lying opposite one another on the several continua of truth concerning the life of God.

B. B. Warfield argued that the full disclosure of God as Holy Trinity awaited, and had to await, the incarnation of God the Son. The Holy Trinity was thus a mystery in that sense, something at first hidden, only later revealed.

> The great thing to be taught the ancient people of God was that the God of all the earth is one person. Over against the varying idolatries about them, this was the truth of truths for which Israel was primarily to stand; and not until this great truth was ineffaceably stamped upon their souls could the personal distinctions in the Triune-God be safely made known to them.[9]

6. Bavinck, *Reformed Dogmatics*, 2:270

7. Bavinck, *Reformed Dogmatics*, 2:269–70.

8. Bettenson, *Documents*, 6.

9. Warfield, "Spirit of God in the Old Testament," 153. Gregory Nazianzen said a similar thing, though with less precision, in his *Fifth Theological Oration*, XXVI,

Here we have the initial paradox: God as one person, then God as three persons. Yahweh, after all, is a singular personal name and Yahweh appears throughout the Hebrew Bible as a person who thinks, who speaks, who acts, who forms relationships with human beings, and so on. It is precisely this that we mean when we use the word *person*.[10] Warfield's point was that anything more than the assertion of the oneness of God, God known to his people as a single person, would have confused the people of Israel in the great battle between monotheism and polytheistic idolatry, an idolatry that for its ubiquity and its sensuality proved a constant temptation to Israel in the ancient epoch. It has been observed that the prohibition of idols in the first two of the Ten Commandments was one of the most unlikely things ever to be found in the ancient world. No wonder then that the process of convincing the people of God that there was but one God proved so tortuous, so painful, and the work of so many years. But once monotheism was firmly fixed in the consciousness and conviction of the Jews, nothing less than the incarnation would suffice to open their minds to the fact that the one living and true God is Father, Son, and Holy Spirit, three distinct persons. And the resurrection fixed that conviction in the minds of the early Christians as firmly as was already fixed the fact that there is but one living and true God. The writers of the New Testament are as fiercely monotheistic as they are unguarded and artless in their confession of the living God as Father, Son, and Holy Spirit.

And so it is that ever since the church has been content with that confession, believing it to be what God has disclosed to us about himself. To be sure, over the several centuries that followed the Lord's resurrection the church struggled to find the most accurate way to represent the revelation of the divine life found in the Word of God, the way least susceptible to misunderstanding, and to represent the Holy Trinity in the most satisfying and helpful form of words. But from Pentecost onwards in baptism, in preaching and teaching, in confession, in worship and prayer, and increasingly in theological definition, the living God was for Christians Father, Son, and Holy Spirit. This was something new, but the history of the incarnation and Pentecost had made plurality in God as inevitable as unity.

---

326. "For it was not safe, when the Godhead of the Father was not yet acknowledged, plainly to proclaim the Son; nor when that of the Son was not yet received to burden us further (if I may use so bold an expression) with the Holy Ghost. . . ."

10. Frame, *Doctrine of God*, 25–27.

The Dialectical Revelation of the Holy Trinity

But the Holy Trinity is a mystery in a still deeper sense than the history of its revelation. The church has always acknowledged that here, supremely, in seeking to comprehend God, whom no man has seen or can see and whose ways are past our finding out, the limitations of the human intellect are revealed with particular force. The truth of the being of God is a truth that the human mind can grasp only at its periphery.[11] To be sure, the biblical revelation of God is clear and sensible. What the Bible says about God is straightforward and its assertions are intelligible one by one. It teaches us what we must know in order to know God now and forever. But uncharted depths and heights lie out of our sight. The full meaning of those assertions and their interrelations are not comprehensible to us. This should hardly surprise us. How little of Almighty God—his eternal existence, his omnipresence, his limitless knowledge, his immeasurable power and insupportable glory—could possibly be grasped by a creature who possesses only decidedly finite powers of thought and comprehension? For example, how little can we even comprehend what an infinite mind would be: a mind that knows all things, past, present, and future, at once and by immediate intuition; a mind that knows everything and so never learns anything (Ps 94:9; Isa 40:27–28)? But it is in regard to God's triune life that the mystery of his being is particularly acute. Our intellectual limitations are not simply numerical; they are intrinsic to our way of knowing and to the very nature of our minds. Here, supremely, as Calvin reminds us, God has accommodated the knowledge of himself "to our slight capacity." He must "lisp" in speaking to us, "as nurses do with infants. . . ." And to reveal himself to us "he must descend far beneath his loftiness."[12]

It is not simply because we are unable fully to measure its brilliance or power or composition that we cannot grasp the glory of God. It also lies beyond our grasp because God is of a different nature, a nature that *transcends the very structures of human understanding.* This is not our

---

11. "I can see no limit to my venture of speaking concerning God in terms more precise than He Himself has used. He has assigned the Names—Father, Son, and Holy Ghost—which are our information of the Divine nature. Words cannot express or feeling embrace or reason apprehend the results of enquiry carried further; all is ineffable, unattainable, incomprehensible." Hilary, *On the Trinity*, II, 5, 53. So Calvin's comment on Psalm 86:8: ". . . the Divine nature is infinitely exalted above the comprehension of our understanding. . . ." *Commentary on the Psalms*, 3:385.

12. Calvin, *Institutes of the Christian Religion*, I, xiii, 1.

loss. It is our privilege and our glory to know and to love the God who inhabits eternity and dwells in unapproachable light (Isa 57:15; 1 Tim 6:16)! John Owen put this point in his own methodical but characteristically prolix and lumbering style.

> For what we call darkness in divine subjects is nothing else than their celestial glory and splendor striking on the weak ball of our eyes, the rays of which we are not able in this life, which "is but a vapour" (and that not very clear), "which appeareth but for a little" to bear. Hence God himself, who is "light, and in whom there is no darkness at all," who "dwelleth in light inaccessible," and who "clotheth himself with light as with a garment," in respect of us, is said to have made "darkness his pavilion."[13]

Indeed, such is the distance between God and ourselves that it is not only in this life that we are incapable of the glory of God; it will always be so. Dante saw this clearly. He reminds us how pleasing it ought already to be and how breathtaking it will someday be to contemplate a divine glory that so far exceeds our powers of comprehension.

> I saw that in its depths there are enclosed,
> Bound up with love in one eternal book,
> The scattered leaves of all the universe—
> Substance, and accidents, and their relations,
> As though fused in such a way
> That what I speak of is a single light.
> The universal form of this commingling
> I think I saw, for when I tell of it
> I feel that I rejoice so much the more. . . .
>   Even thus my mind,
> Enraptured, gazed attentive, motionless,
> And grew the more enkindled as it gazed.
> For in the presence of those radiant beams
> One is so changed, that 'tis impossible
> To turn from it to any other sight—. . . .
>
> How powerless is speech—how weak, compared
> To my conception, which itself is trifling
> Beside the mighty vision that I saw![14]

Once again, this does not trouble us. We understand well enough that we can know something without knowing everything. And this is

13. Owen, *Dissertation on Divine Justice*, 487.
14. Dante, *Paradiso*, Canto 33, 188.

emphatically the case in regard to the Holy Trinity. The more the revelation of God became the revelation of his triunity, the more it was characterized by now-here–now-there assertions not at all obviously consistent with one another, by absoluteness of statement, and by an almost complete lack of abstraction or systematic analysis. Here, in a way typical of the Bible, the assertion of contraries and the tension-laden paradoxes are scattered everywhere and remain beyond our power to reduce to an obvious harmony. We are not given the information necessary to reconcile or resolve the discordant affirmations, no doubt because such knowledge is too wonderful for us; our minds are not capacious enough to comprehend God in the depths and heights of his nature. As Augustine tartly reminded us, "If you can grasp it, it isn't God."[15] In the revelation of the Holy Trinity, at point after point, we are left having to confess two facts—facts in which we are right to invest complete confidence, for they are clearly and repeatedly taught in the Word of God—but facts whose interrelations remain profoundly mysterious to us, if not seemingly the contradiction of one another. Here, supremely, the truth is found not in one extreme but in both extremes. Again, it is not this truth or that that escapes us but the unity of those truths that we cannot conceive. It seems obvious to me that the reason the truth about God is taught in this dialectical fashion, that we are confronted with paradox at every turn, is because this is the only way for us to know the truth *so far as we are capable of knowing it*. The Lord has in this way accommodated himself to the limitations of our intellect.

Indeed, it has been the confession of many believers and theologians that the more we know of God, the more obvious it becomes how much there is that we do not and cannot know. "When God reveals himself to us, he does not thereby decrease his incomprehensibility."[16]

> This self-revelation involves a yet greater self-concealment. There
> will be the manifestation of God in the voluntary condescension

15. Augustine, *Essential Sermons*, 117.5, 197–98. "But you are quite unable to imagine or think of such a thing [i.e., a Being that is no less in his parts than in his totality]. And such ignorance is more pious than any presumption of knowledge. After all, we are talking about God. It says, *and the Word was God* (Jn 1:1). We are talking about God; so why be surprised if you cannot grasp it? I mean, if you can grasp it, it isn't God [si enim comprehendis non est Deus]. Let us rather make a devout confession of ignorance, instead of a brash profession of knowledge. Certainly it is great bliss to have a little touch or taste of God with the mind, but completely to grasp him, to comprehend him, is altogether impossible."

16. Frame, *Doctrine of God*, 201–2.

of his love: and there will be the necessary seclusion within the clouds of his unapproachable glory. When a finite being seeks to understand anything of the Infinite, it must always be so. There will be the fragment of truth which the student has made and is making his own, and the illimitable expanse beneath, above, and beyond him.[17]

The revelation of the Holy Trinity is in fact a litany of discordant propositions, paradoxes, or antinomies.

The Person and Persons of God

My interest is not to defend that doctrine; that has been ably done by many through the ages and into our own time. Still less is it to tell the story of the church's search for precisely that best form of words with which to represent the biblical revelation of God as three persons. That story, stirring, sometimes disheartening, and complex as it is, has also been told many times. But less often is our attention concentrated on *the way in which the doctrine of the three-person God is revealed* in Holy Scripture and how it was, then, that the church came so firmly to believe that Father, Son, and Holy Spirit are the one living and true God. *Here, at the foundation, we encounter the Bible's dialectical or paradoxical method of revelation in a pronounced form.* In one place we are assured that there is but one God and that the numerous gods that various peoples have worshipped throughout history were nothing but the figments of their imagination, "the work of human hands, that neither see, nor hear, nor eat, nor smell" (Deut 4:28; Jas 2:19). The question is asked repeatedly: "Can man make for himself gods?" And as often the same answer is given: "Such are not gods" (Jer 16:20). The living God, the only God (Isa 44:6), on the other hand, made heaven and earth and everything in them (Isa 46:18). Indeed, as J. A. Motyer reminds us, in the Bible, from start to finish, "Salvation is grounded in monotheism."[18]

But in another place, Jesus of Nazareth, who repeatedly addressed his Father in heaven—often addressing him as God (e.g. Matt 26:46; John 20:17)—and who was addressed by the Father as his Son (Mark 1:11), who regularly referred to the one who sent him into the world and spoke of the one who will come after him, is himself identified as Yahweh, the

17. Bickersteth, *Trinity*, 149.

18. Motyer, *Isaiah*, 366.

God of Abraham, Isaac, and Jacob. Indeed, Jesus is identified as the very Yahweh who delivered Israel from bondage in Egypt (Jude 5; Heb 11:26), who gave the law at Sinai (Heb 12:18–29), and whose glory Isaiah saw when he was granted his vision of the Almighty in the temple (Isa 6:1–5; John 12:36–41). Jesus is nothing less than Almighty God, who created the heavens and the earth (John 1:1–3; Col 1:16), who "upholds the universe by the word of his power" (Heb 1:3), the one in whom all men and believers supremely live, and move, and have their being (Acts 17:28; Col 1:17).

And, in the same way in other places, the Holy Spirit is found as a third person, together with the Father and the Son (Matt 28:19; 2 Cor 13:14). We read that he descended upon, accompanied, and empowered the Lord Jesus throughout the course of his ministry (Luke 1:35; 3:22; 4:1, 18); he took the Savior's place when the former ascended to heaven, being sent by the Father as was the Son (John 14:26); and he is the agent of salvation at work in the world (Rom 8:9). I could easily multiply texts that ascribe divine attributes or activities to each of the three persons and texts that distinguish the three persons from one another. It is on the abundance of such evidence that the church founded the doctrine of the triunity of God, which has long been embraced by every Christian who confesses the Bible to be the very Word of God.

> Are there more Gods than one? There is but One only, the living and true God.
>
> How many persons are there in the Godhead? There are three persons in the Godhead, the Father, the Son, and the Holy Ghost; and these three are one God, the same in substance, equal in power and glory.[19]

But nowhere do we find what one can be forgiven for assuming we certainly would find: namely, some explanation or at least consideration of the fact that the one living and true God exists in three persons: Father, Son, and Holy Spirit. Upon reflection, it is startling that this sudden disclosure should not have been made the subject of some deliverance somewhere in the New Testament; that this question of all questions should never have been addressed and answered. To confess and teach that there are three persons in the one God was bound to cause confusion, if not scandal. It should surprise no one that the Jews, who ingested

---

19. *Westminster Shorter Catechism*, questions 5 and 6.

monotheism with their mother's milk, would stumble over the claim that Jesus Christ, the man from Nazareth, is God. Of course they were scandalized by his claim that he is equal with God and by the Christians' claim that he *is* God, no matter that he himself often and emphatically distinguished himself from God in heaven (John 17:3). Jesus performed miracles, to be sure, extraordinary works of divine power; but so did Moses, Elijah, and Elisha, and no one thought any of those prophets was Yahweh himself. It is precisely the obvious paradox that explains why there have continued to be those throughout church history who have found illogical or simply unhelpfully confusing the assertion that the One is three.

The polarities we find revealed in Holy Scripture concerning the nature of God are these: unity or oneness, on the one hand, and three persons, on the other. This is the paradox: that the one God is three persons, each in an I-Thou relationship with the others, each communicating with the others—a divine *tête*-à-tête, if you will. And, as already mentioned, it is entirely predictable that nowhere do we find an explicit examination of the relation between these two poles or an explanation of how both can be true at one and the same time. There is evidence enough in the Gospels that the claim that Jesus *is* God was regarded by many as blasphemous. This makes only the more striking the fact that no explanation was ever offered to allay such offense or to explain how it could be true that, though personally distinct from the Father, the Son is nevertheless the one God himself. As we said, there is very little tendency to abstraction or systematic analysis in the Bible. Rather, we are taught repeatedly that there is but one God; then elsewhere we are taught that the Father is God, the Son is God, and the Holy Spirit is God. We, therefore, can only know God, the one true and living God, by knowing him as Father, Son, and Holy Spirit. We understand that only by embracing discordant polarities.

The Order or Relation Between the Three Persons

The biblical polarities were found to multiply as the biblical data with which to form the doctrine of the Holy Trinity were further examined; as mistakes in theological statement were identified; and as greater precision was found to be necessary as the doctrine was developed in the centuries that followed Pentecost. The Church took note of the fact that there is an order (*taxis*) between the three persons. God is not simply three persons, but three persons in a fixed, original, and essential relationship.

Father and Son

The relationship between the first and second persons of the Godhead is revealed in Holy Scripture to be that of a Father and a Son. Reflection on these titles eventually produced the doctrine of the eternal generation of the Son, which is another way of saying that the Son has always been and forever will be the Son of the Father.[20] But what does that mean? For us a Father comes first, exists before his son, and is the cause of his existence. Moreover, in addition to temporal priority, fatherhood suggests authority and sonship subordination. Throughout the Bible, and regularly in human culture, sons have been taught to be subservient to their fathers. They have owed them honor as inferiors to superiors. Even more in biblical times than today, a father occupied a position superior to his son. It was predictable enough, then, for the Arians to conclude that the Son had a beginning in time as sons do—that is, there was a point at which the Father inhabited eternity alone—and that the Son, therefore, is a creature in a way the eternal Father is not and is subordinate and so inferior to the Father. The names "Father" and "Son," taken by themselves, might very well have led all Christians to think similarly.

Why was it, then, that the church resisted those conclusions? It was not because the nature of divine fatherhood and of divine sonship are carefully defined in the New Testament. It was not because we have, say, in one of the letters of the apostle Paul, a thorough examination of the implications of the disclosure that the first person of the Godhead is to be called "Father" and the second is to be called "Son." It was not because possible misunderstandings of these titles, "Father" and "Son," are forestalled in some careful and explicit analysis of their meaning. It was not because somewhere in the New Testament we are reminded that while "Father" and "Son" identify a particular kind of relationship in human life, in the life of God the terms identify a relationship that, while appropriately described as the relationship between a father and his son, is

---

20. Giles, *Eternal Generation of the Son*. That "Son" is the eternal name of the Second Person and not simply his incarnate name is demonstrated in a number of texts (e.g., Matt 21:37–38; 28:19; Col 1:13–17).

in fact in almost all respects profoundly different from the relationship between human fathers and their sons.

Lacking any such theology or systematic analysis of the revelation of God as Father and Son, the church resisted the conclusions the Arians drew from those divine names only because there was another pole on this biblical continuum of truth concerning the first and second persons of God. Whatever Father and Son mean as titles of two of the three persons, we also are taught in the New Testament that Jesus Christ is himself God, Yahweh, the Creator of heaven and earth. Further, we are taught in a variety of ways that everything that is true of the one living and true God is true of the Son as surely as it is true of the Father: eternity, omniscience, omnipotence, sovereignty, and glory. The Son likewise is to be the object of divine worship as surely as is the Father, though we are taught emphatically to worship the Creator and not the creature. He may be addressed as God, as the Father is so addressed, and must be by believers, no matter their unapologetic and resolute monotheism.

It was the church's conviction that this equilibrium of biblical assertions regarding Father and Son must be respected that led inexorably to the doctrine of the Holy Trinity. Whatever fatherhood (*paternity* is the theological term) entails in regard to the first person—and the Bible does not explain the meaning of that name or title—and whatever sonship entails (*filiation* is the theological term) in regard to the second—and our ignorance is as deep here as it is with regard to the divine fatherhood—we know because we are taught in Holy Scripture that the first person is the Father and the second is the Son, but that each and both together are Almighty God. We are to worship and serve both as God himself.

In other words, here we find a set of polarities that are a subset of the first set: the unity and the threefold personality of God. Here one person is Father and the other is Son. Theirs is a relationship that is to be described as that of a father and a son. That is one end of this biblical continuum of truth. At the other end is all the evidence that teaches us that this Father and this Son are like no father and son familiar to us. This Son has lived as long as his Father. This Son has equal honor, stature, and authority, and possesses all the same divine attributes. Only in this is he to be distinguished: that he is the Son and not the Father, whatever that means. Such was the conclusion of the struggle throughout the fourth century over what Edward Gibbon scornfully dismissed as a controversy over "a single diphthong," the difference between *homoiousios* (of *like* substance) and *homoousios* (of *the same* substance). That controversy over terminology was eventually resolved in the recognition by both sides that while the biblical data in fact does require the confession that the Son of God is of the same substance with the Father, the Son eternally God as the Father is God, the data also made it necessary to ensure that the Son is understood to be, at the same time, a distinct person.[21] This is what biblical polarities do: they require the confession of truths not easily harmonized.

The Holy Spirit

And so it was regarding the Holy Spirit. "Spirit" is not a personal name like Father or Son. We might have expected that the triune life of God would be that of Father, Son, and perhaps "Brother"; or, given that the Spirit is said to be both the Spirit of God and the Spirit of Christ in the New Testament, and the fact that the church has widely confessed that the Spirit proceeds from both the Father *and* the Son, or from the Father *through* the Son, we might have expected the third person of the triune God to be "Grandson." But instead we are told that the third person is the Holy Spirit. That name inevitably tempted the church to depersonalize the Spirit of God, to think of the Spirit as a force or agency—the breath of God, the wind of God, or the power of God at work—rather than a person, such as is so clearly suggested by the names Father and Son.[22] Though some early Christians succumbed to this temptation and others have since, and one would think understandably so, why did the church refuse to do so? Once again, it was not because the obvious question of the significance of the different sort of name for the third person and so the issue of the personality of the Spirit was raised and addressed by one or more apostles. Surely we might well expect that somewhere in the New Testament we would find an exposition of the internal relations of the Godhead, and in that exposition a formula something like the one we are

21. Pelikan, *Christian Tradition*, 1:209–10.

22. Dr. J. Oliver Buswell recollected not only the statement of an influential preacher of his day to the effect that the doctrine of the Holy Trinity was an "absurdity in arithmetic," but that "The president of the theological seminary from which I received my Bachelor of Divinity degree used to say that the Holy Spirit is the name for the influence of Jesus, or the influence of Christianity." *What Is God?*, 91, 96. Modern theology abounds in examples of the same tendency. Cf. Berkhof, *Christian Faith*, 330–37. Berkhof, who denies the historic doctrine of the Holy Trinity, considers the Holy Spirit as "the name for God in action toward the world."

now so well used to: one God in three persons, all three equal in power and glory. Perhaps, given the name, we might all the more have expected some special attention to the personality of the Holy Spirit and his place among the three persons. But as much as we might have expected such attention to the nature of the Holy Spirit and his relation to the Father and the Son, there is none. What we find instead, now here and now there across the face of the New Testament, is more than sufficient evidence of the Spirit's personality, however much in bits and pieces. We must draw the evidence together. We must formulate the biblical doctrine or theology of the Holy Spirit. That was the church's task and she performed it marvelously.[23]

The church fathers noticed, for example, that although the word for "spirit" is a noun of neuter gender in Greek, the Holy Spirit is always referred to with masculine pronouns. Moreover, his personality is obvious in texts such as John 14:26 (". . . the helper whom the Father will send in my name . . . will teach you all things. . . ."), in the title given to him of Comforter or Advocate, in the ascription of emotions to him (Eph 4:30), in identifying him as one who speaks (Acts 8:29; 1 Tim 4:1), in the actions ascribed to him (2 Thess 2:13), in his being numbered together with the Father and the Son, and so on. If his name "Holy Spirit" or "Holy Wind" is one polarity, all of this evidence of his personality is the other. And the church rightly understood that it had not represented the truth about the Holy Spirit unless it had done justice to both poles: both the highly personal account of his being and work and his distinctive *agency* in the Godhead.[24]

23. Chief among the examples of that effort is Basil's *On the Holy Spirit*, in which he deploys a wide range of biblical evidence to demonstrate the full deity of the Holy Spirit as well as his distinction from the Father and the Son. On the other hand, the development of the doctrine of the Holy Spirit "trailed behind the debate about the Son" precisely because neither in the New Testament nor in early Christian practice was the Holy Spirit as clearly set forth as an object of Christian worship or as one to whom believers prayed. Wilken, *Spirit of Early Christian Thought*, 100–106. Gregory will even argue that "The Old Testament proclaimed the Father openly, and the Son more obscurely. The New manifested the Son and suggested the Deity of the Spirit." *Oration* V, xxvi, 326. Over time the biblical evidence proved more than sufficient, but in this way as well the dogma developed from the practice of the faith. For example, from the beginning the Holy Spirit was named with the Father and the Son in the formula of baptism, and the church confessed that the Spirit had been *sent* as had the Son, and that she was living in the power of the Holy Spirit present with her. Pelikan, *Bach among the Theologians*, 6–7.

24. "Power in action is in fact the basic biblical thought whenever God's Spirit is

The Distinction of Persons

And so it is with the distinction of the three persons within the Godhead. The three persons are the one God, but each of the three persons is distinguished from the other two. It was easy enough for some early Christians to seek to solve the problem posed by one God who is also three by coming to think of the persons as simply the person of the one God in various guises, or the one divine person in three different relations to the world. Sabellianism appeared early on and has reappeared times without number since precisely because it offers a simpler and less confusing explanation of the three-person God. But the church rightly concluded that the data of revelation do not permit such a conclusion. In the first place, the personal names themselves suggest intrinsic or essential distinctions. More than that, the biblical account of God's work in the world proves that there are essential and ineradicable distinctions between the three persons. The incarnation, for example, proved that the persons are not only one God but essentially distinct from one another.

Again we have polarities. The three persons are one God, but the Son, who is God and who created the heavens and the earth, took into union with his person a human nature. He became flesh. The Father did not do that, nor did the Holy Spirit. God the Son is now united to humanity in a way that neither the Father nor the Spirit is. But the incarnate Son, now forever God and man, continues to relate to the Father as his Father and to the Holy Spirit as another with him in the Godhead. In the same way, only the Father sent the Son into the world and, after the Son's ascension to heaven, only the Holy Spirit descended at Pentecost. Clearly, the persons are distinct, essentially and eternally to be distinguished from one another.[25] We may not know why it is that such distinctions exist or in what they consist, but each person is different from the others in ways that explain why each did what he did and does what he does. Again, these issues are never addressed as such in the Bible. Attention is never

mentioned." Packer, *Keep in Step*, 57–59.

25. Calvin, *Institutes*, I, xiii, 17–18. As Calvin then goes on to say, ". . . it is not fitting to suppress the distinction that we observe to be expressed in Scripture. It is this: to the Father is attributed the beginning of activity, and the fountain and wellspring of all things; to the Son, wisdom, counsel, and the ordered disposition of all things; but to the Spirit is assigned the power and efficacy of that activity. . . . Indeed, although the eternity of the Father is also the eternity of the Son and the Spirit . . . nevertheless the observance of an order is not meaningless or superfluous, when the Father is thought of as first, then from him the Son, and finally from both the Spirit."

drawn to the fact that each person plays a distinct role in the economy of salvation and that these distinctions arise from the inter-Trinitarian relationships. But what is revealed, now here, now there, once taken together requires such a conclusion.

This was a further refinement of that equilibrium of truths that make up the doctrine of the Holy Trinity, once again a complex of tension-laden polarities. From the assertions of Holy Scripture, it was clear to the church that the Father, the Son, and the Holy Spirit are together the one God. But it was also clear that, given the role that each assumes in relation to the world, in the works of divine providence and supremely in the work of redemption, we are given to see a reflection of or to get a glimpse into the inner life of the Holy Trinity. That is, the work of the three persons in creation and redemption, God's presence and work in the world—what came to be called "the economy"—is a revelation of the inner life of God in the three persons. As it would later be more succinctly put, the church came to realize that the economic Trinity reveals the immanent, inherent, ontological, or essential Trinity. We observe something of the eternal relationships between Father, Son, and Holy Spirit in the revelation of their respective roles in the salvation of the world. It is not mere happenstance that it was the Father who sent the Son, that it was the Son who came into the world as a man, or that it was the Father and the Son who sent the Holy Spirit. This is the reason why salvation is from the Father through the Son and by the Holy Spirit, and why our response to God's grace is by the Holy Spirit, through the Son, to the Father.[26] Again, none of this is explained in the Bible. No biblical writer teaches us to understand in these terms the relationships of love and mutual commitment that define the inner life of God. Rather, such an understanding results from a faithful effort to do justice to everything the Bible teaches us about Father, Son, and Holy Spirit, a great many relevant statements made now here, now there, but statements impossible to systematize into a unity of truth easily comprehended by the human mind.

The Unity of the Persons in the Divine Life

If the persons are distinct, essentially and eternally distinct, the question of their unity becomes more pressing. How can the three, each necessarily to be distinguished from the others, be the one God? Or put the

26. Letham, *Holy Trinity*, 383.

question another way: Given both the unity of God and the clear distinction of persons, are we to understand that each of the three persons, being together the one true and living God, is therefore a third of God, the whole God being made up of the three together? Do we avoid tritheism by maintaining that the three persons together form the one living and true God? To say that there are three persons does not answer the question of the relation of each of the three to God himself, a question made the more pressing by so much evidence of the intrinsic and eternal distinction between the persons. This was a question that bedeviled discussions of the Holy Trinity in patristic Christianity. How are the three persons, how *can* the three persons be one God? Once again, we might well have expected that question to be asked and answered somewhere in the New Testament, but it is not. Instead, we have typical polarities: there is but one God and the Father is God, the Son is God, and the Holy Spirit is God. Still more, the Father is not the Son or the Spirit, the Son is not the Father or the Spirit, and the Spirit is not the Father or the Son.

The way the church found to do justice to these polarities, to this equilibrium of truths—real unity and real distinctions—was in the doctrine of *perichoresis*, a Greek word that literally means "a going round" or "rotation." The term refers to the mutual indwelling of the persons of the Holy Trinity in one another and in the divine life (cf. John 5:19–30; 10:30, 38; 14:9–11; 17:21).[27] One way of saying this is that the persons of the Godhead mutually indwell one another. Another is to say that each person possesses the entire essence, being, or substance of God, or, as Augustine put it, "God is not less in his parts than in his totality."[28] That is, the divine essence or substance is not divided between the three persons. In a famous account of this *perichoresis*, John of Damascus writes,

> The subsistences dwell and are established firmly in one another. For they are inseparable and cannot part from one another, but keep to their separate courses within one another, without coalescing or mingling, but cleaving to each other. For the Son is in the Father and the Spirit: and the Spirit is in the Father and the Son: and the Father is in the Son and the Spirit, but there is no coalescing or commingling or confusion.[29]

27. "This states that the divine modes of being mutually condition and permeate one another so completely that one is always in the other two and the other two in the one." Barth, *Church Dogmatics*, 1/1:370.

28. Augustine, *Essential Sermons*, 117.4, 197.

29. John of Damascus, *Orthodox Faith*, I, 14.

In this way, far from each being a third of God—and, therefore, none of the persons being himself fully God—each is God himself, the whole God, sharing as each person does the essence or nature of God and the nature of the other two. As Robert Letham explains,

> The doctrine of perichoresis affirms that the three persons of the Trinity occupy, in Gerald Bray's words, the same infinite divine space. Since each is wholly God and fully God, no one person is any greater than any other, while the three together are not greater than any one. Thus, the three mutually indwell each other. This is not an indwelling that submerges the particularities of any of the three. It is dynamic, with living relations.[30]

Colin Gunton adds a further thought.

> The central point about the concept is that it enables theology to preserve both the one and the many in dynamic interrelations. It implies that the three persons of the Trinity exist only in reciprocal eternal relatedness. God is not God apart from the way in which Father, Son, and Holy Spirit in eternity give to and receive from each other what they essentially are.[31]

Such was one way found by the church to confess that each of the divine persons is fully God himself and that the distinction of persons does not threaten the oneness or unity of God. A related principle was expressed by the formula "The external works of God are undivided." From his extended demonstration of the fact that, while the three persons are clearly distinguished from one another, the Bible artlessly and repeatedly attributes the same works to each of the three persons, Augustine draws the conclusion that

> . . . with regard to this three the divine utterances have many ways of saying things about them individually which belong to them all, on account of the indivisible operation of their one and the same substance.[32]

---

30. Letham, *Holy Trinity*, 382.

31. Gunton, *One, Three*, 163–64.

32. Augustine, *Trinity*, I, 4, 84. So it is that all three persons are the Creator of heaven and earth (1 Cor 8:6; Col 1:16; Gen 1:3; Ps 104:30); all three brought to pass the incarnation (John 3:16–17; Heb 10:7; Luke 1:35), the crucifixion (Matt 26:39, 42; Mark 10:45; Heb 9:14), the resurrection (Gal 1:1; John 10:17–18; Rom 8:11), and Pentecost (John 14:25; 15:26; 16:7; Acts 1:8; 2:33); and all three are now at work saving the world (John 10:16, 27–30: Acts 1:8; 4:31; 10:44–47; Eph 2:22).

While the Father sent the Son, the Son became a man, and the Holy Spirit descended upon the Son at his baptism and upon the church at Pentecost, since there is but one God and each person is that one God—and so shares the same nature, knowledge, and purpose—the works of God in the world, however different the role of each person may be, are both the works of each person and of all three of them together. Once again, the Bible never formulates such a principle or provides such analysis, but the distinction of persons and works so clearly taught in some places must be held in tension with the incontestable facts that the same works are attributed here and there to each of the three persons and that the Bible teaches both that each person is himself God and that there is a perfect unity of will and purpose within the divine being. Here belongs Augustine's brilliant demonstration that the life of God is a Trinity of love, love given and love received in endless alternation![33]

These different emphases, one by one, are given their day in the revelation of God in the New Testament and so they found their place in the church's theology of the Holy Trinity. But take the point: the Bible doesn't explicitly teach *perichoresis*; Paul or Peter cannot be quoted as saying that the external works of God are undivided. That is the church's way of summarizing an equilibrium of truths, of respecting the polarities of the biblical revelation of God. It is certainly beyond the ability of any human being, no matter how devout, no matter how learned in the Word of God or the theology of the church, to explain how it is that each of the three persons is himself fully God and that God is all three persons at once. *Perichoresis* is simply the church's confession that she knows it is so, deep and impenetrable mystery as this must remain. Taking the biblical data together, this is what must be confessed about the Holy Trinity.

---

33. "Love cannot exist on its own because it is not a thing or an attribute possessed by a thing. In other words, God cannot be love unless there is something for him to love. But if that something were not part of himself, he would not be perfect. The Bible does not teach us that God needed creation in order to have something to love; if he did, he could not be fully himself without it. So Augustine reasoned that God must be love inside himself." Bray, *Augustine on the Christian Life*, 207. This explains the fundamental place of love in human life and experience: the human being is *homo adorans*. We have been made in the image of the triune God!

The Doctrine of the Holy Trinity

It is in these ways and for these reasons that the Son can say, "Whoever has seen me has seen the Father" (John 14:9), that the Father dwells in the Son and does his works through the Son (14:10), and that it can be said of the Son that "in him all the fullness of God was pleased to dwell" (Col 1:19). Once again, this is not an explanation—in fact it adds mystery on top of mystery—but it is a confession of all those truths that together make up the revelation of the Holy Trinity in the Word of God. The Lord Christ is not part of Yahweh; he *is* Yahweh, as is the Father and the Spirit. It took some years of trial and error to find the best, the most precise, and the least ambiguous way of confessing the truth as it was revealed in its polarities in Holy Scripture, but *perichoresis* is nothing else but a faithful witness to the complex of opposites that make up the biblical revelation of God.[34] It is not difficult to see that, in and of themselves, the various assertions of Holy Scripture concerning the nature of the Holy Trinity—one and three, Father, Son, and Holy Spirit, each person with a different name and emphatically distinguished from the other two, all three often being absorbed in reference to the one God but each in an I-Thou relationship with the others—could easily, as in fact they did, lead to endless misunderstanding. And as Augustine famously observed, no doctrine is more difficult to get right—or easier to mistake—and there is no failure more dangerous than getting it wrong.[35] However, so long as the fullness of biblical revelation is respected, so long as the polarities are identified and each is vigorously maintained, so long as the resulting tension is properly felt and preserved, and so long as the final doctrine or teaching is that characteristic equilibrium of truths, truths that can seem discordant if not virtually the contradiction of one another, we will not go wrong.

The doctrine or theology of the Holy Trinity was the remarkable achievement of the patristic church. No statement or formula of this doctrine was provided in the Bible itself. No one put it in quite this way, of course, but it was the church's respect for the dialectical form of revelation—her recognition that everything the Bible said was true and had to

---

34. "The doctrine of the perichoresis links together in a brilliant way the Threeness and the unity, without reducing the threeness to the unity, or dissolving the unity in the Threeness. The unity of the triunity lies in the eternal perichoresis of the trinitarian persons." Moltmann, *Trinity and the Kingdom*, 175.

35. Augustine, *Trinity*, I, iii, 19.

be represented in the finished portrait of God, no matter the apparent antinomies—that led her inexorably to the confession that every Christian makes today: "One God in three persons, the same in substance and equal in power and glory." She happily confessed what the Bible says about the triune God but also that the truth, or rather the truths about God, each clear enough in itself, form a unity deeply mysterious and incomprehensible to the human mind.

That there is but one God who exists in three persons is certainly paradoxical. To be sure, some have argued that it is not, using the conventional explanation that God is one in one respect and three in another.[36] But, as is acknowledged in the historic formulation of the doctrine of the Holy Trinity, to say that hardly does justice to the unresolved tension between the unity and the distinction of persons. Each of the three persons shares the one divine nature or substance. Each of the three coinheres in each of the others. Each is in and of himself the true God. Candidly, no one knows beyond that simple confession what we are talking about.[37] The formulas used to create a theology that does justice to all that the Bible says about God are confessions, not explanations of the truth concerning the divine life. They do not resolve the tension; indeed, in many ways they draw attention to it. *Perichoresis* is not a biblical term; as defined in the dogma of the Holy Trinity, it is not even explicitly a biblical idea. It is a theological confession based upon dialectical assertions concerning the three persons who, each by himself and all three together, are the one living and true God. In order to do justice to these

36. A brilliant teacher of mine, a man I admire greatly, took this view and argued strenuously against the very notion of paradox in biblical interpretation. He once described paradox as a "charley-horse between the ears." He was unwilling "to let allegedly apparently contradictory Scripture passages remain unsystematized. . . ." Douma, *Presbyterian Philosopher*, 117, 125–29, 192. In my view, while Gordon Clark was absolutely correct to emphasize the comprehensibility of the assertions of Holy Scripture at a certain level, he overestimated our ability to comprehend both the meaning of the biblical and theological terminology (e.g., Father, Son, Spirit, Person) and the interrelations of those assertions, including those regarding the triunity of God. He failed to appreciate to what extent biblical doctrine is a confession rather than an explanation. On this point see Frame, *History of Western Philosophy*, 524–25, 718–25. Later we will have occasion to notice that Dr. Clark's exegetical resolution of another biblical paradox, his effort to systematize seemingly discordant assertions, was also unpersuasive.

37. Edmond Hill summarizes Augustine's concession regarding the choice of the term "person" by which to refer to the three subsistences of the divine substance in this way: "It does not matter very much what word we choose to answer this question with, provided we realize that whatever word we do choose it is a pure convention or label, and does not tell us anything real about the three." "Introduction," in *Trinity*, 52.

apparently contrary affirmations a concept was developed that superbly encapsulates the truth about God but does so by asserting a reality that must remain fundamentally incomprehensible to us. What, after all, do we mean when we say that each of the three persons coinheres in the other two and that all three share the entirety of the divine essence? In saying such things we are seeking to do justice to what we have been told, but we are by no means reducing the divine life to something we can understand. We make no claim that the inner life of the Almighty has been rendered intelligible to us in this way! It seems clear to me that we will *never* penetrate the depths of the divine life. The finite is not capable of the infinite. The nature of the relations between the three persons is not revealed for that reason, nor is it revealable to mere human beings.[38]

The simple fact is once again to be observed that the Bible does not teach us the Holy Trinity, this most fundamental of all its doctrines, in any form that remotely resembles the doctrine of God as it came to be formulated from the data of Holy Scripture. This is what Leonard Hodgson meant when he said that there is no "theology" of the Holy Trinity in the New Testament. None of the vocabulary long employed in the church's confession of the Holy Trinity is biblical: not "Trinity," not "essence" or "substance," not even "person." Certainly not *homoousios*, *taxis*, or *perichoresis*. The terminology of the doctrine of the Holy Trinity was developed precisely as a way of representing the various polarities regarding this or that piece of the Bible's teaching concerning the being of God.[39] Augustine famously admitted that the use of such terms was required so as not to say nothing at all.

---

38. Duncan in Brentnall, *Just a Talker*, 72.

39. According to Hodgson, "Of the ancient creeds of Christendom the so-called Athanasian Creed, the *Quicunque Vult*, is the only one which explicitly and unequivocally states the full Christian doctrine of God. In the Nicene Creed the consubstantiality of the Son with the Father, and the association of the Spirit with them in worship and glory, do not necessarily eliminate every trace of subordinationism. . . . The *Quicunque Vult* leaves no room for such misunderstanding. 'In this Trinity none is afore, or after other: none is greater, or less than another; but the whole three Persons are co-eternal together; and co-equal.'" He continues, "The *Quicunque Vult*, moreover, is the standing refutation of the theory that the doctrine of the Trinity represents the perversion of a simple primitive Christian faith by the intrusion of Greek metaphysics. It shows the truth to be the opposite. The logical outcome of Greek metaphysics . . . was the neo-Platonic worship of undifferentiated unity. The doctrine of the Trinity represents the intrusion into Greek metaphysics of a religious faith based on empirical evidence of Divine revelation which the metaphysics of the time could not assimilate. Philosophy had reached one of those points where its categories were inadequate to

For example, we take the use of *person* for granted, but what the term means in its use in the theology of the Holy Trinity—precisely what an I-Thou relation amounts to in the inner life of the living God—no one can say. As has often been pointed out, God does not consist *of* three persons but exists *in* three persons; so the three are not three parts of God. And it is certainly true that "Three human persons could never be one human being just as the Father, the Son, and the Holy Spirit are one God."[40] It is well to remember that the term itself was a choice, for various reasons thought useful in expressing the force of the biblical data. Such a term was not chosen because anyone knew precisely what a divine person is, or because the divine persons relate to one another in ways that we understand because we are persons ourselves, but because, all in all, it was thought to be virtually the only term at hand to identify the three I-Thou instances of the divine substance or essential nature.[41] Calvin agreed with Augustine that "on account of the poverty of human speech in so great a matter, the word 'hypostasis'[42] had been forced upon us by necessity, not to express what it is, but only not to be silent on how Father, Son, and Holy Spirit are three."[43] No wonder then "the tortuous struggles in the fourth century over terminology."[44]

Important evidence of all of this is the simple fact, which any Christian will confess, that we find it necessary to think separately of the divine unity and God's triple personality. At our best we find ourselves as Gregory Nazianzen found himself.

> No sooner do I conceive of the One than I am illumined by the Splendor of the Three; no sooner do I distinguish them than I

---

include new evidence of the actual world of man's experience. All that the church could do was to embody the certainties of its experience in what, from the point of view of the philosophy of the time, were a series of contradictions, and insist that their acceptance was necessary to salvation." *Doctrine of the Trinity*, 102–3. I would add that the Christian doctrine of the Holy Trinity continues to be the assertion of facts that human philosophy cannot assimilate, no matter its development from the days of neo-Platonism.

40. Genderen and Velema, *Concise Reformed Dogmatics*, 153.

41. Augustine, *Trinity*, VII, iii, 224–30.

42. *Hypostasis* was a Greek term first used for the divine essence or substance, only later for the three persons. The Latin *persona* eventually became the term of choice for the three individual subsistences or individual instances of the divine substance or essence. Muller, *Dictionary of Latin and Greek*, 306–10.

43. Calvin, *Institutes*, I, xiii, 5.

44. Letham, *Holy Trinity*, 295.

am carried back to the One. When I think of any One of the
Three I think of Him as the Whole, and my eyes are filled, and
the greater part of what I am thinking escapes me. I cannot grasp
the greatness of That One so as to attribute a greater greatness to
the Rest. When I contemplate the Three together, I see but one
torch, and cannot divide or measure out the Undivided Light.[45]

We do not find it easy; indeed I suspect we are never able to think of God
as one and three in a single, coherent intuition. We must confess the two
truths about God that are revealed to us in Holy Scripture as we think
about them, one at a time, because they remain for us impossible fully
to harmonize or reconcile in our minds. The reality is greater than our
minds can conceive at once, so we confess the polarities in distinction
from one another or one after the other. We see the pieces because we
cannot see the whole! We believe them both to be true but are incapable
of comprehending them in their unity. It is in this way, as we will see,
that we confess, among many other such antinomies, divine sovereignty
and human responsibility. To see a perfect unity of such things would
require us to have an infinite mind. We can confess the consistency of
these discordant affirmations with one another, as we do in the classic
formulation of the doctrine of the Holy Trinity, but they remain discordant and the doctrine remains tension-laden. We do not consider this a
fault. It is the way mere creatures must know the truth that we are incapable of comprehending in its profound complexity, in its entirety, and
in its unity. We can confess the truths that are asserted in the Bible, even
when we cannot comprehend how each of the truths concerning God
relates to one another in perfect harmony. When a finite person seeks
understanding of an infinite life, it must be so: thus far and no further!
The biblical revelation of God is and must be accommodated to human
capacities. Acknowledging this fact, the church's best efforts were always
only to discover how best to confess the truth she had been given concerning the living God, not to explain his nature, still less to imagine
that mere creatures were somehow able to penetrate the divine life and

45. Gregory Nazianzen, *Holy Baptism*, XLI, 375. The translator paraphrases the
second sentence cited above as: "If I think of One Blessed Person, the other Two are
not in my mind, and so the greater part of God escapes me." In Gregory's *Second
Theological Oration* he makes the similar observation that "the Divine Nature cannot
be apprehended by human reason, and that we cannot even represent to ourselves all
its greatness." XI, 292.

explore its secrets. The Almighty has graciously taken us to the limits of our comprehension, severe as those limits are and must remain.

Finally, observing the manner in which the Holy Trinity is revealed to us in the Word of God, it should not surprise us if much else of what we are taught is revealed in the same way: in terms of polarities in equilibrium, in paradoxes beyond our power to resolve. Just as this deepest of all mysteries is the foundation of everything else that is taught us in the Bible and underlies the entire plan of our salvation, so its manner of revelation is paradigmatic. It is the archetype of biblical revelation, the outstanding example of how the faith is communicated to us in Holy Scripture.

4

The Incarnation

He was baptized as man—but he remitted sins as God. . . . He was tempted
as Man, but he conquered as God. . . . He hungered—but he fed thousands.
. . . He thirsted—but he cried, If any man thirst let him come unto me and
drink. . . . He was wearied, but he is the rest of them that are weary and heavy-
laden. He was heavy with sleep, but he walked lightly over the sea. . . . He pays
tribute, but it is out of a fish; yea he is the king of those who demanded it. . . .
He prays, but he hears prayer. He weeps, but he causes tears to cease.

—GREGORY NAZIANZEN

AT THE HEART OF the Christian faith is the claim that God the Son, the
second person of the Holy Trinity, came into the world to give his life a
ransom for many (Mark 10:45). To do this, since God, being eternal and
life itself, cannot die, he had first to add to his person a human nature.
While remaining in every respect eternal God, he was born to his virgin
mother and lived a human life, becoming like his brothers in every way
except for sin (Heb 2:17; 4:15). The term used in Christian theology to
describe the Son of God's becoming a man is *incarnation*, the "in-flesh-
ment" of God, with "flesh" (*sarx* in Greek, *caro* in Latin) being used, as it
sometimes is in the New Testament, for what we today would call human
nature, that constellation of attributes that make up our inherent character or constitution and so define the human being. It was in this way, by
God becoming man, that it was made possible for the Lord Christ to offer

a sufficient sacrifice for our sins (Matt 1:21; Gal 4:4–5), to become our high priest, able to help us in our weakness (Heb 5:1–10), and to conquer death on our behalf (1 Cor 15:20–21).

> In short, since neither as God alone could he feel death, or as man alone could he overcome it, he coupled human nature with divine that to atone for sin he might submit the weakness of the one to death; and that, wrestling with death by the power of the other nature, he might win victory for us.[1]

The Bible teaches the incarnation in many different ways. There are the great prophesies of God's future appearance in the world as a man found in such passages as Isa 9:2–7 (the child to be born will be called "Mighty God"); Jer 23:5–6 (the heir of David, the righteous branch will be called "Yahweh is our righteousness"); Dan 7:13–14 (the son of man came *with the clouds of heaven*, a phrase that in its many uses in the Hebrew Bible is always in reference to God); and a number of others that consolidate a great many other statements forecasting the coming of a redeemer who would save his people and establish the kingdom of God. Throughout the New Testament such prophesies are said to have been fulfilled in the appearance of Jesus of Nazareth. The promise of the coming of this deliverer was ubiquitous in the ancient Scriptures and dominates their proclamation of the consummation of salvation. So it is hardly surprising that the expectation of his coming was firmly fixed in the Jewish mind and heart in the Lord's own day, however little many understood who and what the Messiah would be when he appeared.

Further, in the New Testament there are direct assertions that Jesus Christ is God incarnate in such memorable passages as John 1:1–12; Gal 4:4–5; Phil 2:5–11; and Col 1:15–20. In addition, Jesus of Nazareth is repeatedly identified as Yahweh, either as himself the actor in important events in Israel's history (e.g., Jude 5; 1 Cor 10:1–5; Heb 11:26) or by the application of specific texts to Jesus that in their original context referred explicitly to Yahweh (John 12:37–41; Rom 10:13; Phil 2:10). In fact there is throughout the New Testament what David Wells describes as the "complete linguistic identification of Christ with Yahweh."[2] For example:

1. Calvin, *Institutes*, II, xii, 3. Cf. Francis Turretin's more elaborate demonstration of the necessity of the incarnation for the salvation of sinners. *Institutes*, XIII, iii, 18, 2:302–3.

2. Wells, *Person of Christ*, 64–65. The identification of Jesus with Yahweh, in his presence and action throughout the ancient epoch, is a particular emphasis of the Letter to the Hebrews, an emphasis now receiving new attention. Rayburn, *Yesterday,*

Jesus says of himself that he is the alpha and omega, the first and the last (Rev 1:8), a phrase taken from Yahweh's description of himself in Isa 41:4 and 44:6; and he claims that he alone is the Savior, the way to God (John 14:6; cf. Acts 4:12), repeating what Yahweh says of himself in Isa 45:22. Such examples could be multiplied to great length.

Unsurprisingly, we find throughout the New Testament a host of *obiter dicta* that either assume or directly assert the pre-existence of Jesus Christ, his *coming* into the world, his equality with God even as a human being, and his possessing divine powers and prerogatives. Jesus does what God does: in creation and providence (Heb 1:2–3), as the lawgiver (Mark 2:27–28), and in salvation: whether election (John 13:18), calling (John 10:16), the forgiving of sins (Mark 2:5–7), or the granting of eternal life (John 5:21; 10:28). This abundance of evidence explains why the faith of the Christian church has always rested firmly on the historical fact of the incarnation. The New Testament—its history and its doctrine—is inexplicable without it.

The incarnation *is* the Christian faith and explains why the Gospels are a unique sort of biography, a biography in which believers find the meaning and destiny of their own lives in the personal history of Jesus Christ. The good news, we discover, is the account of an extraordinary person and his utterly exceptional life: his words and deeds, his death for sin, and his resurrection from the dead. The incarnation explains why the gospel is first and foremost not a "way"—a set of teachings about how one ought to think and live—but instead the proclamation of great events that happened in the world some two thousand years ago, together with the consequences of those events. The Christian "way" is simply the inevitable, rational response to this history (Rom 12:1–2).[3] In this the Christian faith is unique. It is the proclamation that God himself, moved by an impossibly great love, entered the world as a man to do for us what only God could do, but could do only as also a man. No wonder then that Christians throughout history have confidently and unashamedly proclaimed that Jesus Christ, the incarnate God, is the only name under heaven by which we must be saved and that by believing in him

---

Today, and Forever, 105, 219–31, 264–65.

3. "For Paul the true worship is rational not in the sense of being consistent with the natural rationality of man . . . but in the sense of being consistent with a proper understanding of the truth of God revealed in Jesus Christ." Cranfield, *Epistle to the Romans*, 2:604–5.

and following him human beings will be saved from sin and all of sin's consequences, now and forever.

> And is it true? And is it true,
> This most tremendous tale of all,
> Seen in a stained-glass window's hue
> A baby in an ox's stall?
> The Maker of the stars and sea
> Become a child on earth for me?
> —John Betjeman, *Christmas*

True indeed and the most beautiful, breathtaking, and consequential of all truth!

I heard John Stott preach only once in person and he was by that time an old man. It was a magnificent address on the missionary emphasis of the entire Bible, but what I remember most is the encomium to Jesus Christ that punctuated the sermon. He reminded us that the Lord Jesus has no rivals; he is utterly unique. He is the Final One because he is the Only One. Historians, he said, speak of Alexander the Great, or Charles the Great, or Napoleon the Great, but never Jesus the Great, because there has always been but one Jesus Christ. He had no precursors and he has never had and never will have a successor. Of course not, if indeed he is God come in the flesh!

The Paradox of the Revelation of the Person of Jesus Christ

But the place the incarnation occupies at the heart of the Christian faith and message makes only the more striking the fact that we are never given anywhere in the New Testament a theological analysis or systematic explanation of the incarnation. After all, never in all human history has there been a more stupendous claim: that God entered the world he had made, the world he rules, the world he will someday judge, entered it incognito as a man to save the world from the sin and death into which it had so willingly pitched itself. If ever there were an event crying out for thorough explanation, it is the incarnation of God! But we are never taught how to define the incarnation, nor with what terms accurately to describe it, and none of the obvious questions it raises are asked or answered. We are taught that God became man in such passages as John 1 and Phil 2 and scattered throughout the New Testament is manifold evidence of both the Lord Christ's humanity and his deity. In the same way that we learn that God is one and that God is Father, Son, and Holy Spirit, we learn that Jesus of Nazareth is eternal God, the Creator of heaven and earth and the Judge of all mankind, *and* a true and authentic human being, a human being as we are human beings, except for sin. But *how* this one person is at one and the same time both God and man or what it means to say that a man could be at the same time the Lord of Hosts is never explained. How we are to understand what precisely happened in the incarnation we are never told. The mystery, impenetrable as it is, *is never even explicitly acknowledged.*

That a single person is both God and man is certainly a paradox! God and man are hardly the same thing! One is eternal; the other is mortal. One has existed forever; the other began to be at a specific point in time: indeed, when Augustus ruled the Roman Empire, Quirinius was governor of Syria, and Herod, near the end of his long reign, was Rome's client king in Judea. One stands above human history; one is firmly situated within it. One is the Creator; the other a creature. One is almighty; the other subject to all the weaknesses of human life. One is omnipresent; the other limited to one small place at a time and must travel from that place to be in some other. One is omniscient; the other ignorant of most things (Mark 5:30; 9:21). One is resplendent in glory that no man has seen or can see; the other is so little possessed of glory that he can be surrounded by crowds of other human beings—pious and impious alike—who never suspect that this person is anything other than a human being like themselves. One cannot die; the other did. How are we to believe that *the same person* is all these contraries at the same time; that he contains within himself these dramatic contradictions?

The Danish philosopher Sören Kierkegaard described the incarnation as "the absolute paradox," a mystery that is beyond the power of human reason to comprehend, certainly to reduce to an explanation intelligible to the human mind. Every human being, no matter his education or the power of her intellect, must accept by faith that God became man because it is impossible to justify this assertion in any other way than by the authority of the Word of God, which repeatedly and emphatically teaches us that God the Son became man for the salvation of the world. No chain of reasoning, however brilliant, could lead us to such a conclusion. We would be seeking to prove something we cannot ourselves understand! But with rare insight Kierkegaard argued that the paradoxical nature of the incarnation is evidence of its truth! Indeed, such a profound mystery is precisely what we should expect in the revelation of the Almighty to man and, all the more, in this utterly unprecedented intervention by God himself on our behalf. However human beings may be offended that it took nothing less than the incarnation of God to rescue them from the fate they deserve, however unwilling they may be to admit that nothing less than God's great stoop down to earth would avail to rescue sinful human beings from themselves, no one who knows the pride of the human heart and the terrible guilt and the deceiving power of human sin is surprised that our deliverance should have required the greatest thing that ever happened in the world. Nor will he or she be surprised that we little and sinful human beings find this thing utterly baffling![4]

The New Testament bears repeated witness to the struggle of many to come to terms with what the Christians were claiming: that the carpenter from Nazareth was the everlasting God! Any Jew could be forgiven for thinking such a claim outrageous. The one thing every Jew knew was that God is not a human being; the Creator is not a creature! Even his disciples, who came only haltingly to a firm and unwavering conviction that Jesus was the Messiah, whose coming the prophets had foretold and for which the Jews had waited for centuries, seem not to have understood that there had been an incarnation until confronted with the resurrection of the Lord. There is no unequivocal declaration of Christ's deity by any disciple prior to his resurrection. His disciples were ready to say that Jesus *came from* God, but not that he *is* God (Matt 8:27; John 16:30).

In a remarkable passage in his work *On the Trinity*, Hilary, the fourth-century father, asks how it was possible for Thomas, a faithful Jew, accustomed to praying the *Shema*—"Hear, O Israel: The Lord our God, the Lord is One"—to cry out to Jesus, the man standing before him, "My Lord and my God!" It was, Hilary explains, "because, in the light of the Resurrection, the whole mystery of the faith had become visible to the Apostle." In other words, it was the resurrection that convinced him that Jesus was not simply the Messiah but God himself, the one and only God. "No longer need he fear that such a confession as his was the proclamation of a second God, a treason against the unity of the Divine nature. . . ."[5] Even though the Lord Jesus had said a number of things that upon later reflection were rightly taken to be assertions of his deity, the obstacle

4. On Kierkegaard regarding the paradoxicality of the incarnation see Evans, *Why Christian Faith*, 104–12, 130–35.

5. Hilary, *On the Trinity*, VII, 12, 122.

to believing that a human being, no matter how extraordinary, could be Yahweh himself was so great for the devout Jewish mind that nothing short of the paradigm-shattering event of his resurrection from the dead could open their minds to the reality of both the Holy Trinity and the incarnation.

Jesus had repeatedly claimed for himself an utterly unprecedented intimacy, mutual understanding, and shared purpose, power, and authority with God. He said things about his relationship to "the Father"— always in the Lord's usage an unmistakable reference to God—that had never been said before by any man and would not be said by any Christian thereafter. These were not statements that could be made by a mere man without blasphemy (John 5:19–23, 26–27; 6:38, 41–42, 62). He said on many occasions that he had been with his Father prior to his appearance on earth, that he had existed before he was born in Bethlehem. He said repeatedly that he *had come* from heaven to earth (John 8:38, 42, 58). These were claims the Jews understandably regarded as blasphemous. So much was his life a mirror of the life of the Father that he claimed nothing less than that, as Augustine put it, in his life "the invisible one was made visible" (John 14:9–11).[6] Indeed, Jesus did not hesitate to claim for himself the divine name, "I Am" (John 8:58),[7] or that he possessed the glory of God (John 17:5). It was the resurrection of the Lord that made the truth of these stupendous claims—still lacking any systematic analysis—not only plausible but irrefutable.

Religious Faith and Theological Dogma

As had been the case with the revelation of the triunity of God, so it was with that of the incarnation: the religious faith came first; the dogma, the doctrinal definition, came later. The fact that Jesus Christ, the man from Galilee, is the living God lies face up on almost every page of the New Testament, written as it was after the fact. But those books were also written after their authors knew full well the difficulties the incarnation posed to both the Jewish and the Greco-Roman mind. Surely, or so we think, we might have expected some helpful analysis of the claim being made that Jesus is God incarnate. But how we are to understand the

---

6. Augustine, *Essential Sermons*, 190.2, 252.

7. "In conformity with John's Prologue, Jesus takes to himself one of the most sacred of divine expressions of self-reference. . . ." Carson, *Gospel According to John*, 358.

incarnation, confess the historical and theological fact of it, formulate the meaning of this stupendous assertion in a manner both accurate and spiritually helpful, and define the boundaries of our knowledge of Jesus Christ the God/man was not the work of the apostles but the hard work of devout intellect through the several centuries that followed the Lord's resurrection. In this way the development of the doctrines of the Holy Trinity and the incarnation proceeded in tandem. To formulate the doctrine of the Holy Trinity required an increasingly biblically sophisticated confession that Jesus Christ is God, the Son of the Father. To formulate the doctrine of the incarnation required the confession, with equal biblical sophistication, that the Father had sent the Son into the world to live and then to die as a human being.

The fact that we do not find such analysis, definition, or explanation—for that matter, that we do not find even the acknowledgement of the inexplicable mystery that is the incarnation of God the Son—is proof, if proof were needed, that the same method of revelation we have already encountered with respect to the Holy Trinity is found here as well. An event so essential to the gospel, so much the presupposition of everything Christians believe about Jesus Christ and salvation by faith in him, deserves, we might have supposed, the most explicit attention and careful definition, together with answers furnished to the many questions that could easily be anticipated from both inquiring and hostile minds. But instead, beside the bare confession that the Word became flesh, we only read here that he is God and there that he is man; here he is the Creator and there he is the creature; here he is Adam's maker and there he is Adam's son (John 1:1–3; Luke 3:23–38).

Collecting the data, what we find is the typically dialectical form of revelation: polarities confronting one another across a number of continua of truth. Here we find Jesus ignorant of many things: whether a tree was bearing fruit, who it was that had touched him, or when he will return to earth and bring history to its consummation. There we find him asserting that he existed before Abraham and that the Father sent him into this world. Here we find him tired and thirsty, sitting beside a well in Samaria. There we find him saying that he himself will one day bring every human life into judgment. Here we find him terrified, the sweat pouring from his face at the prospect of the suffering he was about to endure. There we find even the demons acknowledging his divine authority and obeying his commands. Here he is stymied by the unbelief of those whom he had come to save. There he summons men and women to faith in him by the mere utterance of a word. Here he dies in agony on a Roman gibbet. There he claims authority to forgive sins, something Moses and Elijah never imagined doing. Here he is mocked and belittled. There he is worshipped as God himself. Gregory Nazianzen famously summarized the paradoxical nature of the revelation of Jesus Christ in the Gospels.

> He was baptized as man—but he remitted sins as God. . . . He was tempted as Man, but he conquered as God. . . . He hungered—but he fed thousands. . . . He thirsted—but he cried, If any man thirst let him come unto me and drink. . . . He was wearied, but he is the rest of them that are weary and heavy-laden. He was heavy with sleep, but he walked lightly over the sea. . . . He pays tribute, but it is out of a fish; yea, he is the king of those who demanded it. . . . He prays, but he hears prayer. He weeps, but he causes tears to cease. He asks where Lazarus was laid, for he was Man; but he raises Lazarus, for he was God. He is sold, and very cheap, for it is only for thirty pieces of silver; but he redeems the world, and that at a great price, for the price was his blood. As a sheep he is led to the slaughter, but he is the shepherd of Israel, and now of the whole world also. . . . As a lamb he is silent, yet he is the Word. . . . He is bruised and wounded, but he healeth every disease and every infirmity. He is lifted up and nailed to the tree, but by the tree of life he restoreth. . . . He lays down his life, but he has power to take it again. . . . He dies, but he gives life, and by his death he destroys death.[8]

The narrative of the Lord's life leaves us in no doubt of the Lord's genuine humanity or that those who knew him or who simply observed him never doubted that he was a human being. He looked the part; he behaved as human beings behave; in every obvious way he lived a human life. The Lord himself spoke of his body, bones, blood, head, hands and feet (Mark 14:8, 24; Luke 7:44–45; 22:20; 24:39). The Gospels attribute to him the full range of human emotion: pity and compassion, joy, sorrow, annoyance, surprise, anger, turmoil, disappointment, and fear (e.g., Mark 1:41; 3:5; 6:6; 8:2; 9:19; 10:4; Luke 10:21). Given the abundance of evidence, we may fairly surmise that, like any other human being, he was personally acquainted with confusion and enlightenment, frustration and satisfaction, and ignorance being overcome by discovery and learning. The evidence provided in the Gospels allows us safely to multiply

---

8. Gregory Nazianzen, *Third Theological Oration*, xx, 308–9.

in our minds the characteristic features of his human life beyond those specifically mentioned. Christians almost instinctively hesitate to do this because, being God as they know him to be and the divine Savior they rightly revere, it seems somehow unworthy of him to call attention to the indelicacies of his humanity. But, no matter how unwelcome such thoughts may be to believers, the Gospels' assertion and illustration of the perfectly ordinary features of his humanity being what they are, we can safely extrapolate from their narratives the details they do not mention. As a baby he was suckled at his mother's breast. As a child he only gradually learned to speak. No doubt he bore some resemblance to his mother and then to his brothers and sisters. He would have had to deal with a headache or toothache in days before aspirin and anesthesia. No doubt he shared with us the experience of being sick to his stomach and vomiting. He had dreams when he was asleep and, perhaps especially when he was a child, nightmares.[9] Obviously he had need of the chamber pot or the latrine. He must have belched and suffered from diarrhea, sore feet, and assorted aches and pains. Since we know he was tempted as we are, no doubt some of those temptations were sexual. He laughed at funny jokes and probably groaned at puns as human beings always have. In whatever ways sinlessness must have changed his everyday life—a fascinating question but one the Bible passes over in silence—in every respect in which it could be, his was an ordinary human life. Indeed, it remains a human life! What do you suppose the Lord eats and drinks in heaven? I am famous in my congregation for believing that he drinks no coffee, such is his fondness for iced tea! In any case the Gospels abound in the artless acknowledgment of the Lord's essential humanity (Mark 7:24).

On the other hand, Jesus commanded the winds in his own name and subjected them to his own authority. Unlike the apostles (Acts 10:25; 14:14–15), the Lord Jesus never declined the worship that men offered him. He considered himself the same object of faith as God himself (John 14:1). He didn't hesitate to claim a relationship with his Father that far transcended any claim made before by any prophet of Israel: "The Father is in me and I am in the Father" (John 10:38). In the context of the long march of the grace of God, as that story had unfolded in Holy Scripture from its beginning, for a man to claim to be the Savior of the world, the bringer of the kingdom of God, the sanctifier of sinners, the head of the

9. We know that he was subject to terror on one occasion, why not then on others? "Those who pretend the Son of God was immune from human passions do not truly and seriously acknowledge Him as a man." Calvin, *Harmony of the Gospels*, 3:147.

church, the Judge of all men, and to be himself the only way to heaven was to claim the powers and prerogatives of God himself! So it is that every biblically minded believer accepts the incarnation to mean

> That the eternal Son of God, who is and remains true and eternal God, took to himself, through the working of the Holy Spirit, from the flesh and blood of the virgin Mary, a truly human nature so that he might become David's true descendant, like his brothers in every way except for sin.[10]

But to say that Jesus of Nazareth was and is both God and man— clearly as that fact is either assumed, positively declared, or confirmed by a mountain of evidence in the New Testament—is hardly to explain the incarnation.[11] It isn't even to state the doctrine in a form that helps believers to know at one and the same time what is being asserted and what is not. The fact is the entire personal history of the Lord Jesus, from his conception in the womb of his virgin mother to his ascension to the Right Hand, is shrouded in the deepest mystery. We are taught that as a man he learned many things and so became a merciful and faithful high priest (Heb 2:17–18; 5:8–9). What did he learn, how did he learn it, and when did he learn it? When did he learn as a boy, or as a young man, that he is God the Son? If he were a true human being, he did not know that, could not have known that until he was old enough and intellectually mature enough to comprehend what such an identity actually meant! He must have gained understanding as he spoke with his parents of the circumstances of his birth, as he heard the Scriptures read in the synagogue or recited at home, and as he meditated himself on the prophesies of the coming deliverer. As a prophet he may have received revelation directly. When did he know that he would die for sinners and rise again? We are not told. Precocious as he was, how much more quickly did he learn, how much more fully did he understand because he was without sin (Luke 2:47)? But as God he knew everything already and Jesus is both God and man. How does the Omniscient One learn what he does not already

10. Heidelberg Catechism, question and answer 35 (the translation adopted by the Christian Reformed Church in 1975, revised in 1988).

11. "Everything that is human about Christ he shares with us as the second person of the Trinity, but in the secret recesses of his divine nature he remains, along with the Father and the Holy Spirit, incomprehensible to mortal minds. As Augustine expressed it: 'This is the way. Walk in humility so that you may come to eternity. Christ as God is the country to which we are going; Christ as man is the way by which we get there.'" Bray, *Augustine on the Christian Life*, 81 (citing sermon 123.2).

know? We might at least have expected that such profound mystery might have been openly acknowledged by the Lord or by his apostles, but we don't find even that.

Upon the resurrection of the Lord the apostles came to understand that he is nothing less than incarnate God—would that we had a record of the conversations between Jesus and his disciples during the forty days!— but, if they didn't already, they would soon realize that the incarnation was to become the principal objection to the Christian faith.[12] To believe that the destiny of the human race hangs upon the doings of an amateur Jewish rabbi, who was born and lived his entire life in a backwater of the Roman Empire, and who was executed as an insurrectionist by the Roman state, was always going to be a hard sell. It would be something akin to people hearing today that the Savior of the world had been born in some unheard-of village in Afghanistan, lived a short life as an itinerant guru, and then had been executed as a terrorist outside Kabul. All of that is difficult enough to credit. But then to claim that this individual, who during his entire life was invisible to virtually the whole world and to all its great men, is nothing less than the Living God, the Creator and Sovereign of heaven and earth and the Judge of all men, was inevitably going to produce, as Paul admitted it did produce, either laughter or outrage.

Anyone could have seen that the plausibility of the incarnation was, therefore, essential to the fortunes of the gospel. But, however obvious the necessity may seem to us, neither the Lord nor his apostles thought it necessary to provide the world with a formal and authoritative analysis *or* defense of the incarnation. For that matter, they never even supplied a formal definition of this most important of all developments in the history of the world. The data alone would have to suffice, data that predictably consisted of a large collection of discordant and unsystematized assertions. It would be the church's task to collate the data and describe the result in terms that took us as far as the evidence allowed and no further. That she eventually formulated a definition of such perfection concerning an article of faith so intrinsically complicated yet so fundamental to Christian faith and life, a definition that has successfully stood

12. For example, from his reading of the New Testament Celsus had realized that the incarnation was the distinctive feature of Christianity, and so his attack on the new faith was an attempt to disprove it. His argument depended upon precisely those predictable confusions that the incarnation could be expected to provoke. "What is the purpose of such a descent on the part of God? Was it in order to learn what was going on among men? Doesn't God know everything?" Wilken, *Spirit of Early Christian Thought*, 10.

the test of nearly two millennia of concentrated reflection and hostile criticism, must represent one of if not the greatest achievement of intellectual endeavor in the history of the world.

Edward Irving, the early-nineteenth-century Scottish preacher and theologian, was famous for his captivating rhetorical brilliance—powerful oratory that attracted immense congregations to hear him—for some theological eccentricities, for his love of God, and for the holiness of his life. No less than Robert Murray McCheyne said of Irving upon his death in 1834, "I look back upon him with awe, as on the saints and martyrs of old."[13] In one of his little classics, Alexander Whyte quotes Edward Irving saying apropos the Christology of the *Westminster Shorter Catechism*,

> "I would not give the truth expressed in these words of the Catechism, 'Two distinct natures and one person forever,' for all the truths that by human language have ever been expressed. I would rather have been the humblest defender of this truth in the four Oecumenical Councils than have been the greatest reformer in the Church, the father of the covenant, or the procurer of the English Constitution."[14]

The Two Natures

However easily the words roll off our tongue, "two natures and one person forever," the questions come thick and fast because they are obvious and inevitable. How did, how could deity and humanity dwell together in the same person without the alteration of each into something else? Was Jesus, therefore, two persons, not one? The Scriptures never refer to him in the plural. It is the same Jesus to whom both human and divine characteristics are attributed. Did God surrender his deity in some fashion or respect or, in order to accommodate his deity to his humanity, did he elevate his humanity, becoming something akin to an ancient titan or a modern superman? Were the natures thus merged into a third thing, neither completely God nor ordinary man? Such views appeared early on and have often appeared since. That a great many Christians today, Christians who ought to know better, actually do think of the man Jesus

13. Bonar, *Memoirs and Remains*, 35.
14. Whyte, *Commentary on the Shorter Catechism*, 51.

Christ as a kind of superman is proof enough that such misunderstandings were inevitable.[15]

Or did the natures alternate, only one asserting itself at a time in the life of the Lord? Of the two natures, which exercised the greater influence? In the Gospels we encounter the Lord almost exclusively as a man: a prophet, to be sure, as were the prophets before him, a worker of miracles, as were Moses and Elijah, but definitely a human being; and in most respects an ordinary human being: a walking, talking, eating, sleeping, sometimes happy, sometimes sad human being. In many ways the Bible makes clear that it is essential to the proclamation of the gospel that "there is one God, and there is one mediator between God and men, *the man* Christ Jesus . . ." (1 Tim 2:5). Only three of his disciples ever beheld something of his divine glory and they only once. Where was the invisible God who is the second person of the Holy Trinity throughout the Lord's life on earth, and what was he doing? If Jesus of Nazareth was that *he*, where was that *he*? Had God somehow become captive to the limitations of human life?

It is clear in the New Testament that the church was convinced from the beginning that Jesus was both God and man. That assertion is explicitly made in the New Testament and then confirmed by a vast array of supporting evidence. The strength of the apostolic church's conviction was demonstrated by the fact that while almost immediately, as could have been predicted, the very idea of incarnation struck many as simply incoherent and impossible, in the earliest period of reflection on the incarnation the church disposed quite easily of views that either denied his human nature (Docetism or Marcionism) or denied his deity (whether professing Christians such as the Ebionites or the general run of unbelievers who encountered the Christian message). But from that point onward the search for understanding became increasingly complex as further questions were raised and as the biblical material was weighed, compared, consolidated, and organized.

B. B. Warfield summarized the halting progress of the development of the church's doctrine of the incarnation, the search for an adequate formulation of what Warfield called the church's "vital faith," in this way.

---

15. An accessible but learned survey of the various false steps taken on the way to Chalcedon and the gradual clarity that emerged as one after another was subjected to examination in light of the evidence of Holy Scripture is found in Macleod, *Person of Christ*, 155–88.

To the onlooker from this distance of time, the main line of progress of the debate takes on an odd appearance of a steady zigzag advance. Arising out of the embers of the Arian controversy, there is first vigorously asserted, over against the reduction of our Lord to the dimensions of a creature, the pure deity of his spiritual nature (Apollinarianism); by this there is at once provoked, in the interests of our Lord's humanity, the equally vigorous assertion of the completeness of his human nature as the bearer of his deity (Nestorianism); this in turn provokes, in the interests of the oneness of his person, an equally vigorous assertion of the conjunction of these two natures in a single individuum (Eutychianism): from all of which there gradually emerges at last, by a series of corrections, the balanced statement of Chalcedon, recognizing at once in its 'without confusion, without conversion, eternally and inseparably' the union in the Person of Christ of a complete deity and a complete humanity, constituting a single person without prejudice to the continued integrity of either nature. The pendulum of thought had swung back and forth in ever-decreasing arcs, until at last it found rest along the line of action of the fundamental force. Out of the continuous controversy of a century there issued a balanced statement in which all the elements of the biblical representation were taken up and combined.[16]

That was the church's task and achievement: to take up into an accurate summary or definition of the person of Jesus Christ "all the elements of the biblical representation." It was hardly a simple task. While it may seem straightforward to confess that Jesus Christ is both God and man, without biblical analysis to provide guidance, simply to confess a mystery so profound was to invite errors from every side. And, predictably, they surfaced in those days in precisely the same way they continue to surface in our own. If Christ is God, how could he say that he could do nothing by himself or that his Father is greater than he (John 14:28)? How could he claim to have been abandoned by God on the cross? How could he say after his resurrection that he was returning "to my God" (John 20:17)? Was he not in these ways distinguishing himself from God? Jesus repeatedly represented himself as the Father's servant, as having come into the world to do his Father's will, to fulfill the assignment with which he had been entrusted. In what guise was the Lord speaking: as God the Son, as

---

16. Warfield, "'Two Natures,'" 216–17.

the man Jesus, or as both?[17] Is the Son, as the servant of the Father, therefore inferior to the Father? This was a question with vast implications for an understanding of both the Holy Trinity and the incarnation. But the Bible never answers it. It can only be answered by first identifying and then respecting the equilibrium of truths, paradoxical as they are, that together describe Jesus of Nazareth in Holy Scripture.

How can human ignorance, such ignorance as Jesus confesses in regard to himself on several occasions, coexist with omniscience in the same person? How can weakness and omnipotence be ascribed to the same person at the same time? Did the Lord retain his divine status once he had become a man? There have been some throughout the ages who have denied that he did. They argued that the Lord "emptied himself" of his divine life when he became a man. But Thomas certainly didn't think he had! Nor did Paul, who taught that all the fullness of God was pleased to dwell *bodily* in Jesus (Col 2:9). Rather, taking all the evidence together, we are required to believe that during his earthly life, while the Lord's divine nature was largely hidden, in no way did he cease to be God above all. On the other hand, there were those who argued that Jesus wasn't divine until at some point in his life, perhaps at his baptism, the deity came upon him. But it is clear in the Bible that God became man; no man has ever become God. Some texts explicitly declare that he was Mighty God at his birth and that Jesus himself, though at the time known by another name, delivered his people from bondage in Egypt during the days of Moses.

We have a superabundance of evidence that Jesus is both true God and true man, but Holy Scripture makes no effort to explain how these two natures coexist in a single person. Indeed, though on a few occasions it uses terminology somewhat similar to what would later become standard (Phil 2:6; Rom 1:3), it doesn't anywhere define what is meant by a *nature*. It certainly never tells us how to relate a nature to a person or explains how one person might have two natures. Indeed, a veil is drawn so completely over the inner psychology of the Lord that *we are given not so much as a single hint of how he experienced in his own life the interaction of the two natures.* We are given no help to understand how the same person could know everything and be ignorant of many things.

17. The Athanasian Creed includes the article, "Equal to the Father, as touching his Godhead: and inferior to the Father as touching his Manhood" (verse 33). Such a statement, however obviously true, hardly accounts for every one of the Lord's remarks or the additional data in the rest of the New Testament.

What in the world was going on in Christ's head? As a man he had a mind but then as God he also had what we can only describe as a thinking life. God is represented throughout Holy Scripture as one who has thoughts, however far above our own. A human nature, therefore, being the constitution of the human being, certainly includes the mind. But a saintly man such as Apollinaris can be forgiven for thinking:

> The presence of two minds and two wills would have produced hopeless incoherence. . . . "Two separate principles of mind and will cannot dwell together without one striving against the other"; "such a subject would be in a state of perpetual turmoil, distracted by the conflicting wishes of the elements of which it consists."[18]

But, for all the errors that he was rightly attempting to avoid, Apollinaris thus concluded that Jesus Christ must not be fully "man, though like man; for he is not consubstantial with man in the most important element."[19] In Apollinaris's view the Lord is "a divine spirit united to flesh . . . a mean between God and man, neither wholly man nor wholly God, but a combination of God and man."[20] That is, Christ had a body, but not a human mind. He was only partly human.

Gregory of Nazianzus was perfectly right to reject this interpretation of the incarnation.

> But if he has a soul, and yet is without a mind, how is he man, for man is not a mindless animal? . . . But, says such an one, the Godhead took the place of the human intellect. How does this touch me? For Godhead joined to flesh alone is not man, nor to soul alone, nor to both apart from intellect, which is the most essential part of man. Keep then the whole man, and mingle Godhead therewith, that you may benefit me in my completeness.[21]

18. Macleod, *Person of Christ*, 158. Macleod is citing Raven, *Apollinarianism*, 182, 184.

19. Raven, *Apollinarianism*, 188. "Our confession is not that the Logos of God sojourned in a holy man as happened to the prophets: but that the very Logos became flesh, not assuming a human mind, a mind changeable and the prey of filthy thoughts but being Himself divine mind, changeless, heavenly" 184.

20. Raven, *Apollinarianism*, 204.

21. Gregory Nazianzen, *First Letter*, 440. A similar error was made by the Monothelites, who proposed that Christ had but one will. The Church recognized that the Monothelites had effectively denied the true humanity of Christ as surely as had the Apollonarians. A human being makes choices and determines courses of action as surely as he or she thinks. Clearly the Lord Jesus had a will, even a will that could be

The data of Holy Scripture require us to believe that in the incarnation the Son of God did not become *like a man* but became a true man, that is, a whole man, body and soul, mind and will, a human being as we are human beings. A human being *in the nature of the case* is not omniscient and since Jesus Christ was a true man, he was not omniscient, as the Gospels confirm. He "had a human psychology as truly as he had a human body."[22] God's willingness to submit to these humble conditions and to be subject to the painful limitations they imposed upon him is the marvel and glory of the incarnation!

The Gospels make clear that Jesus knew that he was God, though when in his earthly life he came to that realization remains a fascinating question. But how does a man know that he is God and remain in his daily life a true human being? How are the two natures kept inviolate while coexisting in the same person? All biblically literate Christians affirm, in the words of the Creed of Chalcedon, that the Lord Christ is to be confessed "in two natures, *inconfusedly, unchangeably, indivisibly, inseparably,*" surely the four most famous adverbs in the history of Christian theology. They combine to teach us that both the deity and the humanity were preserved in their integrity in the person of Jesus Christ.

But in so saying we are saying nothing more than that Holy Scripture teaches us that, upon the incarnation, God the Son became and remains a true and authentic human being while not becoming any less the eternal God that he always was, is, and ever shall be. We are saying that Jesus of Nazareth was throughout his human life on earth at the same time the eternal God. We are saying that while remaining the Almighty, the sovereign ruler of heaven and earth, omniscient and omnipotent, the Lord Jesus was nevertheless ignorant of many things, weary, discouraged, frustrated, even afraid. We are saying that while the man Christ Jesus was in Capernaum or Jerusalem, God the Son was everywhere. To be sure, on occasion Jesus of Nazareth made use of what can only be called supernatural knowledge and supernatural presence (John 1:48; 4:18; Luke 5:4–6), but Elijah was given such knowledge as well (2 Kgs 6:12). Such knowledge did not make him less a true man or any less ignorant of a great many things. God can reveal to his prophet things he would not otherwise know and Jesus of Nazareth was certainly a prophet.

distinguished from if never opposed to his Father's (John 6:38). See Robert Wilken's vivid and stirring account of that later controversy in his *Spirit of Early Christian Thought*, 122–35.

22. Macleod, *Person of Christ*, 164.

Are we not, therefore, saying that it was God the Son—given the indwelling of each of the persons of God in the others and the fact that the external works of God are undivided—who, with the Father and the Spirit, abandoned Jesus on the cross? All of which is to say that we are confessing a mystery that defeats our understanding at every turn. All we can do is to seek to remain faithful to each and every assertion made in Holy Scripture concerning Jesus Christ, however seemingly inconsistent the various assertions may be, however paradoxical the result, however impossible it is for us to consolidate them into a unity or harmony of understanding.

> Here is something marvelous: the Son of God descended from heaven in such a way that, without leaving heaven, he willed to be born in the virgin's womb, to go about the earth, and to hang upon the cross; yet he continuously filled the world even as he had done from the beginning![23]

There is no way to do justice to the biblical representation of Jesus Christ but to confess that he is both God and man.

The One Person

But to confess the two natures is inevitably to threaten the single person who is the Lord Jesus Christ. It is not difficult to believe that there might be two persons: one God and one man. That is, in fact, what a great many have believed. Some concluded that Jesus was only God, but made great use of a particular man; or that he was only a man, but a man in whom God made his presence known in a particularly intimate and powerful way. Such views in various permutations are commonplace today as they were in early Christianity. In such views the paradox is resolved and Jesus Christ becomes a person, no matter how remarkable, whose life and influence we can explain in more ordinary ways. Two natures are a severe problem only if we assert a single person at the same time. It is the hypostatic union—the union of two natures *in one person*—that is the problem.[24] The self-same Creator of heaven and earth, the Yahweh of the exodus, became flesh and lived among us!

23. Calvin, *Institutes*, II, xiii, 4.

24. "The term 'hypostatic union' encapsulates three truths: that Christ is one person; that the union between his two natures arises from the fact that they both belong to one and the same person; and that this one person, the son of God, is the Agent

The church fathers and subsequent theologians, seeking to do justice to the full biblical representation of the person of Jesus Christ, taught that the attributes of each nature were communicated to the person (*communicatio idiomatum*). That is, the attributes of each nature remained unchanged—his humanity remained authentic humanity and his deity remained perfect deity—but the Lord Jesus, by the union of the two natures in his person, was and is both God and man at once. After all, natures are not agents, actors, workers, deciders, or speakers. Only persons act and speak. The Lord Christ, being eternal God, was obviously already a person. Therefore, in the incarnation he did not add to himself a person but another nature. This is what the church's doctors meant when they taught that the Son of God assumed an "impersonal" human nature.[25] There was already a person; but that divine person then became also a human being. That second nature now coexists in his eternal person. It is in this way that the same person can be said to be omnipotent and weak or ignorant and all-knowing. The attributes of each nature belong to the person. Leo the Great beautifully articulated that conclusion in this way.

> Without detriment . . . to the properties of either nature and substance which then came together in one person, majesty took on humility, strength weakness, eternity mortality: and for the paying off of the debt belonging to our condition inviolable nature was united with passable nature, so that, as suited the needs of our case, one and the same Mediator between God and men, the Man Christ Jesus, could both die with the one and not die with the other. Thus in the whole and perfect nature of true man was true God born, complete in what was His own, complete in what was ours.[26]

So it was that what was done by the incarnate Son of God was done by this one person, God and man at once. Again, the church was not *explaining* the incarnation in this way; she was *confessing* it in the way most faithful to the entire biblical representation, assertions here and there: one regarding his deity, another his humanity, but all concerning the one and the same person. We understand the words; we understand what is being confessed. But we do not thereby understand the incarnation. We

behind all of the Lord's actions, the Speaker of his utterances and the Subject of all his experiences." Macleod, *Person of Christ*, 189.

25. Macleod helpfully clarifies both the term and the idea in *Person of Christ*, 199–203.

26. Leo the Great, *Letter XXVIII to Flavian*, III, 40.

can know and must know what an immense difference it makes for us that Jesus was and is both God and man, *but we have no idea whatsoever what it meant for him.* We remain baffled before the very idea of a person with two natures, all the more two natures as diametrically different as deity and humanity. We put our hands over our mouths and adore the infinite wisdom, love, and power of God.[27] And with the adoration we consider what would constitute the response of our hearts and lives worthy of such a wonder. No one could do this more wonderfully than Augustine, who often did just this in his celebrated Christmas sermons.

> So let us proclaim the good news of *the day from day, his salvation*; let us proclaim *among the nations his glory, among all the peoples his wonders* (Ps. 96:2–3). He lies in a manger, but he holds the whole world in his hands; he sucks his mother's breasts, but feeds the angels; he is swaddled in rags, but clothes us in immortality; he is suckled, but also worshipped; he could find no room in the inn, but makes a temple for himself in the hearts of believers. It was in order, you see, that weakness may become strong, that strength became weak. Let us therefore rather wonder at than make light of his birth in the flesh, and there recognize the lowliness on our behalf of such loftiness. From there let us kindle charity in ourselves, in order to attain to his eternity.[28]

As before with the terminology of the Holy Trinity, we happily admit that the Chalcedonian definition's four famous adverbs, or *communicatio idiomatum*, are not biblical terms. They are not explicitly biblical teaching. Each is rather a form of words used to summarize the biblical evidence. The Bible does use terms that evoke the idea we express with "nature" (*sarx*, flesh; *morphē*, form), but it never defines them and certainly never combines them in a formula such as "two natures in one person." But, taking the biblical evidence together, who can doubt that the church fathers and many faithful theologians following them were correct to use such terminology to formulate the biblical doctrine of the incarnation? Mystery it remains and must remain, but this *is* the mystery: God and man in one person forever.

Given the limitations of our finite intellects, once again we can think of the Lord Christ as God and we can think of him as a man, but we are

27. As Melanchthon admonished his readers, "We do better to adore the mysteries of Deity than to investigate them." *Loci Communes*, 21.

28. Augustine, *Essential Sermons*, 190.4, 253.

defeated in our attempt to conceive him at one and the same time as the God/man. We must consider the two natures one by one because we cannot comprehend them together in the unity of his person. The incarnation is as surely beyond the grasp of finite intellects as is the Holy Trinity! And so it was that the incarnation was revealed: first in the history of the birth, life, death, and resurrection of the Lord and then in the account of it given us in the New Testament—as it was, in its polarities. The impossibly great truth was broken up into pieces small enough for us to understand.

This fact of the biblical revelation of the incarnation is what is material to the thesis of this book. The progress toward a doctrine of the incarnation, a definition that satisfied the biblical evidence, that successfully incorporated all the data concerning the person of Jesus Christ we find in the Bible, was as halting and complicated as it was *because the Bible itself provides only polarities, only a large set of seemingly contrary assertions.* It took the time it took, it required the sometimes bitter controversies, one after another—a series of false steps painfully and sometimes violently corrected—because it was no simple matter to consolidate the data into a perfect equilibrium of truths. All the various theories eventually rejected were rejected precisely because they embraced one pole on a biblical continuum at the expense of the other. Their advocates could not convince the church that they did justice to both polarities at one and the same time. Some theories minimized or ignored the Bible's unmistakable assertion of the Lord's true deity. Others failed to do justice to the Bible's relentless witness to his authentic humanity. Still others sought to resolve the tension between those two competing emphases by failing to respect the Bible's equally impressive testimony to the unity of the Lord's person. The writings of the fathers bear eloquent witness to the effort they made to weigh the evidence of Holy Scripture and to ensure that all of it was incorporated in their definition of the incarnation, no matter how much mystery and incomprehension was the inevitable result.[29]

There is no biblical analysis of the incarnation that is immediately a contradiction of the Arian or Apollinarian theories or any of the other

29. A typical example is furnished in Gregory's *Third Theological Oration* XVII–XX, 307–9. Or consider Augustine's comment on John 10:30. "'Mark both of those words, *one* and *are*, and you will be delivered from Charybdis and from Scylla. In these two words, in that he said *one*, he delivers you from Arius; in that he said *are*, he delivers you from Sabellius . . . there are both Father and Son. . . . And if *one*, then there is no difference of persons between them." *Tractates on the Gospel of John*, 36.9, 212.

false steps taken on the way to the eventual doctrinal settlement. All of them were, in a general way, efforts to make sense of the data, but all of them fell short of an adequate summary. However, in the case of the incarnation, more so than in the case of the Holy Trinity, the church had at least one biblical example to follow. Already in the apostolic age false views of the incarnation were proliferating. In 1 John one such effort to reduce the mystery to a more "reasonable" understanding is directly addressed. When John writes of Jesus, "This is the one who came by water and blood . . . not by water only but by the water and the blood," it appears likely that he was addressing the views of one Cerinthus, who the evidence suggests was a contemporary of the apostle. According to Irenaeus, Cerinthus distinguished between the man Jesus and the (divine) Christ and taught that the Christ descended upon Jesus at his baptism but left him before his crucifixion.[30] But John categorically rejects this interpretation of the gospel history. Jesus, he says, came by both water (baptism) and blood (crucifixion). The self-same Jesus is the Christ (2:22), is the Son of the Father (4:9, 15), "has come in the flesh," (4:2) and died on the cross. As John makes unmistakably clear in his Gospel, and clear enough again in his first letter,[31] Jesus is God incarnate. But that the one who came from heaven died on the cross was an idea repellent to the sensibilities of that day, in which purity was spiritual and the material world defiling. Cerinthus was accommodating the apostolic message to the prevailing philosophy of the time. Those sensibilities account for various docetic types of early Christology, that is, which held that Jesus Christ only seemed to be a man. As F. F. Bruce observed: "In the particular climate of opinion to which this teaching owed its existence, 'thoughtful men' could not be expected to believe in the 'crude' incarnationalism of the primitive message. . . ."[32]

So John, by his example, taught the church how such corrections are to be done. Any account of Jesus Christ that doesn't do justice to the manifold witness of the apostles and Holy Scripture is to be rejected. And this is what the church did in fact, time after time, until settling on a definition of the incarnation that respected the polarities of biblical revelation—the manhood, the Godhead, and the unity of both in the person of Christ—and presented them as an equilibrium of truths. Those that

30. Irenaeus, *Against Heresies*, I, xxvi, 351–52.

31. Yarbrough, *1–3 John*, 281–82.

32. Bruce, *Epistles of John*, 25.

diminished his deity were rejected for failing to do justice to the Bible's relentless witness to that deity; those that diminished his humanity were rejected for the same reason, a failure to take proper account of the many ways in which Jesus is presented to us as a genuine human being, a man among men. Those that undermined the unity of his person were confronted with the fact that there is in redemptive history and its account in Holy Scripture but one Jesus Christ, to whose person both divine and human attributes are artlessly but equally assigned. Deep mystery it remains, but this *is* the mystery: two natures in one person.

How right then for Dorothy Sayers to write in a newspaper article in 1938 that ". . . The Christian faith is the most exciting drama that ever staggered the imagination of man—and the dogma is the drama."

> The plot pivots upon a single character, and the whole action is the answer to a single central problem: *What think ye of Christ?*
>
> The Church's answer is categorical and uncompromising, and it is this: That Jesus Bar-Joseph, the carpenter of Nazareth, was in fact and in truth, and in the most exact and literal sense of the words, the God "by whom all things were made". . . . This is the dogma we find so dull—this terrifying drama of which God is the victim and the hero.
>
> If this is dull, then what, in Heaven's name, is worthy to be called exciting?
>
> Now we may call that doctrine exhilarating, or we may call it devastating; we may call it revelation, or we may call it rubbish; but if we call it dull, then words have no meaning at all.[33]

---

33. Sayers, "Greatest Drama Ever Staged," 13–15.

5

Divine Sovereignty and Human Freedom

That God works half and man does the other half is false;
that God works all, and man does all is true.

—JOHN DUNCAN

THE DOCTRINES OR DEFINITIONS of the Holy Trinity and the incarnation, hammered out as they were over several centuries by extraordinarily devout and powerful intellects, have ever since satisfied and unified the whole of believing Christendom. No doubt this is due in large part to the continual resifting and reanalyzing of the biblical data and the gradual perfecting of the doctrines' form of words under the influence of repeated false steps taken in search of a faithful summary. With precious few exceptions all who make a serious profession of faith in Jesus Christ as King of Kings and the Savior of the world confess that faith in harmony with the Nicene-Constantinopolitan and Chalcedonian Creeds. Alas, the same cannot be said of the various attempts to represent the biblical teaching regarding the interaction of divine and human agency in the salvation of sinners. The same devout intellect, the same history of controversy, and a similar sifting and analysis of the biblical data over long periods of time have not produced a similar consensus.

Perhaps no area of doctrine has been more consistently debated throughout the twenty centuries of Christianity's life than that of God's sovereignty and man's responsibility. This debate has waxed warmer since the Reformation.[1]

The polarities of divine sovereignty and human responsibility or accountability are encountered everywhere in the Bible's anatomy of human life—and so surface equally in Christian theology in regard to the larger subject of divine providence—but for the purposes of the present argument we can restrict ourselves to the causation of salvation, the most important dimension of the interaction of divine and human agency. Unlike our faith in the Holy Trinity and the person of Jesus Christ, believing Christendom has not found rest in *any* creedal statement. It has never agreed that any theological tradition has succeeded in summarizing accurately the entire biblical representation. Polarities there certainly are and only polarities, however differently each polarity may be defined.[2]

More than that, every theological tradition, whether strongly predestinarian or emphatically voluntarist,[3] has had to deal with skeptics from the other side. Such is the state of the biblical evidence that no one should find this particularly surprising. Roman Catholic scholars typically consider Augustine a doctor of their church, so much so that you will sometimes read one of them arguing that the great African's strongly predestinarian reputation rests on a misunderstanding! But Calvinists rightly regard Augustine as the first and perhaps greatest champion of their soteriology. Seventeenth-century Jansenism, a movement within

1. Carson, *Divine Sovereignty*, 219.

2. For example, in the excellent Lutheran theologies of Francis Pieper and his disciple, John Theodore Mueller, the polarities are identified as *gratia universalis* and *sola gratia*. They attempt no reconciliation between the two but accept both to be true: those who are saved are saved by grace alone while those who are lost are lost through their own fault. Mueller, *Christian Dogmatics*, 251. Mueller's work is an epitome of Pieper's larger work, *Christian Dogmatics*; see, e.g., 2:465. Calvinists would not speak of a universal *grace* but of God's desire that all men be saved, on the one hand, and his sovereign and discriminating grace on the other. ". . . His redeeming grace is not universal but particular." Heppe, *Reformed Dogmatics*, 172.

3. Here "voluntarist" is used, not in its philosophical sense, but more generally to describe those views that understand the beginning of saving faith to be solely an act of the human will, however divine grace may have helped to prepare the way beforehand or helps to strengthen faith immediately thereafter. Such views are typically described as either semi-Pelagian (pejoratively) or semi-Augustinian (approvingly). Election in such views is typically understood in terms of divine foreknowledge. Another set of terms used to describe the difference between these accounts of the causation of salvation is that of *monergism* and *synergism*, God the sole cause or God and man cooperative causes of salvation.

French Catholicism, was a return to Augustine's predestinarian views and resulted eventually in the Roman Church's condemnation of both. Among the early Lutherans, Philip Melanchthon's gradual move away from his mentor Martin Luther's uncompromising emphasis on sovereign and particular grace—in Luther's views "predestination stands in the closest relation to justification"[4]—can be charted in the successive editions of his *Loci Communes*. The seeds of Arminianism were sown and bore fruit in Reformed soil and Arminianism or similar views have resurfaced in Reformed communions repeatedly through the centuries. Comparatively few Anglicans have been outspoken Calvinists as were most of their founding fathers in the sixteenth century, the Puritans in the seventeenth, George Whitefield in the eighteenth, J. C. Ryle in the nineteenth, and J. I. Packer in the twentieth, even though *The Thirty-Nine Articles* articulate a Calvinist conception of divine grace and the origin of saving faith. The early Methodist leaders, the princes of the Great Awakening, were divided, often bitterly, over the question of divine grace and human freedom. Many evangelical churches today have within their membership ministers and lay people who embrace one or the other of these different conceptions and not infrequently after having first held the contrary view. As has often been observed, perhaps the easiest way to start an argument among Christians is to ask the obvious and vital question: Why is one person saved and another not?[5]

The Polarities

Again, that should surprise no one. The Bible teaches the absolute dominion of God in salvation in terms, one would think, impossible to mistake. It is because of the Bible's relentless assertion of the sovereignty of God that the biblical mind is alive to the unqualified rule the Creator exercises over his creation and the divine will that is the cause of everything that comes to pass. And so biblically minded men and women are everywhere conscious of their absolute dependence upon the good pleasure of God for the fulfillment of their hopes for life in this world and the next. The thought that the Almighty is subject to the whims of his creatures or can be defeated in his hopes and plans by the rebellion of human beings is an

---

4. Bromiley, *Historical Theology*, 242.

5. Pieper repeatedly refers to that question as the *crux theologorum*, the puzzling or difficult problem of the theologians. *Christian Dogmatics*, 3:502; 4:203.

affront to these convictions, frequently and emphatically asserted as they are (Isa 55:10–11; Eph 1:11; 3:11). Yahweh is never surprised; his plans are never overthrown by the schemes of human beings (Isa 46:8–11), for "he does according to his will among the host of heaven and among the inhabitants of the earth; and none can stay his hand or say to him, 'What have you done?'" (Dan 4:35; Ps 47:8). The history of the world and of every human being in it is a story written first in the eternal counsels of the Almighty (Ps 139:16). He is the one in whose hand is every person's breath (Dan 5:23; Gen 20:6). He is the one whose purposes and plans direct the history of each individual human life: from his formation in the womb, to the number of hairs on her head, to the destiny of each at the consummation of history. The faithful know to say "that the way of man is not in himself, that it is not in man who walks to direct his steps" (Jer 10:23; Prov 16:9; 20:24). Indeed, the Bible does not scruple to say that the thoughts, intentions, and undertakings of people with no thought whatsoever of the living God, who imagine themselves sole masters of their own acts, are all, unbeknownst to them, the will of God. He or she may say, "By the strength of my hand I have done it, and by my wisdom," but in fact it was God all along (Isa 10:5–15; Acts 4:25–28). In the matter of salvation, God knows who will be saved before they do because he has determined their salvation long before (Matt 13:11; 15:13; 22:14; Acts 13:48; 18:10; Rom 11:5; Eph 1:11; 1 Thess 1:4–5). The prophets and apostles forecast both catastrophe and restoration, the Day of Judgment and the Day of Salvation, for God is the Lord of both. And, in the matter of salvation, when he roars, they will come (Hos 11:10). The great illustrations of salvation in redemptive history, the exodus, the healing miracles of the Lord, and the conversion of the apostle Paul all emphasize the result as solely the accomplishment of divine initiative and divine power, utterly beyond the will of man to achieve. We were dead and God made us alive (Eph 2:4).

But, at the same time, the Bible is equally relentless in its appeal to men and women to believe and be saved, in its warning that they will have no one to blame but themselves should they refuse to respond in obedience to the gospel summons, and equally emphatic and unmistakable in the way in which it repeatedly suspends the issue of salvation on the exercise of the human will. If destiny is writ large in Holy Scripture, so is contingency (Deut 30:11–20; Ps 103:17–18; 2 Chr 6:14, 16; Isa 59:1–2; Jer 17:20–27; 18:7–10; Dan 9:4; Matt 23:37; Acts 10:34–35; Rev 22:17). "Abide in my love. If you keep my commandments, you will abide in my love" (John 15:19–20). "Do good, O Lord, to those who are good, and to those who are upright in their hearts" (Ps 125:4; 1 Sam 26:23). Whatever else that is, it is contingency. Salvation is suspended upon an exercise of the human will.

However perfect God's knowledge of everything that will come to pass, having himself determined from eternity past the course of history down to its smallest details, he not only grieves over mankind's sinfulness and rebellion; he is offended by it (Gen 6:5–6; Isa 1:11–14; 43:24). Indeed, we read in Holy Scripture that the Lord "cannot endure" the evil men do (Isa 1:13–14; Jer 44:22), even that he had confronted them "in vain" (Jer 2:30) and hoped for their repentance (Jer 3:19), extraordinary things for the Almighty to say. The God of love pleads with human beings to repent and turn to him for salvation from themselves, the world, the devil, and, supremely, from divine judgment. His prophets and apostles cajole with warnings, threats, promises, encouragements, and appeals, as did the Lord Christ himself (Isa 55:1–3, 6–7; Jer 18:7–10; 36:3; Ezek 18:30–32; Matt 11:28–29; 21:28–33; 2 Cor 5:10–11). No holy book in the world is remotely as tenacious and searching in its demand that human beings accept full responsibility for their lives. No book so solemnly lays every human life under the specter of a final judgment rendered in strict accordance with an infallible record scrupulously kept of a man or woman's words and deeds, attitudes and actions, loves and hatreds (Jer 17:10; Rom 2:16; 14:10; 2 Cor 5:10; Rev 2:23; 20:11–12). And no book makes such extraordinary promises to the unworthy, *if only men and women will believe, receive, turn, follow, and persevere in gratitude and obedience to Jesus Christ.* Even the most outspoken advocates of divine sovereignty among the prophets and apostles inveigh against the sins of their readers, warn of horrific consequences if they remain unrepentant, and urge upon them faith in the Lord and perseverance in obedience lest they fail to obtain the salvation God graciously offers them, or if already believers, lest, God forbid, they receive the grace of God in vain (1 Cor 15:1–2; Heb 10:26–27; 12:25–29; Rev 22:19).

The Bible is one very long and urgent address to the human mind, heart, will, and conscience. The Lord Jesus himself rested the salvation of his congregations upon their willingness to put their trust in him and live lives of obedience to him (John 6:29; 8:24; 17:6). He repeatedly insisted that those who do the will of God and *only those* will enter the kingdom of heaven (Matt 7:21). One solemnizing address to the human will after another litter the pages of Holy Scripture (Heb 2:3). In a hundred ways we are told that "everyone who calls on the name of the Lord will be saved" (Rom 10:13) and that others, alas, "forsake their hope of steadfast love" (Jonah 2:8).

Such are the grand polarities, though they certainly can be and have been divided and subdivided. We encounter the issue of agency in salvation in regard to the divine will in eternity past (election), in regard to the capacity of the fallen human mind and will (original sin), in regard to the atonement, in regard to the beginning of spiritual life (calling, regeneration, and faith), and in regard to its continuance (perseverance). Monergistic and synergistic views collide as well at the intersection of Christ's death and resurrection (*historia salutis*) with the individual experience of salvation (*ordo salutis*). In regard to every dimension of the biblical teaching of salvation we are confronted with this characteristically and emphatically dialectical pedagogy: divine sovereignty here, human responsibility there.

Divine election is in one place the ultimate explanation of anyone's salvation (Eph 1:3–10); in another it increases the severity of the punishment of those who fall away (Isa 1:2–9; Amos 3:2). In one place the Lord distinguishes precisely between those he will save and those he will leave in their unbelief (John 10:25–28; Acts 18:10; Rom 11:7). In another place he laments that he was "ready to be found by those who did not seek me" and complains, "I spread out my hands all the day to a rebellious people" (Isa 65:1–2), while in still another he acts *so as to prevent* the salvation of those who have rejected him (Mark 4:11–12; John 12:18–20; 2 Thess 2:11–12). In one place Christ's death makes certain the salvation of those whom the Father gave him to save (Matt 1:21; John 10:11–18, 25–30; Rev 5:9). In another place the church is warned against teachers who deny "the Master who bought them, bringing on swift destruction" (Heb 10:29; 2 Pet 2:1; cf. Heb 6:6). In one place God opens the mind to the truth and turns the rebellious heart toward him, granting repentance and faith (Ezek 36:25–27; John 1:11–13; 10:16; Acts 16:14). In another place human beings are summoned to make themselves new hearts and find salvation by an exercise of their will (Deut 10:16; Jer 36:3; 39:18; Ezek 18:31–32; Rom 10:5–13; 1 Pet 1:22). In one place faith in Jesus Christ is a divine gift (John 6:44; Acts 18:27; Eph 2:8–10; Col 2:11–13; 2 Tim 2:25). In another faith in Jesus Christ is the commendable act of a man or woman (Luke 5:20; 17:15–19; Acts 17:11–12). In still another place the want of faith is a tragic moral failure for which men and women have no excuse (Gal 3:3–4; Heb 4:1–2; 10:34–35). In one place a believer's perseverance in faith is the guaranteed result of his or her election, regeneration, and union with Christ (Rom 8:28–35; Phil 1:5; 1 Pet 1:3–5, 23). In another believers who began, even who began well by the power of the Holy Spirit, fall away never to be recovered to faith and salvation (2 Chr 15:2; Ezek 16; Matt 13:20–21; John 15:1–11; Acts 11:22; Heb 6:4–8; 1 John 5:16).

Indeed, as anyone knows who makes it his or her regular practice to read the Bible with attention, the artless interweaving of divine and human agency in salvation is a feature found on every page, and even in many places found in virtually every paragraph of Holy Scripture. No wonder that this welter of biblical polarities, relentlessly emphasized but never systematized, has churned up disagreement that remains unresolved after centuries of concentrated reflection, sometimes bitter controversy, and the best efforts of devout minds to forge a theological consensus regarding divine and human agency in the salvation of sinners.

Indeed, these polarities raise a constellation of issues that, after all these years and endless discussion, still succeed in provoking intense heat but little light. Does a predestinarian understanding defame God by making him the author of sin and represent him as willfully indifferent to, if not callously desirous of, the damnation of vast multitudes of human beings? Does a voluntarist understanding rob God of his glory as the Savior of sinners since, while certainly an indispensable helper to our salvation, it is not his grace and power but the independent exercise of the human will that tells the tale? After all these years and endless controversies, it seems safe to say that so long as we read in Holy Scripture that God "loved Jacob and hated Esau," or "that it depends not on human will or exertion, but on God, who has mercy," or "as many as were appointed to eternal life believed," the church will always have her Calvinists. Similarly, as long as we read in the same Bible, "I have set before you life and death, blessing and curse; therefore choose life, that you and your offspring may live . . . ," or "whoever does not believe is condemned already, because he has not believed in the name of the only Son of God," or "[Christ] became the source of eternal salvation to all who obey him," the church will always have her Arminians.

Dialectical Revelation Once Again

Still, it should be obvious to any thoughtful and well-read believer that whenever polarities as diametrically contrary as are an absolute divine sovereignty and a responsible and causative exercise of the human will confront one another across a biblical continuum, and when these polarities and their implications are scattered everywhere across the face of Holy Scripture, we should at least willingly acknowledge the Bible's characteristically dialectical form of revelation. It is quite easy to demonstrate that the history of this debate is, in too many cases, a history of embracing one pole at the expense of the other, wrapping one's arms around one biblical perspective and finding some way, any way, to reinterpret its contrary. Far too easily and far too often the truth has been found in one extreme, not both, and the equilibrium of truths has been lost as harmony has been forcibly imposed on the discordant biblical data.

I appreciate that no defender of one of the several systems of interpretation will admit that this is what has been done. Who will confess that his or her theological tradition has enthusiastically championed one biblical emphasis and minimized, ignored, or redefined the other at significant cost to the obvious meaning of words? But it is not difficult to demonstrate that this is precisely what has been done and the more easily done given the investment of powerful emotion in the controversy. The existence of the other systems is some proof that it is so. Why else have the defenders of one system proved incapable, no matter the centuries of effort, no matter the assistance of powerful and devout intellects, of persuading devout defenders of other systems that at least *they* have laid proper weight on *everything* the Bible says in explaining the causes of salvation?

Agreement After All

But, even more obvious, the Bible speaks so clearly, defines the polarities—a discriminating divine sovereignty, on the one hand, and a morally responsible and causative exercise of the human will, on the other—so transparently, and emphasizes and illustrates them both so comprehensively that at the critical point, at that point where every thoughtful Christian reckons with the cause of his or her own salvation, *each one understands salvation in much the same way.* That there is a long history of admiration on the part of the representatives of one theological tradition for the faith and life of many advocates of another tradition can only be explained because there is greater agreement than might at first appear. For the same reason Arminians pray urgently for the salvation of others and Calvinists shake their heads in frustration and mourn the intransigent unbelief of those they long to see come to Christ. We all know that the triune God saved us and that we owe our hope of everlasting life entirely to him and not in the least degree to ourselves. From first to last and in all the links of the chain we honor Father, Son, and Holy Spirit as our Savior from sin and death. Guilty and helpless, he did for us and in us what we could and would never have done for ourselves. We also know that we are responsible for the decisions that we make, that they are our decisions, that we are obliged to make the right ones, that such decisions are eternally consequential, and that those who refuse to believe and obey cannot blame God for the judgment that must follow. And we who believe in Christ know that we must continue to follow him in faith and obedience or it will be our fault if, having begun our pilgrimage, we fail at last to attain the heavenly country.

As staunch an Arminian as Charles Wesley accounted for his own salvation in a way entirely satisfying to any Calvinist.

> Long my imprisoned spirit lay,
>   Fast bound in sin and nature's night.
> Thine eye diffused a quick'ning ray;
>   I woke; the dungeon flamed with light.
> My chains fell off, my heart was free,
> I rose, went forth, and followed thee.[6]

Charles Wesley never dreamed of suggesting that, with God having done all that he could and would do, it was Wesley himself, by the exercise of his will, who effected his transition from sinner to saint; that it was he and not God who made himself a member of Christ's body. Arminians likewise love to sing the Calvinist John Newton's "Amazing Grace," with its lines

> 'Twas grace that taught my heart to fear,
> And grace my fears relieved . . .

They never suppose that in singing such words they are repudiating their own faith. Similarly, as unashamed a Calvinist as Joseph Alleine

---

6. If possible, John Wesley, Charles' brother, was a still more determined Arminian, but "And Can It Be" was one of the hymns he sang on his deathbed. *Works of John Wesley*, 7:68. Another Wesley verse often used by Calvinistic preachers in addressing the unsaved is "O God, my inmost soul convert, / And deeply on my thoughtful heart/ Eternal things impress; / Give me to feel their solemn weight, / And trembling on the brink of fate, / Wake me to righteousness!"

could summon the unsaved in terms fully agreeable to the most ardent Arminian.

> Accept an offered Christ now, and you are made forever. Give your consent to Him now, and the match is made; all the world cannot hinder it. Do not stand off because of your unworthiness. I tell you, nothing can undo you but your own unwillingness. Speak, man; will you give your consent? Will you have Christ. . . ?[7]

Alleine would never have imagined telling the readers of his spiritual classic that, given the fact that salvation is of the Lord, all they could do was wait in the expectation that they would eventually discover if God had plans to save them.

Charles Simeon famously illustrated this perhaps unwitting coalescence of theological viewpoint in his account of his first encounter with John Wesley, once again describing himself in the third person.

> A young Minister, about three or four years after he was ordained, had an opportunity of conversing familiarly with the great and venerable leader of the Arminians in this kingdom; and, wishing to improve the occasion to the uttermost, he addressed him nearly in the following words: "Sir, I understand that you are called an Arminian; and I have been sometimes called a Calvinist; and therefore I suppose we are to draw daggers. But before I consent to begin the combat, with your permission I will ask you a few questions, not from impertinent curiosity, but for real instruction." Permission being very readily and kindly granted, the young Minister proceeded to ask, "Pray, Sir, do you feel yourself a depraved creature, so depraved, that you would never have thought of turning unto God, if God had not first put in into your heart?"—"Yes," says the veteran, "I do indeed."—"And do you utterly despair of recommending yourself to God by any thing that you can do; and look for salvation solely through the blood and righteousness of Christ?"—"Yes, solely through Christ."—"But, Sir, supposing you were first saved by Christ, are you not somehow or other to save yourself afterwards by your own works?"—"No; I must be saved by Christ from first to last."—"Allowing then that you were first turned

7. Alleine, *Alarm to the Unconverted*, 113. Or consider this from the arch-Calvinist, John Calvin himself. "Therefore since no man is excluded from calling upon God the gate of salvation is set open to all. There is nothing else to hinder us from entering, but our own unbelief. It is, I say, all men, to whom God reveals Himself through the Gospel." *Acts of the Apostles, 1–13,* 62.

by the grace of God, are you not in some way or other to keep yourself by your own power?"—"No."—"What then, are you to be upheld every hour and every moment by God, as much as an infant in its mother's arms?"—"Yes; altogether."—"And is all your hope in the grace and mercy of God to preserve you unto his heavenly kingdom?"—"Yes; I have no hope, but in him."—"Then, Sir, with your leave, I will put up my dagger again; for this is all my Calvinism; this is my election, my justification by faith, my final perseverance: it is, in substance, all that I hold, and as I hold it: and therefore, if you please, instead of searching out terms and phrases to be a ground of contention between us, we will cordially unite in those things wherein we agree." The Arminian leader was so pleased with the conversation that he made particular mention of it in his journals; and notwithstanding there never afterwards was any connexion between the parties, he retained an unfeigned regard for his young inquirer to the hour of his death. Doubtless either of these points may be injudiciously stated, or improperly applied. If the doctrines of Election and Predestination be so stated as to destroy man's free agency, and make him merely passive in the work of salvation, they are not stated as they are in the Articles and Homilies of our Church, or as they are in the Holy Scriptures. On the other hand, if the doctrines of free-will and liableness to final apostasy be so stated as to rob God of his honour, and to deny that he is both "the Author and the Finisher of our faith," they are equally abhorrent from the sentiments of our Established Church, and from the plainest declarations of Holy Writ.[8]

It is a fact not cheerfully enough acknowledged or the cause of which not often enough carefully considered that Arminians and Calvinists share so much in common at the very point where the issue of the agency of salvation matters most: *the explanation of one's own salvation.* Surely the first reason for this is the testimony of the renewed conscience. But a second reason must be the fact that the Bible speaks so repeatedly, so unmistakably, and so insistently both to the sovereign grace of God and to the exercise of the human will as the causes of salvation that it is very difficult for any biblically literate Christian not to believe both.

As a Calvinist myself, I take pleasure in the fact that many representative Calvinists have openly acknowledged and ardently defended almost all the truths that devout Arminians are most concerned to protect: that in the gospel salvation is offered to all, that God desires the salvation

8. "Preface," in *Horae Homileticae*, 1:loc. 312–26 of 36288.

of all, and that human beings are responsible to avail themselves of the offer of eternal life through faith in Jesus Christ.[9] Charles Spurgeon was an unrepentant Calvinist, but he was equally a great pleader with men.

> I believe in predestination, yea, even in its very jots and tittles. I believe that the path of a single grain of dust in the March wind is ordained and settled by a decree which cannot be violated; that every word and thought of man, every flittering of a sparrow's wing, every flight of a fly . . . that everything, in fact is foreknown and foreordained. But I do equally believe in the free agency of man, that man acts as he wills, especially in moral operations—choosing the evil with a will that is unbiased by anything that comes from God, biased only by his own depravity of heart and the perverseness of his habits; choosing the right too with perfect freedom, though sacredly guided and led by the Holy Spirit. . . . I believe that man is as accountable as if there were no destiny whatever. . . . Where these two truths meet I do not know, nor do I want to know. They do not puzzle me, since I have given up my mind to believing them both.[10]

9. Alas there have been Calvinists who have denied both that the gospel is sincerely offered to all and that God desires the salvation of all. But the fact remains that their exegetical evasions are so unimpressive that they have always remained a small minority. Gordon Clark, following John Gill, the eighteenth-century hyper-Calvinist (a technical term identifying someone who denies, perhaps among other things, the free or well-meant offer of the gospel to all), explains the Lord's lament over Jerusalem (Matt 23:37–39) in this way: by Jerusalem only the leadership was meant; that the gathering the Lord wished for was the opportunity for them to hear him preach; that his desire was that of a man and not of God, and so on. Quite apart from the fact that God's desire for the salvation of all is mentioned repeatedly and in various contexts in the Bible, this is a reading of the Lord's words that would have occurred to no original reader of the Gospel and is not today either obvious or likely. As Gill makes clear with commendable honesty, it is an interpretation thought to be made necessary by the sovereignty of God in salvation. Clark, *Predestination*, 136–39. Cf. Gill's similar treatment of Paul's remark in 1 Tim 2:4 that God desires all people to be saved. Paul must mean *all sorts of people* since what God wills must come to pass. *Exposition of the New Testament*, 4:526. Regarding some modern advocates of such interpretations, see De Jong, *Well-Meant Gospel Offer*. To be fair, this was also Augustine's interpretation of "all" in 1 Tim 2:4. *Rebuke and Grace*, 44, 47, 489, 491. It is the thesis of this book that attempts completely to *eliminate* the apparent conflict between the "all" in such a text and Paul's emphasis on God's discriminating grace are almost inevitably misguided. Such "contraries" are a feature of the biblical pedagogy.

10. *Metropolitan Tabernacle Pulpit*, 15:458, cited in Murray, *Spurgeon v. Hyper-Calvinism*, 82–83. Speaking of Spurgeon's evangelistic preaching, Murray observes, "The point at which he diverged from both Hyper-Calvinism and Arminianism is that he refused to rationalize *how* men can be commanded to do what is not in their power." Murray, *Forgotten Spurgeon*, 99. Typical of Spurgeon is the magnificent peroration of

And John Duncan spoke with even greater emphasis on the importance of doing justice to the entire biblical representation. "That God works half and man the other half is false; that God works all, and man does all, is true."[11]

I don't mean to minimize the difference between Calvinistic and Arminian conceptions of divine sovereignty or human freedom. Reformed teaching differs dramatically from Arminian in regard to divine election, the bondage of the sinful human will, the nature and consequence of Christ's atonement, and the *ordo salutis*, or how it happens that individuals experience the saving grace of God. But who can deny that the Bible speaks in ways that are not easily reconciled to one another?

> I will sprinkle clean water on you, and you shall be clean. . . .
> And I will give you a new heart, and a new spirit I will put within
> you. And I will remove the heart of stone from your flesh and
> give you a heart of flesh. And I will put my Spirit within you and
> cause you to walk in my statutes. . . . (Ezek 36:25–27)

That is one message, often repeated in Holy Scripture. But here is another from the same book of the Bible.

> Cast away from you all the transgressions that you have com-
> mitted, and make yourselves a new heart and a new spirit! For
> why will you die, O house of Israel? For I have no pleasure in the
> death of anyone, declares the Lord God; so turn and live. (Ezek
> 18:31-32)

Commentaries have some helpful things to say about the contrast between the indicative in Ezekiel 36 and the imperative in Ezekiel 18, but

---

his sermon on 2 Thess 2:13–14. He challenged his hearers not to let the truth of God's election of some to eternal life prevent them from acting on the summons to believe and be saved. "Go to God. . . . Besides, supposing thou be damned, thou wouldst have the satisfaction at least of being able to lift up thine eyes in hell, and say, 'God, I asked mercy of thee and thou wouldst not grant it; I sought it, but thou didst refuse it.' That thou never shalt say, O sinner! If thou goest to him, and askest him, thou shalt receive. . . ." Spurgeon, *New Park Street Pulpit*, 1:322.

11. Duncan, *Colloquia Peripatetica*, 29–30. Duncan was an avid reader of Jonathan Edwards and I wonder if he took his turn of phrase from the great colonial theologian. "In efficacious grace we are not merely passive, nor yet does God do some, and we do the rest. But God does all, and we do all. God produces all, and we act all. . . . We are, in different respects, wholly passive and wholly active." *Works*, 2:557 Anthony Hoekema spoke similarly. In speaking of sanctification, one principal dimension of salvation, he wrote that it is "one hundred percent God's work and one hundred percent our work." *Saved by Grace*, 5.

they cannot and do not deny that, as Duncan put it, "God does all and man does all."[12] Here is my point. This dialectical revelation of the agency or cause of salvation is characteristic of the Bible from beginning to end.[13]

As I have argued, given the biblical penchant for the assertion of seemingly incompatible ideas, for absolute statement, and for the lack of systematic analysis; given the Bible's high tolerance for tension; and given the ineffable nature of reality *as it is known to God*, it is only to be expected that we should find such paradoxical contraries here at the very heart of the Bible's message of divine grace and the salvation of sinners. The problem, very obviously, is not that we do not know what the Bible is saying. It is perfectly clear in what it teaches about salvation. Sentence after sentence in Hebrew, Greek, and the languages into which the Bible is translated speak the truth in words that in themselves are easy to understand. It is precisely their clarity that produces the sense of discordance in our minds and that has led to the temptation to make a choice between the contraries, to redefine the other, and somehow to escape the paradox.

Paradox

The sovereignty of God in salvation is writ large on the pages of Holy Scripture.[14] "Our God is in the heavens; he does all that he pleases" (Ps 115:3).

> I thank you, Father, Lord of heaven and earth, that you have hidden these things from the wise and understanding and revealed them to little children; yes, Father, for such was your gracious will. (Matt 11:25–26)

But equally emphatic is the Bible's punishing assertion of the moral accountability of every human being and the life and death consequences of

12. Cf. Eichrodt, *Ezekiel*, 245–46; Block, *Ezekiel*, 1:587–89.

13. In his foreword to Leonhard Goppelt's influential *Typos*, xvi, E. Earle Ellis criticizes Karl Popper for having no place for either revealed truth or the truth of logical antinomies. "He apparently is not aware that in a theistic view of history divine sovereignty and human freedom and responsibility operate as a *concursus* in which neither is sacrificed and neither forcibly conformed to the other. . . . But a proper Christian attitude toward history affirms the biblical revelation that both are true and that here, as in other matters, reality transcends the reasoning of autonomous man."

14. "In one word, the sovereignty of the Divine will as the principle of all that comes to pass, is a primary postulate of the whole religious life. . . ." Warfield, "Predestination," 275.

the choices he or she makes.[15] How does the great apostle to the Gentiles summarize his message?

> Believe in the Lord Jesus, and you will be saved, you and your household. (Acts 16:31)

And how does Paul speak to those who rejected his message?

> Since you thrust [the word of God] aside and judge yourselves unworthy of eternal life, behold, we are turning to the Gentiles. (Acts 13:46)

That is undeniably contingency and, of course, "if . . . then" statements such as these are found everywhere in Holy Scripture. What are we to do with these contraries? "The religious mind chooses both, confesses both, and confirms both by the faith of piety."[16] The fact is, there is no obvious way neatly to harmonize these contrary emphases, ubiquitous and emphatic as they are in Holy Scripture. Is it not then far wiser to accept that both are true but that the unity of truth lies beyond our comprehension; that to see and understand the interrelationship of divine and human agency in any dimension of human life and supremely in the salvation of sinners would require an intellect far more powerful than that possessed by human beings? That God does all and man does all is a paradox, to be sure, but then there is, as we have argued, a great deal that is paradoxical in biblical revelation, a great deal that must remain mysterious to us given the limited capacities of our finite minds. It is possible, after all, to weep over one's sins and to regard oneself as utterly undeserving of the least of God's mercies. We have such confessions often enough in the Bible (Job 42:6; Ps 51:3–5; Ezek 20:43; Luke 5:8; Rom 7:24). But we also find righteous men appealing to God for favor on the strength of their own obedience and service (Neh 5:19; Ps 18:20–26; 2 Tim 4:7–8; Heb 6:10) and an entire class of texts in which heaven is said to be the reward of the faithful (e.g., Rom 2:6, 13; Rev 2:7, 11, 26; 3:4–5, 12).

---

15. ". . . there is never the least doubt expressed of the freedom or moral responsibility of man. . . ." "We are never permitted to imagine . . . that God is the author of sin, either in the world at large or in any individual soul—that He is any way implicated in the sinfulness of the acts performed by the perverse misuse of creaturely freedom." Warfield, "Predestination," 282, 283.

16. Augustine, *City of God*, V, 9–10 as translated in Bavinck, *Reformed Dogmatics*, 2:198. Typical of much Reformed preaching, Spurgeon spoke similarly. "Both are true; no two truths can be inconsistent with each other; and what you have to do is to believe them both." *New Park Street Pulpit*, 4:343.

Theologoumena

Theologoumena are doctrinal opinions, shared by some but not all representatives of a theological tradition. Typically, they are thought by their advocates to be a way of unifying the biblical data, but they lack overt biblical demonstration or authority. They may be popular within a tradition, but they do not rise to the level of fixed or authoritative dogma. Theologoumena abound in this area of Christian theology as one hypothesis after another has been proposed either to explain the discordance between the polarities or to define them in ways that eliminate or reduce the tension produced by their seeming incompatibility. These are not—for example, with *perichoresis*—ways to express and so preserve the tension, but ways to ameliorate if not eliminate it.

The so-called middle knowledge (*scientia media*) of Luis de Molina, later adopted by the Arminians, Roman Catholics, and some Lutherans, is such a theologoumenon.[17] So is the distinction between God's decretive and permissive wills, adopted by some Calvinists and rejected by others.[18] A third example would be the distinction between first causes and second causes: the will of God being the first cause, the will and actions of human beings second causes, real causes but not ultimate causes.

17. The *scientia media* is not God's knowledge of himself and all possibilities that omniscience bequeaths to him. Nor is it that knowledge of everything that he has determined to bring to pass. *Ex hypothesi* the middle knowledge lies between those uncontroversial dimensions of God's knowledge and is that knowledge God has of contingent events that will occur because of the will of others, of events that he himself has not determined to bring to pass. This theory underlies synergistic theories of salvation by attributing foreknowledge to God concerning events he did not decree and for which he is not responsible. The belief or unbelief of human beings would be something that belongs to God's middle knowledge. In this understanding, at the key point, human beings are independent of God. Or, as Bavinck tartly puts it: "God looks on, while humans decide." *Reformed Dogmatics*, 2:201.

18. According to this distinction God has made everything that happens certain by his decree, but in regard to human sin, which includes human unbelief, God's decree is only permissive, which is to say that he does not bring sin to pass by his own direct action or by exercising immediate control over the human will to produce a sinful effect. This has been thought to be a way to protect God from the accusation that, by his all-encompassing predetermination of events, he becomes the author of sin. It is a distinction, Bavinck wisely observes, that "offers no solution whatever to the problem of God's relation to sin." Almost everyone can see in a moment that if God has determined the result and made it certain, the means by which the result comes to pass are largely irrelevant. *Reformed Dogmatics*, 3:62. Calvin himself had serious doubts as to the usefulness of the distinction. *Concerning the Eternal Predestination of God*, X, 10–11, 174–77.

Again, I don't decry the effort to confess in some helpful way the biblical representation of divine and human agency in salvation. But everyone should at least readily admit that such distinctions are nowhere found in Holy Scripture. Indeed, the distinction of causes is drawn from philosophy, not from the Bible. Each of these theological opinions is an invention intended to impose some consistency or intelligibility upon the biblical contraries, and none of them has succeeded in a way satisfying to anyone not already disposed to the interpretation of biblical teaching that the particular theologoumenon is intended to explain or defend.

The middle knowledge has been rejected outright by Calvinism as failing to do justice to the emphatic declarations of Holy Scripture that God does not simply know the future; he orders and rules it in every part. The distinction between God's decretive and permissive wills has been rejected by Arminians and many Calvinists alike as a distinction without a useful difference. And to distinguish between first and second causes, while perhaps useful as a bare confession of the obvious, offers very little in the way of an explanation. This distinction, enshrined in the *Westminster Confession of Faith*, a distinction that most theologians accept in some form, proves of very modest utility because it fails to explain what must be explained: why human beings who do not believe are justly and often ferociously condemned for that unbelief, why God grieves as he does over human sin and unbelief, why God desires the salvation of all human beings but does not secure it, and how it can be said that God is not the author of sin. It isn't particularly controversial to say that God is the ultimate cause of history and that the human will is a secondary cause.[19] But in saying such what has been said? In fact, in the *Westminster Confession* itself the assertion of first and secondary causation has more the character of a confession of paradox than of its resolution. After all, how is the biblical tension relaxed by saying,

> God from all eternity, did, by the most wise and holy counsel
> of His own will, freely, and unchangeably ordain whatsoever
> comes to pass: yet so, as thereby neither is God the author of
> sin, nor is violence offered to the will of the creatures; nor is the
> liberty or contingency of second causes taken away, but rather
> established (III, i)?

19. "No doubt all history in the last resort must be held by Christians to be a story with a divine plot." Lewis, *Discarded Image*, 176.

DIVINE SOVEREIGNTY AND HUMAN FREEDOM 109

That is more a repetition of the biblical polarities than an explanation, still less a harmonization or resolution of them.

Finally, among the theologoumena relating to sovereignty and human accountability there are the various definitions of free will (*liberum arbitrium*) that are used either to absolve God of any moral responsibility for human evil, including human unbelief, or to render man's freedom consistent with an absolute divine rule. Is human freedom simply the freedom to act voluntarily, in keeping with one's desires, so that the acts of human beings are their own acts and so acts they are morally responsible for? Since Holy Scripture seems clearly to teach that human beings by nature are defiantly and incorrigibly rebellious and would never and could never willingly submit themselves to God absent the re-creative work of the Holy Spirit, on this definition human beings remain entirely free in their unbelief nevertheless since they continue to do *as they please*.[20] Or, contrarily, must human freedom entail the power to choose the contrary? In such a view human beings can be said to be free only if they have the power within themselves and by themselves to believe *or* refuse to believe, to submit to God *or* refuse to do so. We generally associate the former view with Reformed theology (though its foundation was laid in what Martin Luther himself regarded as his *magnum opus*, *The Bondage of the Will*[21]) and the latter view with Roman Catholic and Arminian theology. The situation is actually more complicated, given that neither Lutheran nor Reformed theology is monolithic in its understanding of the powers of the human will. There are in those traditions both weaker and stronger views of the contingency of life, more or less deterministic, or more or less willing to define the freedom of the will in terms of the power of contrary choice. More robust views of human freedom are found even among Reformed theologians committed to absolute divine sovereignty in both providence and salvation.[22]

20. The Reformed theologian Johannes Maccovius defined human freedom in this way. "Liberty does not consist in this, that what you do, if you wish you are able not to do, but in this, that what you do you do willingly. . . ." [My translation] This he and others call the liberty of spontaneity. Kuyper, *Johannes Maccovius*, 291.

21. For Luther's own construction of free will, see his *Bondage of the Will*, 102–3. And for Packer and Johnston's account of Luther's doctrine of man's will, see 48–49. They write: "Are there problems raised by this Biblical doctrine of the absolute sovereignty of God in providence and grace? Of course there are. Everything that God reveals of Himself transcends man's comprehension; every doctrine, therefore, must of necessity terminate in mystery, and man must humbly acquiesce in having it so." 54.

22. Muller, *Divine Will*, 247–57. These discussions are punishingly complex and

Again, Holy Scripture neither uses the term "free will" nor defines human freedom in one way or another.[23] It teaches the bondage of the human will to sin in the strongest possible terms (Gen 8:21; Jer 13:23; John 15:5; Rom 3:10–18; 8:7–8; Eph 2:1–5), but at the same time everywhere appeals to the will of man to believe and be saved, asserts the obligation of human beings to answer the summons of the gospel, and blames them for the failure to do so (Deut 30:19; Ezek 18:30–32; John 3:16–18; Acts 13:38–46; 28:23–28). This is why such interpretations are theologoumena, opinions and not dogma.[24] No Christian is obliged to find such opinions persuasive or agree that they solve the problem created by the Bible's parallel assertions of divine sovereignty and human accountability. There will always be reasons leading many to doubt they are of much use in helping us to understand the biblical contraries. Such theologoumena are understandable efforts to make sense of the discordant assertions we find in Holy Scripture concerning causation in this world and especially in the salvation of sinners. But they lack explicit biblical demonstration and certainly have not proved convincing to enough devout intellects to enable the church to find rest in consensus as she has in the cases of both the Holy Trinity and the incarnation of God the Son. In those cases the paradoxical and ineffable nature of the revelation is more readily admitted.

Everyone should at least admit that such explanations have never proved particularly successful in addressing the standard problems posed by the biblical polarities. They certainly have not put the typical

---

difficult and depend heavily on the philosophical tradition. For example, Francis Turretin, a representative Calvinist, admits that "free will" is not a biblical term, it derives from philosophy, but argues that "freedom is a fundamental characteristic of the rational creature, belonging to it by nature," and that this freedom involves "potencies to the opposite effect," but, at the same time, "the lack of power to the good is strongly asserted, but the essence of freedom is not destroyed." The human will, in both sin and grace, remains "the mistress of its own acts." Or, in other words, "although [the will] determines itself, nevertheless this does not prevent it from being determined by God, since the determination of God does not exclude it from human determination." These "explanations" are manifestly more philosophical than biblical.

23. Calvin was so uncomfortable with the term "free will," susceptible as it was and is to so many different definitions, that he said not only that it "cannot be retained without great peril" but that it would be "a great boon for the church if it [were] abolished." *Institutes*, II, 8. Cf. the fine discussion of human freedom in Berkouwer, *Man*, 310–48.

24. Cf. Carson's discussion of the various ways in which theologians have attempted to domesticate this paradox. *Divine Sovereignty*, 206–9.

questions to rest. If God is sovereign, if he determines who will and will not be saved, even more, if he fashions from the same lump of clay both vessels for honor and dishonor, is he then morally responsible for the unbelief and so the damnation of the lost? If so, why does Holy Scripture so relentlessly lay the responsibility for their rebellion and the judgment it deserves at the feet of the unbelieving? If salvation is of the Lord, can we continue to believe that human beings have no one to blame but themselves should they not be saved? In the matters of both divine providence and a person's own salvation, are human beings thus reduced by an inexorable logic to the status of puppets, dancing to the invisible strings God holds in his hands? Is the holy, just, and loving God as morally accountable for the damnation of sinners as he is for their salvation? Was the defiantly Calvinistic Charles Spurgeon thus wrong to declaim to his great congregation in terms such as these?

> I charge you by the living God, I charge you by the world's Redeemer, I charge you by the cross of Calvary, and by the blood which stained the dust at Golgotha, obey this divine message and you shall have eternal life; but refuse it, and on your own heads be your blood for ever and ever![25]

If, on the other hand, men and women in sin are capable in and of themselves of believing in Christ or refusing to do so, and so solely accountable for their choice, is it the free exercise of the human will, not divine grace, that separates the saved from the lost? However we may seek to disguise the fact, is the human being, at the critical point, his or her own savior? Does salvation, therefore, finally depend upon the intelligence, the humility, or the moral perception of human beings dead in their transgressions and sins? Is faith then a work, a human achievement, however much assisted by the help God provides to everyone, the saved and the unsaved alike? And, if so, what then of those human beings who never heard of Christ, were never invited to come to Christ and be saved, and so never had the opportunity to exercise their wills on behalf of their own salvation? Must we create a separate category of human beings to account for people that were never given a gospel summons, a category admittedly unknown to Holy Scripture?

---

25. *Metropolitan Tabernacle Pulpit*, 8:408, cited in Murray, *Forgotten Spurgeon*, 101. This was a frequent emphasis in Spurgeon's preaching. "If he be lost, damnation is all of man; but, if he be saved, still salvation is all of God." Cited in Murray, *Spurgeon v. Hyper-Calvinism*, 86.

If God is sovereign and effects the salvation of only some, must we then find some other way to read the impressive number of statements to the effect that he desires the salvation of everyone (e.g., Isa 30:18–19; Ezek 18:23, 31–32; 33:11; Rom 10:20–21; 1 Tim 2:3–4; Heb 2:9; 2 Pet 3:9; Rev 22:17)[26] or the Lord's many and various statements to the effect that he is disgusted with death?[27] On the other hand, if the human will, independent of God's rule, tells the tale, must we find some other way to read the vast collection of biblical assertions and illustrations to the effect that sinful human beings are reborn not of the will of the flesh nor of the will of man, but of the will of God? How many times, after all, does Holy Scripture say that it is God who makes the dead to live! It takes very little time in the literature to learn that it is precisely these questions, one set or the other, that continue to be raised as the principal arguments against one or the other understanding of divine and human agency in the salvation of sinners. Efforts to harmonize the biblical data to the satisfaction of most Christians, on one side or the other, have proven uniformly unsuccessful.

A Way Forward

It would advance the discussion considerably if everyone were simply to acknowledge the fact, obvious as it is, that the Bible never explains the interrelation of divine and human agency in human history or in salvation. Obvious as the questions are to us, they are neither asked nor answered in Holy Scripture. The Bible asserts in turn that God wants everyone to be saved; he has chosen only some for salvation; he summons all to drink freely of the living water; those who refuse are culpable for their unbelief; God is not the author of sin and cannot be blamed for the unbelief of human beings; those he has chosen to save he makes able and willing to confess that Jesus is Lord; he preserves his elect in faith and eternal life; and some who begin to follow Christ apostatize by their own will and to their own ruin. That all these assertions are true is certainly paradoxical, all the more obviously since Holy Scripture never provides the means to resolve the asymmetry between them.

26. Typical of a great many who make the same point, Calvin, in his comment on Hosea 13:14 writes, ". . . God . . . does not simply promise salvation, but shows that he is indeed ready to save, but that the wickedness of the people . . . was an impediment in the way." *Commentaries on the Minor Prophets*, 1:476.

27. Moon, *Hosea*, 214.

Romans 9 and 10

Even in Romans 9, the only place where we find a prophet or an apostle wrestling with the interplay of divine rule and human responsibility in anything like an abstract or systematic way, no attempt is made to harmonize them.[28] There Paul raises *arguendo* the typical objections to an absolute divine sovereignty in salvation. But, having done so, Paul simply defends his assertion of that sovereignty. He does not relate it to human responsibility or accountability. He says the fact that God shows mercy to some and not to all does not impugn God's justice, since the gift of salvation is explicitly an exercise of divine mercy not justice. He goes on to say that God's absolute rule is also not a crime against the constitution of a human being made in his image, a human being who thinks and chooses, since the Creator has an absolute right to do with his creatures as he pleases. "Who are you to answer back to God?" However appropriate a reminder of the creature's place before the majesty of the Almighty, Paul's rhetorical question is hardly an explanation or a resolution of the polarities. But take the point: *Paul will brook no diminishment of God's absolute rule in the matter of the salvation of sinners!*

However, what Paul does not do is offer any explanation of how that divine sovereignty relates to or interacts with the responsible exercise of the human will. Indeed, without any such explanation, without any suggestion that he is contradicting himself or speaking in a way inconsistent with what he has just said, Paul immediately and artlessly proceeds to assert in the strongest and most unqualified terms the exercise of the human will as a cause of salvation. The Jews were *willfully* ignorant of the gospel and defiant rebels against God. This is a fact the Bible relentlessly asserts against all comers (Ezek 2–3; 1 Thess 2:14–16). They had failed to find salvation, no matter God's appeal to them to believe and be saved, because they were, he says, a disobedient and contrary people (10:21). The Gentiles, on the other hand, were now being summoned to the very salvation the Jews had rejected. But their salvation absolutely requires an act of the will by which they would answer the gospel summons and call upon the name of the Lord. This they can do, says Paul, only if Christians

28. I remain unimpressed by the attempts made by many somehow to remove personal salvation from Paul's argument in Romans 9. The issue under discussion, its context, the argument itself, the vocabulary employed, the Scripture cited, and the objections anticipated all conspire to prove that Paul is talking about how it is that some are saved and others are not (Rom 9:6, 8, 27; 10:1; 11:14, 20).

bend every effort to ensure that the unbelieving world is evangelized. If Romans 9:1–29 is one of the Bible's most emphatic assertions of destiny, Romans 9:30—10:21 is an equally urgent assertion of contingency. Indeed Romans 9 and 10 are as perfect an example of biblical parataxis, the side-by-side arrangement of assertions or ideas, of absoluteness in their statement, and of the absence of any analysis of their systematic interrelation as are Romans 6 and 7 in their assertion first of the Christian's liberation from sin and then his or her continuing bondage to that same sin.

Paul's anticipation of objections in Romans 9 is evidence enough that he knew that the interaction of divine and human agency in salvation was going to provoke confusion, if not objection. The fact that he did not then explicitly address the interrelation of the two agencies; the fact that, having so emphatically asserted the sovereignty of God, he promptly asserted the responsibility of the human will; and the fact that he refused to raise the issue or even acknowledge the mystery in Romans 9, where his discussion provided the perfect opportunity to do so, is certainly some proof that it was neither his nor the Holy Spirit's intention *ever* to address the question. Rather he moves, as the Bible invariably does, seamlessly and with a striking lack of self-consciousness, from absolute divine sovereignty to the responsibility of human beings to exercise their will in obedience to the gospel *or else*. This is what the Bible *always does*: ". . . constantly mingles ultimacy and human responsibility without mutual dilution."[29] If we may personalize the Bible, we might say that it is unashamed to assert both divine rule and human accountability in the most unqualified terms and to never engage the question how both can be true at one and the same time. John Duncan was only being faithful to the biblical representation, therefore, when he said that to say that God does half and man does half is wrong; to say that God does all and man does all is right!

So What?

What that means, then, is simply this: we must believe in an absolute divine sovereignty and an absolutely responsible exercise of the human will, however much the harmony of those two truths eludes our

29. Carson, *Divine Sovereignty*, 203. Holy Scripture, Carson goes on to say, juxtaposes "divine sovereignty and human responsibility at every turn, manifesting little if any awareness of the theoretical difficulties which later thinkers discover in such a juxtaposition" 206.

comprehension. Once again, it should neither surprise nor depress us that reality in its scope and complexity exceeds our understanding. Why is one person saved and another not? The Bible answers that question in more than one way. Certainly, first and foremost, a gracious God is saving his people from their sins. But the devil and his minions are also at work doing their nefarious will. Human beings themselves are at work for good or for ill. What person supposes that we could understand or explain precisely how these agencies in their interaction produce the intricate and complex circumstances that make up the human story and the story of every individual human life?

One thing is certain: the Bible makes no effort to dissipate the mystery. One would need a mind as powerful and capacious as God's own to see the infinite number of connections between one thing and everything else, the influence that one person or thing bears upon another, and the pathway by which any series of events leads to an eventual and final outcome. We know that God is a person and we know that he is a transcendent person, whose nature, thoughts, and acts must remain in many respects profoundly mysterious to mere creatures. How God interacts with human history; how eternity interacts with time; how the laws he has established to direct both inanimate and animate life function to bring his plans to pass; how his immediate and direct intervention relate to those laws; how love, justice, holiness, and omnipotence combine in his rule of human affairs; and how the intellect and will of the creatures made in his image are woven into the fabric of history are matters about which we must see only very dimly. He is an absolute ruler of time and history, but he is also a person engaged with us, who grieves over our sins, who pleads with us to come to him, who rejoices when we do and grieves when we do not, and who loves us and wants the best for us, all of us (Isa 16:11).[30] Who, with a Bible in his or her hands and a willingness to acknowledge the mystery of life, can deny any of this? Once again, the truth is broken into pieces small enough for us to grasp because we are not able to see the whole.

What we *know* is that God is in absolute control of history and of our history; that it is the outworking of a plan that he formed in eternity past, a plan so comprehensive that absolutely nothing was or is left to

---

30. "... the Lord too grieves over the pride of Moab and its consequences. In 15:5 he wept for Moab, but now he weeps *with* Moab ... making its tears his own. He is no onlooker at the world's sorrow but identifies with the mourners even though it is the weight of his own justly imposed punishment that he feels." Motyer, *Isaiah*, 154.

chance.[31] Even the evil that men do, even their unbelief accomplishes, however unwittingly and mysteriously, the purposes of God (Josh 11:20; Judg 14:1–4; 1 Sam 2:25; 16:14; 1 Kgs 12:15; Isa 6:9–10; 63:17; Ezek 14:9; John 9:39; Acts 2:23; 4:28; 2 Thess 2:11–12; 1 Pet 2:8; Rev 17:17), no matter that God "cannot be tempted with evil, and he himself tempts no one" (Jas 1:13) and that his eyes are too pure to "look at wrong" (Hab 1:13).[32] We know that Adam, by an act of his will, fell from the holy condition in which he was created and became, with all his descendants, inescapably sinful and rebellious in thought, word, and deed. Only divine power can overcome such rebellion. We also know that human beings must exercise their will in obedience to God if they are to be saved. We know that they bear a moral responsibility for the outcome of their lives. We know that God is right to blame them and to punish them for their refusal to submit to his will. We must call upon the Lord; we must repent of our sins; we must obey his commandments; we must seek his forgiveness throughout the course of our lives; and we must persevere in faith and love until the end of our lives. All of this we must do in active dependence upon the grace of God. We must do all of this or, by our own fault, we will fail to obtain the heavenly country.[33]

The immense practical importance of the embrace of the biblical dialectic of divine sovereignty and human responsibility, that is, an active confidence in the truth of both *without qualification*, is that it is this paradox that is *the foundation of an authentically biblical life*. Such a life is one of active and unqualified dependence upon God's grace and power, his sovereign plan—in every respect and at all times—*and* one of uncomplaining acceptance of responsibility for one's faith, hope, love, and obedience. It is a life of the deepest humility in the recognition of the fact that the *only* thing we have contributed to our salvation is the sin and the

31. Jerome's suggestion, in his commentary on Habbakuk, that it belittles the majesty of God to suppose that he knows each moment how many mosquitoes are born and how many die, how many bugs, fleas, and flies there are in the world, etc. finds no support in the Bible and was uniformly rejected by Christian theology. He knows everything because he brings everything to pass! Bavinck, *Reformed Dogmatics*, 2:196–98.

32. William Still, my honored pastor during my years of study in Scotland in the 1970s, used to confess the mystery by saying that God "uses sin sinlessly."

33. "D.M. Baillie refers (*God was in Christ* [London, 1948], p. 114ff.) to what he calls the 'paradox peculiar to Christianity' that man has a sense of genuine ability to participate creatively in the work of God and yet must acknowledge that everything he does is to be ascribed only to God." MacGregor, *Corpus Christi*, 209n.

bondage to sin from which we needed to be delivered. It is also a life of zealous and determined activity in obedience to the divine summons to believe in the Lord Jesus Christ and to put our faith to work, not only out of boundless gratitude for God's love and grace pitched upon us in defiance of our ill desert, but in the expectation that our lives will be subject to review and judgment on the Great Day. This life, as we find it taught and illustrated in the Bible, is a life of affiance and activity; of waiting upon God and of working and wrestling; of undying love for eternal life given and of constant watchfulness that we be found not to have received the grace of God in vain. It is fundamental to our understanding of life and salvation that we know both that "we love *because* he first loved us" (1 John 4:19; Eph 1:4–5) *and* that God loves us *because* we love Christ and have believed that he came from God (John 14:27).

The moral consciousness of the Christian soul rises in protest against any thought that we are our own saviors, but equally against any suggestion that we are not responsible for the lives we live before God and man. We know our need for the grace of God. We know the greatness of our sin and the weakness of our faith. We know we are not autonomous. We are not simply mere creatures, subject to many factors beyond our control; our lives are hemmed in by God on every side. Our consciences, catechized as they are by Holy Scripture and informed by our daily experience of life, instinctively repudiate both the thought that we are puppets—that we make our own decisions is what it means to be made in the image of God—and the thought that we are the captains of our own fate. We *know* that we are neither! Though we cannot explain how it is that God is an absolute sovereign in both providence and salvation and yet that we are creative and accountable actors in both, it has never proved impossible or even especially difficult for God's people to understand that the Christian life is a life of working out our salvation in fear and trembling because it is God who is working in us both to will and to work for his good pleasure (Phil 2:12–13). Our work depends upon his; we must work for God is at work in us, but it is not for that reason any less our responsibility to work or any less absolutely necessary, hence the "fear and trembling." We grasp each truth—so clearly, repeatedly, and emphatically taught— separately, even if we cannot grasp their unity.

6

The Doctrines of the Bible

You have all heard of the difficulty the voyager had in steering between Scylla and Charybdis in the Latin adage. Well, the true preacher's difficulty is just like that. Indeed, it is beyond the wit of man, and it takes all the wit of God, aright to unite the doctrine of our utter inability with the companion doctrine of our strict responsibility; free grace with full reward; the cross of Christ once for all, with the saint's continual crucifixion; the Savior's blood with the sinner's; and atonement with attainment; in short, salvation without works with no salvation without works. Deft steersman as the devil is, he never yet took his ship clear through those Charybdic passages.

—ALEXANDER WHYTE

I HAVE ARGUED THAT the method of revelation by and in polarities is found everywhere we look in Holy Scripture. It is characteristic of the revelation of doctrine, of the Bible's theological teaching. In this chapter I propose to demonstrate this phenomenon with three further examples that serve to illustrate both the ubiquity of this biblical pedagogy and its genius. The three dialectics I have chosen to consider cluster around the salvation of sinners, as do many of the biblical paradoxes. That should surprise no one. The Bible's principal theme is salvation and it addresses this theme in many different respects: its origin, its principles, its accomplishment in history, its experience by individuals, its dependence on both divine and human agency, and its consummation at the second coming and in the world to come. In regard to all of this we are given a welter of polarities and only polarities.

I have also argued that a principal reason for this dialectical method of revelation is that it enables finite minds to grasp the truth to the extent that they are able to do so. But, ubiquitous as this pedagogy is in Holy Scripture, there are other reasons for it than that the human mind is incapable of comprehending the truth in its breadth and depth. The limitations of creaturely intellect explain the manner in which certain doctrines are revealed, but this is not invariably the case. There are other advantages to parataxis, paradox, absoluteness of statement, and the lack of systematic analysis. One of them, no doubt, is the way it serves to emphasize truth, to force it upon the consciousness, and to prevent that indifference, especially to some truth, that is a fatal tendency of the sinful mind.

I. The Assurance of Salvation

Given the nature and history of salvation and the sometimes tumultuous and confusing experience of it in any individual life, how can one know that he or she is saved? How does any Christian know that he is not indulging in self-deception? How does she know that her interest in Jesus Christ is genuine, that her sins have really been forgiven, that she has her feet safely planted on the straight and narrow way that leads to everlasting life? Over the years of my pastorate I baptized both infants born to Christian parents and adult converts who, after living for some time not only as professing Christians but, by all accounts, faithful Christians, forsook the faith and now live as unbelievers. How does one know that he or she will not do the same?

In times of the Spirit's powerful working, when people in great numbers are taking biblical teaching seriously and considering the issues of eternity in deadly earnest, the lack of assurance is not infrequently an existential crisis and gaining it the source of peace, joy, and spiritual power. At such times ministers have had to apply themselves to the challenge both to be able to instruct their congregations in the biblical grounds of a well-founded assurance and to warn them of the errors typically entertained even by the well-meaning. The saints are often confused in such heady times precisely because spiritual experiences are typically powerful but sometimes come to nothing (Mark 4:16; Heb 6:4–5). So, for example, both the English Puritans and the preachers of the Great Awakening made the assurance of salvation a subject of careful study and one that frequently surfaced in their preaching.[1] As part of its teaching of the nature of salvation and in light of the complexity of human responses to the gospel, the Bible has much to say about assurance: about how a person can *know* that he or she has eternal life.

The Need for Assurance

In an antinomian day, in a time such as ours when even believers by and large have little fear of the judgment of God and far too many consider the certainty of their own salvation with blithe self-confidence or active indifference, assurance rarely surfaces as a subject requiring careful thought or discrimination in preaching and pastoral care. I can chart, even over the course of my own forty years of ministry, a decline of interest in the question.[2] But since it is a subject to which Holy Scripture devotes considerable attention, Christians' indifference to it is no sign of spiritual health and vitality. A properly founded assurance is not only the sure protection against fatal self-deception; it is the foundation of a more than ordinarily faithful, fruitful, and happy Christian life. As the seventeenth- and early-eighteenth-century Scottish divine Thomas Halyburton put it, ". . . the most effectual inducement to obedience is, a constant improvement of the blood of Christ by faith, and a sense of forgiveness kept on the soul. Lord, bear home truth!"[3] A "sense of forgiveness" is simply assurance in other words. The lack of the joy of one's salvation, of living assurance, is a chief cause of weak faith.

1. According to Martyn Lloyd-Jones, ". . . assurance . . . in many ways was the distinguishing mark of Methodism." *Puritans*, 198.

2. "I have not conducted a scientific poll to establish changing patterns over the last few decades. My impression, however, is that in many churches Christian assurance is not a major topic for sermons or discussion groups, largely because popular eschatology has become so realized that there is very little futurist element left, except at the merely creedal level. If we do not long for the consummation of our salvation in the new heaven and the new earth, for the *visio Dei* that is the believer's inheritance, then there is little point in talking about our assurance of gaining it." Carson, "Reflections on Christian Assurance," 7.

3. Halyburton, *Memoirs*, 193. "In giving assurance, [God] convinces the Christian that the absolute promises of Scripture include him in their scope . . . and moves him to make the appropriate response, i.e., to rejoice." Packer, *Quest for Godliness*, 185.

The Bible, after all, leaves us in no doubt that multitudes have supposed themselves saved when they were not. The history of Israel proved
to be more often than not the history of unbelief *in the church* and of
Israel's indifference and inattention to her danger. The prophets warned
Israel, "Prepare to meet your God," but their warning repeatedly fell on
deaf ears. Our Lord's congregations included many people at ease in Zion.
Church history is not only the story of the long march of living faith in
the world, but of the believing community's struggle to drag along behind
her immense numbers of merely nominal Christians, Christians whose
faith was a poor imitation, often a very poor imitation of the real thing.
The Bible both teaches and illustrates the reality of both counterfeit faith
and apostasy. Both the Lord and his apostles regularly address these realities. One of the Twelve, who witnessed the Lord's miracles and heard all
his sermons, who had his own experience of powerful ministry in the
Lord's name, proved himself at last a reprobate. One of the apostle Paul's
inner circle, likewise a witness of gospel power, eventually decamped. Indeed, some of the Lord's most solemn teaching addresses this mournful
phenomenon of faith that is appearance only, not substance. No wonder
then that we find in the Bible explicit instruction how to make our calling
and election sure (2 Pet 1:10–11).

The Grounds of Assurance

To summarize a great deal of biblical teaching and theological reflection
on the subject, a well-grounded assurance of salvation may be said to
rest on three pillars: 1) the promises of the gospel believed and embraced
with mind and heart (John 1:12; Acts 16:31; 2 Tim 1:12), 2) the witness of
the Holy Spirit to our spirits (Ps 73:15–26; Rom 8:14–17; 14:17), and 3) a
life that demonstrates love for and loyalty to God (Rom 8:4, 13; Eph 2:10;
1 John 1:6; 2:4).[4] Think of them as the legs of a three-legged stool; each is
essential and the lack of any one of them can cause even the most devout

---

4. ". . . a firm assurance of salvation [can be] obtained . . . by the testimony of the
Holy Spirit from the nature and fruits of faith." Bavinck, *Reformed Dogmatics*, 4:228.
John Duncan, a careful student of Christian assurance, said he never found a better
mark by which to examine himself than this from Thomas Halyburton's *Memoirs*. "I
never wish the law to be changed to meet my heart; but that my heart may be changed
to meet God's law." Duncan went on to observe that if we can say that even at our worst
time, bondage has become liberty! *Just a Talker*, 91.

Christian's confidence to totter. In any case, there is without question in the Bible a *theology of assurance*.

The Lord and his brother James are among the many biblical voices that reject the possibility of true faith without obedience. Throughout his public ministry the Lord also dealt with those who rested their confidence in obedience but were lacking faith in one who would save them from their sins.[5] And the entire Bible protests against the very idea of an impersonal faith and obedience, without the motivations of knowledge, love, and gratitude instilled by the Holy Spirit.

Contraries Once Again: A Changed Life

However, each of these foundations of assurance happens to lie at one end of a biblical continuum. With its opposite pole, each forms a complex of opposites. Any pastor who has sought to comfort a troubled soul, a soul that is troubled by fears of self-deception, knows only too well how easily the counter-positions to the three grounds of biblical assurance can bedevil the believer's search for a sense of security. An obedient life? The sensitive and thoughtful believer knows only too well how little changed his or her life actually is, how much it remains enslaved to self and to uncounted sins of both commission and omission. More than that, the believer has no excuse; he or she knows better and should do better! For all that we hope for the transformation of life, surely Augustine was correct to admit that "in this life [our righteousness] consists rather in the remission of sins than in the perfecting of virtues."[6] And what honest believer does not see the truth in Bishop William Beveridge's painful admission?

> I cannot pray, but I sin: I cannot hear or preach a sermon but I sin: I cannot give an alms, or receive the sacrament, but I sin: nay, I cannot so much as confess my sins, but my confessions are still aggravations of them. My repentance needs to be repented of, my tears want washing, and the very washing of my tears needs still to be washed over again with the blood of my Redeemer.[7]

5. Despite the great effort expended recently to rehabilitate the theology of Second Temple Judaism as a theology of grace, Paul Billerbeck's conclusion remains incontestable that the religion of the scribes and Pharisees had no place for a Redeemer-Savior who would die for the sin of the world. *Kommentar zum Neuen Testament*, 4:6.

6. Augustine, *City of God*, XIX, 27, 419.

7. Cited in Ryle, *Old Paths*, 130n. "Alas! I have never done a sinless action during it

Every Christian should know very well, and the sensitive Christian conscience most certainly knows only too well how true it is that "my iniquities have overtaken me, and I cannot see; they are more than the hairs of my head; my heart fails me" (Ps 40:12). So when the Christian with a scrupulous conscience reads that we are called to be perfect as our Heavenly Father is perfect (Matt 5:48), that without holiness no one will see the Lord (Heb 12:14), that our righteousness must exceed that of the scribes and Pharisees (Matt 5:20), that to be Christ's disciple one must take up his or her cross to follow him, hating even his own life (Luke 14:26–27), that many confess Jesus as Lord and try to get into the banquet only to encounter his peremptory rejection because they did not obey and serve him (Matt 7:21–23; 25:12, 41–43), and that real Christians purify themselves and no longer sin (1 John 3:3, 9), it should surprise no one that his or her faith can be shaken and assurance lost. Indeed, who can read those texts and not feel a shiver? In fact, if such statements *never* shake a Christian's confidence, can he or she be taking them seriously? There can be no doubt that Holy Scripture insists in many different ways that God's grace, by the working of the Holy Spirit, will transform the heart and life. But how easily some believers find it difficult to see persuasive evidence of this transformation. The antinomy of a Christian life that is at one and the same time radically delivered from bondage to sin and yet remains its slave has held hostage the assurance of multitudes of devout Christians. This equilibrium of truths—liberation from sin and continued bondage to it—has been lost through a failure to believe two seemingly contrary truths at the same time. It is no easy work to believe oneself both free and a slave!

The faithful pastor will remind fearful Christians that even their worry, their conviction of their many great sins sets them dramatically

---

all; I have never done a sinless action during the seventy years. I don't say but by God's grace there may have been some holy action done, but never a sinless action during the seventy years. What an awful thing is human life! And what a solemn consideration it should be to us, that we have never done a sinless action all our life, that we have never done one act that did not need to be pardoned." John Duncan, quoted in Moody Stuart, *Life of John Duncan*, 150. "Happy is that man who can comfort himself with having employed any one day of his life so perfectly well, as he might, and ought to have done." Kempis, *Imitation of Christ*, 58. "I never did anything which might not and ought not to have been done better." Richard Baxter, *Penitent Confession* (London, 1691), 28, cited in Murray, *Evangelicalism Divided*, 316. Of course, we encounter in such confessions still another complex of opposites, for the Bible does not hesitate to acknowledge the obedience and virtue, even the blamelessness, of those who know very well how disobedient and unvirtuous they are.

apart from the unsaved. Contrition of that kind is true virtue! He will remind them that Christ died for our sins, that there is forgiveness with God, that we are justified by faith and not by works, even that the Bible repeatedly acknowledges and illustrates the continual sinfulness of genuine believers. But for some that proves little comfort. The struggling Christian—the direct descendent of the apostle Paul's "wretched man"—will reply, "How do I know that *I* am not among those described in those terrifying scenes of repudiation? After all, the foolish virgins in the Lord's parable (Matt 25:1–13) went out to meet the Lord, expected to be welcomed by him, but were shut out of the banquet nevertheless. There will be those on the Great Day who could claim that they drove out demons in the Lord's name and performed other mighty works, which I have never done, but they were rejected for their failure to do the will of God, a failure of which I too am guilty (Matt 7:21–23)." Satan is an acute theologian and, as he did in tempting the Lord, the accuser of the brethren often deploys with devastating effect the Bible's teaching in his effort to undermine living faith (Matt 4:4, 6).

Contraries Once Again: The Gospel Embraced by Faith

Well, what then of the promises God has addressed to believers? Believe in the Lord Jesus Christ and you will be saved! Alas, they know only too well how weak their faith actually is, how little their hearts and lives are what they know they ought to be if they *really believed* in the majesty of divine love for deeply undeserving sinners; the terrible suffering and sacrifice of the Son of God on the cross; his triumphant resurrection from the dead; and his summons to his disciples to adorn the teaching of God their Savior, to seek first the kingdom of God and leave the rest to God's wise and faithful provision, and to conduct themselves at all times alive to the looming realities of divine judgment, heaven, and hell. "Wouldn't one who *really believed* these things live a far, far better life, more devout, more useful than mine? There were many who 'believed' in Jesus during his ministry whose faith was temporary, hypocritical, and a mere imitation of the real thing (John 2:23–25). How weak can faith be before it is no longer faith at all? Paul was well aware that some of his converts might fail the test of faith (2 Cor 13:5). The number of those who have 'made shipwreck *of their faith*' (1 Tim 1:19; Rev 3:2–3) is not small!" This fact is turned often enough into solemn warning (2 Pet 2:20–22).

Contraries Once Again: The Testimony of the Holy Spirit

Well, what of the testimony of the Holy Spirit? "What testimony?" he or she is likely to ask. "I find prayer difficult work. Why should that be so if the Lord is near to me and promises to hear and answer? I have lived for months, if not for years without a bracing, soul-arresting, empowering experience of the love of God shed abroad in my heart, without the ecstasy with which God's grace ought to fill my heart. I can go for weeks without a chill once traveling up and down my spine at the thought that I was going to hell, blissfully unaware, and in the nick of conversion God placed my feet on the path to that place where everlasting joy rests on everyone's head. He might so easily not have done so; he has not done so for multitudes no more sinful than I. How could I really be a believer in these stupendous realities and feel them so little, be so little moved and changed by them? Can the testimony of the Holy Spirit be thought to mean so little? I can experience some sense of the Lord's majestic presence when singing in church or under the influence of a powerful sermon, but then Judas excitedly rejoiced at the power he wielded over demons and he too had been moved by the Lord's preaching. So must Ananias and Sapphira once have been, and Demas!" Such a reply is hardly surprising given the number of times in Holy Scripture we are given to see believers struggle under a silent heaven or mourn God's having seemed to have hidden himself from his people (Isa 45:15; Ps 42:3, 9–10; 69:1–5; 74:1–11; 77:1–9), or the number of times we ourselves have seen believers return to the world as a dog to its vomit. *Each of the foundations provided for the assurance of salvation has its emphatic counterpoint in the Bible's own teaching!*

Assurance: A Tangled Skein

Once again, the Bible presents its teaching in polarities, each stated in an absolute form, but does not account for or systematize their interrelations. The grounds of assurance are said to be realities the Scripture itself acknowledges are not easy to measure. Precisely how much holiness is required to see the Lord? The Holy Spirit's testimony is seemingly sometimes missing or has been experienced by or possessed to some degree by hypocrites. What true assurance of salvation could David have enjoyed during the nine months between his terrible sins and his repentance? The Bible furnishes us with examples of believers who at certain times in their

lives were bereft of any living sense of the love of God (Psalm 73).[8] Here
is assurance: the Spirit testifies, the promises are believed, and the obedient life confirms—all of this on the one hand. On the other, however,
believers know, because they are taught in the Bible, that they remain
deeply selfish and sinful, that even the works of Christians can amount
to very little (1 Cor 3:14–15), that their faith regularly must be taken to
be even smaller than a mustard seed since it appears incapable of moving
any mountains, and that while they may pray for the powerful witness of
the Holy Spirit many do not experience it for long periods of time. No
wonder J. I. Packer called the problem of assurance "a tangled skein, if
ever there was one!"[9] The Scottish theologian James Denney famously
remarked that whereas assurance is a sin in Romanism, and a duty in
much of Protestantism, in the New Testament it is simply a fact. But fact
though it may be—and there are certainly multitudes of faithful believers
who have never or only very rarely seriously struggled with doubts about
their own salvation—as a teaching of the Bible the assurance of salvation is complicated precisely by the dialectical assertions concerning the
evidences of a person's being in a state of grace.[10] No wonder a wit once

8. Complicating a thoughtful believer's search for assurance is the fact that the
Christian life is composed of peaks and valleys, of times of spiritual progress and re-
gression, times of the softening of the heart and times of its hardening. As Bavinck
observes, "So, whereas election and reprobation may culminate in a final and total
separation, on earth they continually crisscross each other." *Reformed Dogmatics*,
2:398. It should not be difficult to see how this complicates making one's election sure:
the evidences themselves wax and wane!

9. Packer, *Knowing God*, 223. "Certainly the question of Christian assurance is
raised by what appear to be tensions within the biblical documents themselves." Carson, "Reflections on Christian Assurance," 2. It is precisely these tensions that account
for the dramatically different accounts of assurance—its nature, its grounds, even its
possibility—one finds in the theological literature. No wonder then that some have
argued that the assurance of salvation cannot be found in this life and that others have
argued that assurance is an indispensable mark of salvation!

10. It is to be admitted that certain personalities have a greater difficulty putting
their hearts to rest in the confidence of their salvation. Regarding people who suffer
serious doubts even deep into their Christian lives John Duncan observed, "There is
no dealing with such persons; for if you give them signs of grace, they will ask for signs
of the signs." *Just a Talker*, 56. Assurance is a grace and like every grace it is sovereign.
The Lord gives it to some in greater measure than to others. Each theological tradition,
likewise, has its own peculiar problems with assurance, a further demonstration of the
influence of the Bible's dialectical revelation of salvation and its evidences. Abraham
Kuyper acknowledged that Reformed theology, with its doctrine of divine election,
had a penchant for creating an unhealthy obsession with the state of one's soul, pay-
ing greater attention to oneself than to Christ's triumph over sin and death. This he

observed, "A Methodist knows he's got religion, but he's afraid he'll lose it. A Presbyterian knows he can't lose it, but he's afraid he hasn't got it."[11]

No Christian believer or Christian minister can solve the problem of assurance of salvation because neither has access to information sufficient to prove that at any moment or under any or all circumstances a professing Christian is saved now and forever. No human being knows what God alone can know. After all, he promises to judge according to the principle that to whom much is given much is required (Luke 12:48). How much has any Christian been given? And would not the very attempt to answer that question inevitably increase his or her responsibility? More than this, no one knows the future as God does, and so none of us can with certainty identify, in the midst of another Christian's manifold spiritual experience, his or her name in the Book of Life. The divine work of salvation and its experience in human life is simply too complex for us, involving too many factors, only some of which can be identified and they only partially and from time to time.

Surely, had the Lord wanted to do so, he might have ordered that regeneration by the imperishable seed of the Word leave some visible mark, but he did not. How little can we understand how such a mark would alter the very nature of believing life in the world! So it may not be intellectual incapacity, pure and simple, that accounts for the biblical polarities upon which the believer's assurance of salvation is suspended. The relevant truth in its polarities, the summons to believe it all without qualification, and the lack of any means by which to render the conclusion objectively obvious and inescapable produces a distinct and specific result. That result is that we must live our lives *in wary confidence*, taking comfort from the evidences of salvation—not least the fact that it concerns us greatly *to know* that we are saved and disturbs us when we are unsure—while at the same time being alert to the devil's wiles and our own weakness and hypocrisy. We are to live our lives aware of what distinguishes the life of a follower of Jesus Christ in this world and determined to be his faithful follower until the end. The Lord will order our ups and downs as he will, but the safest place for Christians is always to live in the tension between liberation and slavery to sin, between confidence in the promises of God

---

rightfully and scornfully referred to as "navel gazing," a form of self-centeredness he labeled the "holy despair of the sect." Bratt, *Abraham Kuyper*, 181.

11. The citation is from a newspaper clipping, cited first in Helm, *Faith with Reason*, 159, then in Lane, *Justification by Faith*, 43. I'm grateful to Prof. Robert Letham for drawing my attention to the quotation.

and a healthy awareness of the weakness of our faith, and between the joy of our salvation and the peace that passes understanding, on the one hand, and, on the other, the lifelong struggle with God's silence and unanswered prayer. Such is our calling to live by faith and to walk the straight and narrow way to everlasting life. It invariably wends its way between the most wonderful promises and the most solemn warnings, between victories and defeats. The apostle Paul is himself our example of one who was both confident of his own salvation—founded as that confidence was on God's promise, his irrevocable gifts, the joy of his salvation, and the apostle's astonishingly impressive faithfulness to his calling as an apostle and as a Christian man—and, no matter his extraordinary privileges and experiences, was taking great care not to lose it (1 Cor 9:1, 26–27). Here was a man who could not fail to be saved, nevertheless making a concentrated, spirited, even painful effort not to receive the grace of God in vain! *How else could such a state of mind be achieved than by requiring Christians to embrace the paradox of new life in the Spirit beset on every side by the vigorous expression of the old life?*

II. How Many Will Be Saved?

The question of the number of the elect is one that has usually been addressed superficially in the manuals of Christian theology but has in the modern era taken on new importance. Christians are now more immediately aware not only of how vast is the population of the world but of the immense number of human beings who are not Christians. We see the teeming masses of humanity on our television screens. In an antinomian and theologically unserious age, when it is already difficult to believe in divine judgment, the idea that vast multitudes would be damned is increasingly unbelievable even to people who consider themselves devout and serious Christians. For this reason alone it is hardly surprising that doubts should surface regarding a salvation that comparatively few seem to share.

Historically, it was not uncommon for theologians to teach that the number of the saved, while large considered by itself, is nevertheless smaller, perhaps much smaller, than the number of the damned.[12]

12. This was true of both Reformed and Lutheran theology. Among the Reformed, typical examples are easily found. *The Leiden Synopsis*, a standard manual originally published in 1652, accepts that the damned will outnumber the saved, though it also acknowledges that the elect nevertheless form a multitude no one can number (Rev

Indeed, in some influential manuals of theology one "attribute" of the elect is their fewness (such even became a doctrine with a Latin name, *paucitas salvandorum*) and of the reprobate their multitudinousness![13] However, especially from the eighteeenth century onwards, a growing number of theologians and influential preachers have argued that the number of the saved will in fact far exceed that of the lost. Among the advocates of this position were Jonathan Edwards, the Presbyterian theologians Charles Hodge and Benjamin Warfield, and Charles Spurgeon. By this point in the argument it should surprise no one that this difference of opinion results from the fact that in describing the number of the saved the Scripture says both that they are few and that they amount to an innumerable company; that they represent a small minority and that the day is coming when the whole world will worship the King of kings.

The Narrow Gate and the Few Who Find It

Chief among the texts typically used to prove that the number of the elect is smaller than that of the damned are Matt 7:14 ("For the gate is narrow and the way is hard that leads to life, and those who find it are few"); Luke 13:23–24 ("For many, I tell you, will seek to enter and will not be able"); Matt 22:14 ("For many are called, but few are chosen"); various texts that refer to believers as comprising a small company (e.g., Luke 12:32's "little flock"); and the Bible's repeated prophesy of human unbelief and rebellion at the time of the second coming (e.g., 2 Thess 2:1–8; cf. the Lord's statement, "Nevertheless, when the Son of Man comes, will he find faith on earth?" Luke 18:8). And when to such assertions as these is added the evidence of biblical history, throughout which the people of God have comprised a small fraction of the world's population, and even within Israel the believing community was often a mere remnant, a small minority of a small nation, it appears beyond question that the community

7:9). Bavinck, ed., *Synopsis Purioris Theologiae*, XXIV, xxx, 228. Another popular manual simply observes that "The elect are fewer [*pauciores*] than the reprobate." Marck, *Christianae Theologiae Medulla*, VII, xxiv, 82. This assumption was often made the basis of warning in preaching. "The world of unbelievers is like a flock of goats, very numerous, whereas the elect of God are but like sheep scattered here and there upon the mountains." Love, *Preacher of God's Word*, 163.

13. Heinrich Schmid considered the "paucity" of the elect and the "plurality" of the reprobate a commonplace of Lutheran dogmatics in the scholastic period. *Doctrinal Theology*, 273–74. See Warfield's summary in "Are They Few," 334–35. This was also Augustine's view. *City of God*, XXI, 12, 463.

of believers has been from the beginning a distinct minority. In history since Pentecost, even as the community of faith has grown substantially, even as now it includes hundreds of millions if not billions of human beings, the Christian church remains only a fraction of the human race, a still smaller fraction if significant deductions are made for her nominal membership.

Every Tongue Shall Swear Allegiance

On the other hand, the Bible frequently speaks of the number of God's elect with extravagant hyperbole: as many "as the stars of heaven and the sand that is on the seashore" (Gen 22:17) and "a great multitude that no one could number" (Rev 7:9). The Lord Jesus is described as the Savior "of the world" (John 4:42; 1 John 4:14), who will "draw all people to [himself]" (John 12:32). Indeed, the apostles do not scruple to say that the Lord Christ is the propitiation not only for our sins, but also for the sins of the whole world (1 John 2:2). And the prophets repeatedly spoke of the day when "the earth will be full of the knowledge of the Lord as the waters cover the sea" (Isa 11:9; Rom 11:32) and when the nations of the earth will worship the Lord (Isa 2:2–4; Zech 8:20–23; Mal 1:11; Rev 15:4). Indeed, so much was the future triumph of the kingdom of God a feature of Israel's eschatological expectation that it became a typical argument for the veneration of God's power and goodness (Ps 86:9; 87:4; 102:15). The gospel has world conquest in its future! If the kingdom of God is likened to a grain of mustard seed or to leaven, the point of the comparison is precisely that what was once very small will eventually become immense (Matt 13:31–33). Even in the mid-eighteenth century Jonathan Edwards could calculate that the immensely greater population of mankind at the time of the consummation, together with the triumph of the kingdom of God predicted in Holy Scripture, would result in a number of believers compared to which all the number of human beings who had existed previously would be but a fraction.[14] Or, as Warfield put it, "We are a 'little flock' now: tomorrow we shall be the world."[15]

In other words, there is a universalizing tendency in the Bible's account of the fortunes of the salvation of God. Its implication is that

14. Marsden, *Jonathan Edwards*, 485.

15. "Jesus Christ the Propitiation for the Whole World," Warfield, *Selected Shorter Writings*, 1:177. Paul Helm adds further arguments in "Are They Few," 257–81.

the company of the elect is far from being, in Mark Twain's caricature, a number so small as to be scarcely worth saving. Rather, it is so large that it may fairly be taken to represent a reconstituted world, a mankind reborn and remade. The prophets and the apostles plainly do not mean that the entire human race is saved, or that Christ by his atonement saved each and every human being. But their penchant for speaking in such expansive terms confirms that they saw a future in which the entire world and the nations of the world would fall under the spell of the gospel.[16]

An Unanswered Question

But observe once more Scripture's characteristic failure to harmonize or rationalize the counter-positions. The Bible does not itself explain how we are to relate the few who are chosen to the innumerable host. It does not tell us in anything resembling explicit or arithmetic terms whether the number of the elect will at the consummation of history be smaller, the same, or larger than the number of the damned. Indeed, when this very question, "Will those who are saved be few?" was put to the Lord, he virtually rebuffed the one asking the question, apparently refusing to satisfy his merely theoretical curiosity, and exposed the lack of self-involvement in his question by turning to the crowd around him and using the occasion to urge them to take with utmost seriousness the issue of their own salvation (Luke 13:22–30). The question, he said, is not how many others will be saved; the question is whether *you* will be! The question was perhaps prompted by the fact that the company of the followers of Jesus amounted, even in his own assessment, to a little flock, a fact he affirmed in his answer. By this point in his ministry it was obvious that the Lord had multiplied his enemies and that many of those who had once seemed to be his friends had deserted him.

Clearly there have been times and places in the history of the gospel's advance when many were being saved as well as times when only a few were entering by the narrow door. It is doubtful, for example, that in the heady days following Pentecost when thousands were streaming into the church (Acts 5:14; 6:7) anyone would have asked, "Lord, will those

16. Even if such a text as Isa 45:23 (Phil 2:10–11)—"To me every knee shall bow, every tongue shall swear allegiance"—does not mean that in those latter days *everyone* will be a true believer, since a typical biblical hyperbole may be at work and a true universalism is denied in the larger context (e.g., 60:12; 66:18–24), the universal scope of the promise is emphatically the point.

who are saved be few?" It is equally doubtful that such a question would be asked today in Sub-Saharan Africa. But it remains the case that the Bible's only answer to this important question is found in its polarities: few in one place, a great host in another.

Surely the Lord might have taken the occasion to say that, however small at present, the company of the saved would be incomparably larger in due time, perhaps even far larger than the company of the unbelieving. Instead, when asked, he used the occasion to press home the necessity of making full use of the opportunity provided by the offer of salvation through the gospel. "Strive to enter through the narrow door. For many I tell you will seek to enter and will not be able" (Luke 13:23–24). However large the number of those who will *not* enter, it is unquestionably "many"! It would twist his words to conclude that he meant that the gate would not always be narrow or that the way that leads to life would not always be hard (Matt 7:14). But that is not itself an answer to the question. For in the day of the Spirit's power "violent" men and women take the kingdom of God by force (Matt 11:12)! And what are the prophecies of the gospel's triumph in the world but forecasts of such holy violence on the part of both God and man on a scale yet unprecedented in history?

A Useful Ignorance

In this case, it does not seem that this is knowledge too wonderful for us, as if we could not comprehend the revelation of the respective numbers of the saved and unsaved. Holy Scripture knows how to say "more" or "less." Here the discordant assertions, here the juxtaposition of contraries, here the lack of systemization or abstraction seem rather to serve another purpose. Here the point is not to instruct us as far as we are capable of being instructed, but rather to leave us knowing the two things we must know, the truth necessary for us to weave into the fabric of a faithful Christian life.

God knows—he has always known—those who are his. But he has told us both that they are few and that they are a great host. He has not, even in general terms, revealed the total number of the saved and the damned, nor the percentage of each company. His silence is instructive because obviously intentional! More information, it seems, would be counterproductive, if not positively harmful! It is hardly uncommon in human life that too much information can confuse, distract, even mislead us. Had we been told when the Lord would return, for example, it is not difficult to predict the deleterious effects on Christian faith, hope, and obedience! By repeating these contraries in such emphatic ways and by refusing to rationalize them, we are exhorted both to take salvation with deadly seriousness, for great multitudes fail to obtain it, *and* to live in the confidence of the worldwide vindication of the gospel of Jesus Christ. How else could caution and hope, enthusiastic evangelistic effort and perseverance in the face of disappointment, be combined than to be faced with these contraries again and again? Struggle, disappointment, even doubt; but great victory looms on the distant horizon! What is this but the dialectic of faith!

III. The Necessity of Good Works

Justification by Faith Alone

After the account of the life, ministry, death, and resurrection of the Lord, the most detailed, sustained, and dramatic piece of history in the New Testament, and the most consequential for the church's conception of her faith, is that of the apostle Paul's struggle for the grace of God against the furious effort to reinsert, in imitation of the Judaism of the day and in deference to the pride of the sinful human heart, human performance as an essential prerequisite for the forgiveness of sins. The story is told both in Acts and in several of the letters of Paul and the consistent lesson is that justification—the forgiveness of sin and the obtaining of peace with God—is and must be by faith in Jesus Christ and the power of his cross and cannot in any respect be thought the achievement of the sinner's obedience, however imperfect, whether liturgical (Acts 15:1) or moral (Rom 2:17–29; 3:9–20). It is the Lord "who blots out your transgressions" and he does so *for his own sake* (Isa 43:25).

Paul's mighty polemic against the introduction of the Pharisaic spirit into the Christian gospel has rightly left an indelible mark on the believing Christian mind as it has on Christian worship. The repeated loss of this conviction and then its recovery are respectively the tragedies and triumphs of Christian history. Accordingly, this is what the devout, biblically minded Christian, whatever his or her theological tradition, understands the gospel to be: the thrilling proclamation of deliverance from sin and death as the free gift of God to the enslaved and undeserving. It is precisely this message that has continued to bring peace with

God and the joy of salvation to untold millions in our time. Justification is by faith—which is to say by grace and so the act and the gift of God—and not by works (Acts 13:38–39; Rom 4:1–6, 13–16; Gal 1:6–7; 3:7–14; Phil 3:1–11).[17] As Paul is at pains to demonstrate, justification by faith or by grace is the consistent teaching of the ancient Scriptures, the lesson of Israel's history, the logic of Christ's atoning work, Paul's own personal experience, and was powerfully demonstrated by the progress of the gospel throughout the Gentile world after Pentecost. In the Christian mind and heart the hope of everlasting life is suspended from beginning to end on the love of God, the sacrifice of Christ, and the renewing work of the Holy Spirit, not the performance of the sinner, however obedient that performance, however enabled as that performance may be by the grace of God. Whether the thief on the cross, the congregation at Pentecost, Saul on the road to Damascus, Lydia and the jailer in Philippi, or Dionysius and Damaris in Athens, the crossing from death to life was made by faith, not by works. It is by God's initiative and power over the heart; it is by Christ's righteousness, not the sinner's, that peace with God is found (Rom 5:6–11, 18–19). The gospel is precisely the announcement that through faith in Jesus Christ God justifies the ungodly.

The Judgment According to Works

However, it is precisely this conviction—made ineradicable in the believing heart by Paul's polemic against justification by works and sustained and strengthened by the church's hymns and history of gospel preaching—that has virtually inoculated the evangelical mind against the also impressive emphasis on the necessity of obedience we find in the Bible from beginning to end.[18]

Over the years of my pastorate I have found that many Christians seem never to have noticed that all the scenes of the Last Judgment

17. That this struggle for the purity of the gospel of grace had implications for Christian unity across the Jew/Gentile and other social divides is obvious. Equally obvious is that the fundamental question was always by what means a person is saved (Acts 15:1; Rom 4:7–8; Gal 5:2–6; 6:8). Gaffin, *By Faith*, 44–52.

18. For all the hymns that beautifully celebrate *sola gratia* and *sola fide*, in even the best hymnals one struggles to find even one hymn with equal emotive power that raises the believer's eyes to the distant horizon and the judgment of life according to the measure of one's obedience to God. But this too is a theme that is given persistent attention in the Word of God and, not least, in the writings of the apostle Paul.

painted for us in Holy Scripture describe the weighing of works of either obedience or disobedience, or that it is a promise of the gospel that "each one of us will give an account of himself to God" (Rom 14:10–12; 2 Cor 5:10), or that God, "who searches mind and heart," will give to each of us "according to [our] works" (Rev 2:23).[19] Again and again the evangelical mind, schooled as it has been in justification by faith alone, passes over without recognition Paul's own insistence that God "will render to each one according to his works" and that it is "the doers of the law who will be justified" (Rom 2:8, 13; cf. 6:16, 22). They do not expect that Paul would say such a thing and so they hardly notice that he did, or that the Lord himself said that "an hour is coming when all who are in the tombs will hear his voice and come out, those who have done good to the resurrection of life and those who have done evil to the resurrection of judgment" (John 5:28–29).[20]

They expect that justification—after all, an act of divine judgment— being by faith and not by works, the separation of the sheep from the goats, will be made solely and explicitly on the basis of the former's faith in Jesus Christ and the latter's lack of such faith. But again and again it is not said to be so; the separation is effected by the judgment of behavior (Jer 17:10; Ezek 24:14; Matt 12:36–37;[21] 16:27; 25:31–46[22]; Rev 20:12).[23] How commonplace are such expressions of piety as "For the Lord is righteous;

19. That statement is clearly a thematic summary of the letters to the seven churches in Rev 2–3. It is found in the middle of the middle letter and is the only statement addressed to all the churches.

20. It is striking how the necessity of works is so artlessly asserted even in the Bible's principal manifestoes of *sola gratia* and *sola fide*, such as John, Romans, and Hebrews (12:14–17).

21. "The idle words of which account must be given on the day of judgment (Matt 12:36) are not, as the NEB would have it, 'thoughtless' words, such as a carefree joke, but deedless ones, loafers which ought to be up and busy about what they say, the broken promise, the unpaid vow, words which said, 'I go, sir' and never went (Matt 21:29)." Caird, *Language and Imagery*, 21–22.

22. The lack of oil that condemns the foolish virgins in the parable in Matt 25:1–13 may be, in part, a reference to the lack of good works. Silva, *Biblical Words*, 156–57.

23. This fact perhaps explains why the accounts of the second coming in the New Testament are characteristically as solemn as they are celebratory. The warning note is prominent. In the dramatic narrative of the Lord's return in Rev 19 there too the "righteous deeds of the saints" are prominent. For thoughtful, serious believers the thought is not entirely consoling that "their deeds follow them" (Rev 14:13). "What we weave in time, we wear in eternity." Ryle, cited in Murray, *J.C. Ryle*, 129. But in a typical complex of opposites, we are to fear this judgment (2 Cor 5:11) and not to fear it (Rom 8:1; 1 John 4:7).

he loves righteous deeds; the upright shall behold his face" (Ps 11:7; cf. Ps 24:3–6). Through the years I have heard in too many sermons on Matt 5:20 the argument that righteousness better than that of the scribes and Pharisees, righteousness sufficient for entry into the kingdom of heaven, could only be that perfect righteousness of Jesus Christ obtained by faith. In the context of the Sermon on the Mount, however, what the Lord was referring to as the prerequisite of heaven was manifestly not the verdict of acquittal through the righteousness of Christ received by faith but a better life, a holier life than that lived by the Pharisees (Matt 5:27–30; 6:1; 7:19–23). Once again truth has been found in one extreme only, not in both. It was our Lord, after all, who said *both* "I give them eternal life and they shall never perish" *and* "every branch in me that does not bear fruit shall be cut off and thrown into the fire."[24]

An Impressive Emphasis

True enough, Christian obedience is faith working through love (John 14:15; Gal 5:6), made possible only by the presence of the Lord Christ by his Holy Spirit (John 15:5; Phil 2:13), the inevitable fruit of living faith (Rom 8:1–8; Jas 2:14–26) and the outworking of the divine plan of salvation (Eph 2:10; Titus 2:11–14).[25] True enough, justification and

24. In ways both predictable and typical, various efforts have been made to resolve the appearance of conflict between John 15:1–6 and the doctrines of justification by faith and the security of the believer. One such interpretation was made popular by A. W. Pink, the influential biblical expositor of the first half of the twentieth century. In his work on the Gospel of John Pink argued that the fruitless branches mentioned in v. 2 were not cut off, but, rather, "lifted up," so that they could get that exposure to the sun that had been denied them and so that, as a result, they could become fruit-bearing branches also. Another interpretation popular in evangelical preaching in the twentieth century was that the branches that were cut off referred to Christians who were taken out of the world by death and sent immediately to heaven because they were not bearing fruit on earth. That such interpretations are desperate evasions is demonstrated not only in v. 6, but by the fact that the same warning is given in many texts and in various ways in Holy Scripture. Once again, the truth was being found in but one extreme, not both, and paradox was avoided by the unlikely reinterpretation of one of the polarities.

25. "... I cannot, by direct moral effort, give myself new motives. After the first few steps in the Christian life we realize that everything which really needs to be done in our souls can be done only by God." Lewis, *Mere Christianity*, 165. Making allowances for his characteristic overstatement, Luther was right to say, in his "Introduction to St. Paul's Letter to the Romans" in the 1522 edition of his German Bible, that "... faith is God's work in us. ... It kills the Old Adam and makes us completely different

sanctification may be distinguished, but they may never be separated. But, as the thoughtful Christian conscience will readily confess, too often the necessity of obedience is compromised by reference to these facts. Obedience thus becomes only the evidence or fruit of faith and so, for the believer, less important in its own right. It is easier—far easier—to think oneself a believer than honestly to acknowledge the poverty of one's obedience to God and bend every effort to put one's sins to death. True enough, obedience is both the fruit and the evidence of faith (2 Cor 9:13). But that is hardly a sufficient explanation for the Bible's impressive and consistent witness to the necessity of obedience for salvation, the intrinsic importance of obedience, and the differing measure of it in believers' lives—and that for three reasons.

The first is that again and again faith itself is declared to be an act of obedience (Deut 9:23; John 6:29; 17:6; Acts 10:35; Rom 1:5; 6:17; Gal 5:7; 2 Thess 1:8; Heb 3:18–19; 5:9; 1 Pet 3:1; 4:17). Holy Scripture does not carefully and consistently distinguish faith and obedience as simply cause and effect or root and fruit in the way they are often distinguished in Christian preaching and sometimes in Christian theology.

In the second place, the Bible does not teach that obedience is significant only as the evidence of something else. The judgment of human life, whether believing or unbelieving, is invariably according to behavior. The Bible is repeatedly insistent on this fact. Men and women are condemned and punished for their sinful acts and vindicated and rewarded for their obedience to God (1 Sam 26:23; Ezek 18:1–32; Matt 5:12; 10:41–41; Luke 6:35; 1 Cor 3:8; 2 John 8). It is those who have done good who will rise to live forever (Ezek 14:14–20). Moreover, both the saved and the lost are accorded positions in the world to come *according to what they have done* (Dan 12:3; Matt 11:23–24; 16:27; Luke 19:15–19). In other words, in the Final Judgment there will be an *exact* reckoning of the lives human beings have lived in this world (Jer 17:10; Matt 16:27; 2 Cor 5:10; Rev 2:23; 20:12–13), and both the righteous and the wicked will receive more or less *according to their due.*[26]

---

people. It changes our hearts, our spirits, our thoughts and all our powers. It brings the Holy Spirit with it. Yes, it is a living, creative, active and powerful thing, this faith. Faith cannot help doing good works constantly. It doesn't stop to ask if good works ought to be done, but before anyone asks, it already has done them and continues to do them without ceasing. Anyone who does not do good works in this manner is an unbeliever." *Luther's Vermischte Deutsche Schriften*, 63:124–25.

26. It is the teaching of Holy Scripture that due to their unfaithfulness some true believers will "suffer loss" though saved, while more faithful saints will "receive a

Third, the measure of Christian obedience, being *the fruit of faith* as it certainly is, is determined by *the measure of faith* (Mark 9:23–24; Luke 12:28–31; 17:5–6). If our obedience is less than it ought to be, it is because our faith is weaker than it ought to be (Matt 14:31). But *we are responsible* for the strength of our faith. We are summoned to instruct and inspire it with the Word of God, to pray for it, and to strengthen it by practice. In this way as well we are responsible for our obedience, both root and fruit, and for this reason we cannot complain that God will pass judgment upon it.

It is, of course, true that God in Christ mercifully takes his people's very little for a lot; true that he freely forgives what is sinful in our good works; true that our works are the fruit of the Holy Spirit's work within us; and true that by God's patience our continuing sinfulness does not make worthless the seriously imperfect obedience Christians offer to God. All of this is so plainly taught in Holy Scripture that Augustine is surely right when he says that when God rewards his people for their obedience he is "crowning his own gifts, not [their] deservings."[27] There can be no thought of believers claiming that the rewards lavished upon them are their own achievement. They are themselves the grace of God to us. The biblical writers unashamedly assert all those facts and no one should ever take our crown in confessing them. Nevertheless, the apostle Paul is also our example in the deadly earnestness with which he took his responsibility to obey the commandments of God and serve the interests of Christ's kingdom *so as to receive an imperishable reward* (1 Cor 9:19–27; 2 Cor 5:10–11; Acts 24:15–16)! It is only to take seriously the plain speaking of the Bible to believe that we will be judged according to our behavior and by that judgment Christians will be received into glory and according to that judgment receive the proper measure of reward.

---

reward" (1 Cor 3:10–15). "That this passage speaks about a reward which some believers receive and others do not seems obvious. That reward will be directly proportional . . . to the quality of his Christian life." Hoekema, *Bible and the Future*, 262–63. Note the artless way in which the Bible regularly refers to the *reward* of the faithful and the obedient (Matt 16:27; 2 John 8), a reward greater or lesser depending upon the measure of one's obedience. By faithful obedience we gain a greater reward in this world (Mark 10:29–30; Luke 6:38; 18:29–30) and "lay up treasure in heaven" (Matt 6:19–20; Luke 6:38). There is everywhere a direct relation between what is done in this life and the reward granted in the life to come (Matt 7:2). "This emphasis is fully in keeping with the common use of eschatology in the NT as a motivation for ethics." Hagner, *Matthew 14–28*, 484.

27. Augustine, *Expositions on the Book of Psalms*, CIII, 7, 505.

Our Savior, who is also our King, is likewise our Judge (Rom 14:10; Heb 10:30). Invariably, those works are understood to be *our* works for which *we* are responsible.

Paradox Once Again

In other words, in considering these contraries—justification by faith and not by works, on the one hand, and final judgment according to works, on the other—we face a paradox or antinomy similar to, indeed part and parcel with that of divine sovereignty and human responsibility, of salvation by God's decision and gracious and powerful working alone and salvation that requires the dutiful exercise of the human will. It is striking and deserves to be pondered how clearly and emphatically the Bible teaches both justification by faith alone *and* the absolute necessity of good works for entrance into eternal life.[28] Faithful to this paradox, Francis Turretin, whose credentials as an evangelical authority are impeccable, wrote, "although works may be said to contribute nothing to the acquisition (*salutem acquirendam*) of salvation, still they should be considered necessary to the obtainment of it (*eam obtinendam*), so that no one may be saved without them. . . ."[29] That statement is certainly paradoxical!

Throughout the Bible, now here, now there, are emphatic assertions that God justifies the ungodly, together with dramatic illustrations of his doing so, on the one hand, and, on the other, the declaration that we will receive on the Great Day *what is due us* in reward or punishment (2 Cor 5:10)—a way of speaking many evangelicals, thoroughly catechized in the doctrine of justification by faith alone, do not expect to find in Holy Scripture. Is there anything good that God should give us miserable sinners *as our due*? The Bible's studied disinterest in the analysis of this complex of opposites—never does it address or explain the relation of

28. The paradox is heightened by reference to recompense or an appropriate reward for work done in both Rom 4:4 and 2 Cor 5:10. In the first, such recompense is explicitly repudiated. Justification is precisely *not* our receiving what is due us; indeed, it is the granting of peace with God *in defiance of our ill desert*. In the latter, however, it *is* precisely what is due us for the measure of good we have done that will be given believers in the Last Judgment. The principle of recompense is deeply engrained in the biblical worldview (2 Sam 22:25; Zech 1:6; 1 Cor 16:18).

29. As used here the verbs in participial form are synonyms! Turretin, *Institutes of Elenctic Theology*, XVII, iii, 4, 2:703.

the polarities—together with the unqualified emphasis Holy Scripture repeatedly places on both assertions certainly should command our attention. The way in which theologians, desiring to be faithful to the teaching
of the Bible, describe the relationship between *sola fide* and the necessity
of good works for salvation serves only to draw attention to the paradox.
They may say, for example, that good works are not "an efficient necessity" but only "a cause *sine qua non*,"[30] but in so saying they neither deny
that such works are the believers' works for which they are responsible
nor that they are necessary for entrance into the kingdom of heaven. The
Bible rings the changes on Milton's acknowledgment that the Christian
must live his or her life "As ever in my great Taskmaster's eye" (Sonnet 7).

Once again we encounter a dialectical biblical pedagogy, a paradoxical revelation of biblical soteriology. The Bible asserts emphatically and
without qualification that our peace with God rests upon the righteousness of Christ received by faith, a faith that is itself the gift of God, and asserts those facts against all comers, controversially and unapologetically.
It also teaches that we must keep God's commandments or we will not and
cannot be saved and that behavior in this life will determine the measure
of reward or punishment received in the world to come. It invariably sets
this prospect before us as motivation for a holier life. It holds us accountable for the fidelity of our thoughts, words, and deeds.[31] We must entrust
ourselves to the God who both justifies and sanctifies the ungodly, but we
will be judged according to what we have done. The man whose work is
burned up (1 Cor 3:14–15) certainly cannot complain that God was not
sufficiently gracious to him any more than the one who is placed over ten
cities (Luke 19:16–17) can bask in any sense of personal achievement.
But the fact remains that the difference between them, to which Scripture
invariably draws our attention, is precisely that the one served the Lord
more faithfully and fruitfully than the other. Each received what *was due
him*, notwithstanding that God "does not deal with us according to our

30. Hurd, "Dei Via Regia," 14–15. It is obvious that such a distinction is drawn
from philosophy, not directly from the Bible, which makes no use of such terminology.

31. "Everything a person has done is an expression of the basic direction of his
heart, and thus will be taken into account on the Day of Judgment. This includes a
person's deeds, words, and thoughts. . . . It is sometimes said that the sins of believers,
which God has pardoned, blotted out, and cast into the sea of forgetfulness, will not be
mentioned on the Day of Judgment. If it be true, however, that there is nothing hidden
which will not then be revealed, and that the judgment will concern itself with all our
deeds, words, and thoughts, surely the sins of believers will also be revealed on that
day." Hoekema, *Bible and the Future*, 258.

sins, nor repay us according to our iniquities" (Ps 103:10). Everywhere we find this tension between what Christ has done and must do *for us and in us* and what we must do *for him* or else. Dramatic polarities indeed!

The Happy Effect

And, once again, however troublesome this pedagogy has proved through the ages, however many times Christians have been tempted to prefer one truth to the other, to wrap themselves around one pole at the expense of the other, however often the equilibrium of truths has been lost,[32] who can deny that it is precisely this complex of opposites that has throughout the ages nurtured the Christian conviction that our salvation is the free gift of our loving Heavenly Father, the purchase at terrible cost of God the Son, and comes to us through the recreative work of the Holy Spirit, on the one hand, *and*, on the other, that we must believe in him and live for him or suffer the consequences?

What the Bible's way of teaching produces in the believing mind and heart is precisely this double conviction, instinctive, ineradicable, and powerfully at work. In the same mind and heart *we find both truths* ardently confessed, deeply felt, and made the foundation of life.

> Let it be counted folly, or phrensy, or fury, or whatsoever, it is our wisdom and our comfort, we care for no other knowledge in the world but this: that man hath sinned and God hath suffered: that God hath made himself the sin of men, and that men are made the righteousness of God.[33]

> Whatever I do, I think I still hear the sound of these words in my ear: 'Arise you dead, and come to judgment.'[34]

32. "I remember Luther says, that in his time, if they taught in a sermon, that salvation consisted not in our works or life, but in the gift of God, some men took occasion thence to be slow to good works, and to live a dishonest life. And if they preached of a godly and honest life, others did by and by attempt to build ladders to heaven." "Evangelista" in Fisher, *Marrow of Modern Divinity*, cited in the edition of Boston, *Complete Works*, 7:236.

33. Hooker, *Discourse of Justification*, 243.

34. This sentence has long been credited to Jerome, even to his *Commentary on Matthew*, but I have been unable to verify the reference in that or any other of Jerome's writings. However, who can deny that it is an entirely biblical sentiment and, in particular, Pauline in the form of its words (2 Cor 5:10–11; Rom 14:12; 1 Cor 9:25–27; Eph 6:8; Phil 4:17; 1 Tim 6:19; cf. Heb 13:17; Luke 19:17; Rev 2:23). John Flavel summarized the biblical data in a similarly emotive way. "It is true, our actions, physically

Here the unsystematized polarities serve the purpose of unrelenting empha-sis! By this paradox we learn to love God and rest in that love but never to take his love for granted; to be ceaselessly grateful for his mercy to us but never to allow that mercy to become an excuse for sin; and to live in a constant state of active dependence upon the Lord while at all times rousing ourselves to the difficult work of loving him and our neighbor, obeying his commandments, and serving his kingdom. It is by this em-phasis of contraries that we become champions of God's grace, Christ's atonement, and the Spirit's renewing power *to the backbone* and, at the same time, live each day solemnized by the prospect of giving an account of our lives before the great throne. Not affiance *or* obedience, but always both. This is how Holy Scripture teaches us to "Trust in the Lord and do good . . ." (Ps 37:3).[35]

---

considered, are transient; how soon is a word or action spoken or done, and there is an end of it? But *morally* considered, they are permanent, being put upon God's book of account. O! therefore take heed what you do: so speak, and so act, as they that must give an account." *Fountain of Life*, 306.

35. Anthony Hoekema describes the significance of the Last Judgment in four particulars. Among them are that "The Day of Judgment will reveal that salvation and eternal blessedness will depend on one's relationship to Jesus Christ" and that "The inescapableness of the Day of Judgment underscores man's accountability for his life, and asserts the seriousness of the moral struggle in the life of every person, particu-larly in the life of the Christian." *Bible and the Future*, 264.

7

The Christian Life

You say you are more disposed to cry, Miserere! than Hallelujah! Why not both together? When the treble is praise and the heart-humiliation for the bass, the melody is pleasant and the harmony is good. However, if not both together, we must have them alternately.... But though we change, the Savior changes not. All our concerns are in his hands, and therefore safe.

—JOHN NEWTON[1]

SO FAR WE HAVE been occupied with what are typically referred to as "doctrines," the themes or subjects that make up the Bible's definition of the Christian faith, the teachings that are enshrined in the great creeds and theological confessions of Christendom. We have observed that the Bible never teaches its doctrines in the way they are found in the creeds and confessions or defined, organized, and elaborated in a systematic theology. Rather, Holy Scripture supplies the raw data that, when consolidated and summarized, become the principal themes of Christian theology. The data themselves, we have argued, typically represent various polarities, an assertion now here, now there, that regularly seems to be incompatible with if not virtually the contradiction of another.

All biblical doctrines have vital implications for a distinctively Christian way of life; some, for example the doctrines of assurance or

1. Newton, *Works*, 1:631.

the Last Judgment, explicitly so. But such implications are not typically found in creeds and manuals of theology. They are, however, spelled out in detail in the teaching of the Bible, teaching that is found in a wide variety of forms: from history and biography to law and wisdom, from hymns and prayers to the profiles of the faithful life we find in the sermons of the prophets and the Lord himself and in the letters of his apostles. This teaching has also been consolidated and summarized in the great manuals of spiritual or practical theology—from Augustine's *Confessions*, to à Kempis's *Imitation of Christ*, to John Bunyan's *Pilgrim's Progress*, and many others—in the memoirs and biographies of the saints, in Christian poetry and hymnody, and in Christian preaching. As with its doctrine, the Bible's anatomy of the Christian life and its variegated experience is likewise severely dialectical.

As much as is the case with the Holy Trinity and the incarnation, the account of believing experience is characterized by polarity, paradox, absoluteness of statement, and an almost complete lack of systematic analysis. This pedagogy has led believers through the ages to a marvelously many-sided practice of their faith, indeed to the contemporaneous expression of virtually contradictory experience, but it has also produced, as might well be expected, a great deal of spiritual confusion, a confusion as commonplace today as it has ever been. The Christian life is and must be a welter of contradictions. This is obviously God's intention, for in push and pull the life of faith takes wing.

Some Examples

Every earnest follower of Jesus Christ lives and must live in the tension between deliverance from the power of sin and one's continuing bondage to it. The hunger and thirst for righteousness and the real moral transformation of our lives lie both in the Bible's teaching and in the believing life cheek to jowl with the dismal moral failure of even the most committed Christians. One has only to read Christian autobiography and biography to learn that victory and defeat collide repeatedly in the experience of even the most devout. We have said that the product of this tension is both hope and humility, both courageous striving and patient dependence upon both the forgiveness of God and the help of the Holy Spirit.

Similarly, the calm confidence of faith in our all-powerful and loving Heavenly Father and his perfect plan for our lives—the knowledge that if God be for us, who can stand against us and that all things work together for good for those who love God—competes for hegemony in our hearts with a full set of fears, for ourselves and others, that Holy Scripture itself urges upon us. We are called to serve God without fear (Luke 1:74); we are told that God has not given us a spirit of fear (2 Tim 1:7) and that perfect love casts out fear (1 John 4:18; Luke 12:32); but the dangers that threaten spiritual life in this world inevitably churn up perfectly reasonable, even responsible fears (Rom 11:20; 2 Cor 5:11; 11:3; Phil 2:12). Who can deny that sturdy confidence and real fear not only have always been but must always be together the experience of God's people? By asserting both, by describing believing life as subject to both, and by refusing to reconcile the two poles, Holy Scripture relentlessly impresses upon us the necessity of living in calm assurance and dutiful apprehension at one and the same time. The love and power of God, on the one hand, and, on the other, both our own weakness and the high stakes for which we are playing require it to be so.

In any case, it is simply a fact that what we find in Holy Scripture is the unqualified assertion and illustration of such contraries—victory and defeat, peace and worry—with virtually no instruction as to how to relate the one to the other. Never does the Bible teach us how to reconcile victory over sin and continuing slavery to it or explain how peace and fear can together cohabit the same heart. And so it is with respect to virtually every dimension of Christian experience as it is described in the Bible. In this chapter I will consider two further examples of the paradoxical revelation of Christian experience found in Holy Scripture.

I. The Promises of Blessing and the Life of Troubles

Given both the rise of the so-called prosperity gospel, on the one hand, and the suffering and martyrdom of immense numbers of Christians in our time, on the other, perhaps no biblical dialectic requires more intelligent acceptance and appreciation than the emphatic promises of the Lord's blessing to his faithful servants—both temporal and eternal blessing—and the afflictions, deprivations, and sorrows that the followers of Jesus encounter in this world.

Surely no one who suddenly experiences the thrilling deliverance that comes with the discovery of new life in Jesus Christ expects that the Christian life will disappoint in so many ways or prove so punishingly difficult to live well! Many statements can be found in the Bible that suggest that Christians will experience sustained victory; a life of joy, peace, and abundance; and be daily buoyed by the eager expectation of still more of the same in the world to come. Surely the Bible gives us reason to believe that we all, with unveiled face and beholding the glory of the Lord, will be transformed into the same image from one degree of glory to another (2 Cor 3:18). How quickly the young Christian discovers that it is not obviously so; that believing life is troubled in many ways, too often in ways of our own making; and that it is the often painful testing of our faith that produces the deeper godliness that God is after in the lives of his children. What biblical exemplar of the Christian faith, of devotion to God, and of a life of real worth to the kingdom of God did not live with disappointment and with the confusion that resulted from the fact that God seemed to have promised one thing and delivered another? I have lived long enough and been a pastor long enough to know how often the conflict between expectation and actual experience can seriously trouble the faithful followers of the Lord Christ. It troubled the lives of the psalmists long before!

The Saints and Their Sorrows

The Lord made most of us for marriage and there is in most human beings and so most Christians a deep-seated longing for that unique companionship and the life of love and family that it makes possible. The Bible both celebrates married love and rings the changes on its importance. What is more, we are taught to praise God because "he settles the solitary in a home" (Ps 68:6) and "gives the barren woman a home, making her the joyous mother of children" (Ps 113:9). But what of the growing number of young men and women who cannot find a wife or husband? What of those spiritually serious young adults who long for such love and who have sought to delight themselves in the Lord, but to whom he has not given the desires of their heart (Ps 37:4)? This is hardly an uncommon occurrence. When my wife and I lived in Scotland in the mid-1970s we noticed almost immediately how many older never-married women, delightful and godly Christian women, there were in our congregation. The explanation met our eye at every service. When we looked toward the high pulpit from which Mr. Still's scintillating and powerful sermons were delivered every Lord's Day morning and evening, we couldn't help noticing the two panels on the woodwork immediately below him with the names of the war-dead from that small parish inscribed in letters of gold. Two panels, one for each world war. On the first were inscribed the names of twenty young men, including two sets of brothers; on the second an additional thirteen—thirty-three young men from that single parish who would never be a young woman's husband. The Lord never settled those solitary women in their own families. It was not their desire to live a single life, but the Lord never joined them together with a man (Matt 19:6).

Then there are those who find that happy love only to lose it. When I came to my pastorate in 1978 I found there was in the congregation a dear woman, a faithful Christian who had lived most of her life as a widow, as had Anna long years before (Luke 2:36–37). Born in 1895, she married in 1915. Two years later, just after her only child was born, her husband was killed in an industrial accident. She remained a widow for the rest of her life and died in the faith of Jesus Christ in 1988. Where does the Bible explain the relation between those promises of happy companionship and that heartbreak?

What of the death of an infant? That crushing disappointment is known in my family and in many Christian families. I'm not sure there is a man of church history I admire more than the seventeenth- and eighteenth-century Scottish pastor and theologian Thomas Boston. Here was a man who loved and trusted God if ever anyone did. But he lost six of his children in infancy, or, as he put it in his *Memoirs*, "I travelled that gloomy road six times." Did not the Lord promise that his faithful people will "abound in the fruit of your womb" (Deut 28:11)? What of the early death of a promising Christian man or woman? In my Presbyterian tradition, one of the chief exemplars of true godliness is the nineteenth-century Scottish pastor Robert Murray McCheyne, a man still famous not for what he did but for what he was. But he died before his thirtieth birthday. He honored his father and mother, he "held fast to the Lord in love," but the Lord did not satisfy him with long life (Ps 91:16), nor did he "live long in the land" (Eph 6:2–3). And what of believing parents who mourn for the unfulfilled life of a disabled child, or faithful disciples who are condemned to live in ill health much of their lives? Where does the Bible teach us how to relate God's wonderful promises of fulfillment to the actual experience of believing life?

Will God's favored people, those who trust in him and walk with him, be rich or poor? Well, perhaps by now unsurprisingly, we read in

Deut 15:4 that "there will be no poor among you," and later in the same chapter (v.11) "that there will never cease to be poor in the land." There is no help to be found by supposing, as too many have, that this is a problem that no longer confronts us in the new epoch established by Christ and his apostles. We have the promise of prosperity, the promise of full provision as well in the New Testament (Matt 6:25–35; Mark 10:29–30), but equally evidence of Christian poverty and want (Matt 25:35–40; Acts 6:1; 1 Cor 16:1; Rev 2:9). The Lord's faithful servants, indeed his apostles, were promised a hundredfold return in houses and lands in this life (Mark 10:29–30), but none of them ended his life as a real estate mogul! Again, nowhere is this discordance examined or explained; everywhere the tension remains.

And what of scandal and public disgrace that befall real Christians, devout Christians, on account of their sins? It is surely not the case, as any humble, observant, and thoughtful Christian knows, that it is only those saints who have done things deserving of such painful consequences. It was saintly John Newton himself who acknowledged that about himself.

> The Lord makes some of his children examples and warnings to others, as he pleases. They who are spared, and whose worst deviations are only known to the Lord and themselves, have great reason to be thankful. I am sure I have: the merciful Lord has not suffered me to make any considerable blot in my profession during the time I have been numbered amongst his people. But I have nothing to boast of herein. It has not been owing to my wisdom, watchfulness, or spirituality. . . . But I hope to go softly all my days under the remembrance of many things, for which I have as great cause to be abased before him, as if I had been left to sin grievously in the sight of men.[2]

But if this is so, how are those who have fallen to read the promise, made so often and in so many ways in Holy Scripture, that the Lord "will not let your foot be moved" and "will keep you from all evil . . . your going out and your coming in" (Ps 121:3, 7–8)?[3] As any Christian knows only too well, I could multiply illustrations of the seeming contradiction

2. Newton, *Works*, 1:208.

3. In this case, we have an interesting instance of at least a measure of resolution. In Prov 37:23–24 we read, "The steps of a man are established by the Lord, when he delights in his way; *though he fall, he shall not be cast headlong, for the Lord upholds his hand.*" The Lord's care mitigates the severity of the trial and its otherwise possibly spiritually lethal effect.

between God's promises of help, safety, prosperity, growth in grace, and the fulfillment of life, on the one hand, and, on the other, the bitter disappointments of even the holiest of saints in respect of all those things.

Our Father Told Us It Must Be So

But, as any reader of the Bible also knows, Holy Scripture itself prepares us for just such disappointment and heartbreak. As often as it promises prosperity and happiness to the faithful, it warns that life will prove difficult in many ways for the children of God. Even the godly may lose a measure of the Lord's blessing when he disciplines his children to correct their errors and every Christian stumbles repeatedly (Num 20:12; Ps 32:3–4; 1 Cor 11:30–32; Heb 12:4–11). Moses and David serve as examples of believers who suffered greatly on account of their sins or whose sins caused the suffering of other saints.

But, more than this, as a general rule the faithful will not be spared the troubles of life, even the heaviest of afflictions. We are told explicitly that even God's generous provision will be accompanied by persecution (Mark 10:30), indeed that it must be so if we are to live godly lives (2 Tim 3:12). Many psalms record the keen disappointments of the godly, of those who had various reasons to say to the Lord, "all your breakers and your waves have gone over me" (42:7) or "my soul is full of troubles" (88:3). So much is sorrow a fact of believing life that Paul was careful to make sure that his new converts expected it. A persevering faith was required, he told them, because "through many tribulations we must enter the kingdom of God" (Acts 14:22). Indeed, it is the Christian's calling to share in the sufferings of Christ (Phil 2:10).[4] No one with a Bible in his or her hand can accuse Luther of exaggeration when he described suffering as the seventh mark of the church.

> . . . the holy Christian people are externally recognized by the holy possession of the sacred cross. They must endure every misfortune and persecution, all kinds of trials and evil from the devil, the world, and the flesh . . . by inward sadness, timidity,

4. There is another dialectic hidden within that between the promises of prosperity and those of affliction. The Bible is unapologetic in asserting that God orders the sorrows of his people's lives precisely to secure holy ends (Ps 42:7; Jonah 2:3; 1 Cor 11:19; 2 Cor 4:7–12; 12:7–9; Heb 12:5–7; Jas 1:2), but the same Bible declares that the Lord "does not willingly afflict or grieve the children of men" (Lam 3:33), and grieves that his children have such troubles (Isa 63:9).

fear, outward poverty, contempt, illness, weakness, in order to become like their head, Christ. . . . In summary, they must be called heretics, knaves, and devils, the most pernicious people on earth, to the point where those who hang, drown, murder, torture, banish, and plague them to death are rendering God a service. No one has compassion on them; they are given myrrh and gall to drink when they thirst. And all of this is done not because they are adulterers, murderers, thieves, or rogues, but because they want to have none but Christ, no other God.[5]

Faithful Jeremiah was compelled to live his life unmarried and to end it in Egypt, where no true Israelite wished to be, not because he had betrayed the Lord but precisely because he had been so steadfast in honoring his name and his Word. James the apostle and brother of John died an early death for no other reason than his public and unrepentant association with Jesus of Nazareth. The suffering of the saints is prophesied in the Bible, its various purposes are explained, and it is comprehensively illustrated in the historical narrative, the wisdom literature, and the Psalms. The reality of suffering and crushing disappointment in the lives of the saints is what imparts poignancy and deep feeling to Holy Scripture and has made it the source of hope and comfort it has always been to God's people. They find in the Bible not only their world as they have come to know it but the divine affirmation of their pain and its holy purpose. They have found hope in the realization that "the receiving of this world's good with no admixture of its evil, the course of an unbroken prosperity, is ever a sign and augury of ultimate reprobation . . ." (Ps 17:13–14; 73:4–12; Luke 6:24–25).[6] Indeed, the Bible so relentlessly portrays human life and believing life as a life of suffering—Augustine says somewhere that God had one Son on earth without sin, but never one without suffering—that the also ubiquitous and impressively forceful promises of blessing and prosperity of every kind create a dialectic of terrible emotional power. Through the ages God's people have sought with tears to understand how a life of such promised blessing could possibly be so painful, how such a kind and generous Father could lay such heavy burdens on his children.

---

5. Luther, *On the Councils of the Church* (Luther's Works 41:164–65), cited in Trueman, *Luther on the Christian Life*, 77–78.

6. Trench, *Notes on the Parables*, 465.

The Mystery of Suffering

This confusion has prompted through the ages the saints' urgent examination of God's Word, a study that has shed and continues to shed much light on both the blessing and the suffering of the saints. We learn to find a proper place for both, however mysteriously their juxtaposition. That suffering is a means to holy ends, that it is, as Bonhoeffer put it, nothing less than a holy angel, becomes clearer the longer one lives with Holy Scripture and the providence of God. Not only does suffering produce a depth of godliness and usefulness beyond the reach of those who live in comfort and ease (Rom 5:3; Jas 1:2–3), so much so that even the sinless Savior had to suffer to be able to fulfill his calling in the world (Heb 2:18; 5:8), but prosperity unmixed with deprivation and sorrow is itself a lethal threat to living faith (Mark 10:25).

> Count each affliction, whether light or grave,
> God's messenger sent down to thee; do thou
> With courtesy receive him; rise and bow;
> And, ere his shadow cross thy threshold, crave
> Permission first his heavenly feet to lave;
> Then lay before him all thou hast.
> —Aubrey de Vere

Further, the Bible teaches us to find in the more explicitly temporal promises of blessing a metaphor for the higher and deeper blessings of the heart: the knowledge of God and his love and the hope of everlasting life. The writer of Psalm 73 suffered a crisis of faith because of the prosperity of the wicked: unbelievers seemed to be doing better and living happier lives than the faithful. When in church one day, he came to his senses and left the sanctuary six inches off the ground, thrilled by the realization that the Lord was his *portion forever.* "Portion" was the term used for an Israelite's holding in the promised land. The faithful in Israel always understood that the promised land was not primarily real estate in Canaan but loving fellowship with God and supremely that fellowship as it will be enjoyed in heaven (Heb 11:13–16, 35). The psalmist might have just as well said, "The Lord is my rain; the Lord is my victory in battle; the Lord is my husband, my wife, my child." The earthly blessing was the sign and seal of the still higher, greater thing (Lam 3:24).

Nevertheless, this does not mean that the promises were not to be understood as actual promises of the blessings described. When Israel was faithful to the Lord, prosperity *as it was defined in Deut 28:1–14* was very much her lot: she "lived in safety . . . every man under his vine and under his fig tree . . ." (Josh 23:9–11;1 Kgs 4:25; 8:66; Ps 144:12–15; Acts 4:32–35). Israel's prophets regularly reminded her of those very blessings she had forfeited and the punishments that she had suffered precisely because of her infidelity to God's covenant (Isa 5:1–17; Lam 1:1–13; Joel 1:1–20).[7]

We also now know that in the covenant material in the Pentateuch both the language of promised blessing and prosperity and the language of threatened curse is formulaic rather than original. The list of covenant blessings in both Leviticus 26 and Deuteronomy 28 resemble in wording similar lists found in the ancient Near Eastern secular or political covenants or treaties, whose literary form is now recognized to have been employed in the revelation of the covenant Yahweh made with Israel at Sinai and renewed on the plains of Moab. The rhetoric of both blessing and cursing is fairly standardized.[8] This does not mean that such promises were not well meant, but it suggests we should understand them in a more impressionistic rather than literal way. Here too the Bible's penchant for absoluteness of statement must be recognized and appreciated. It is not the case, for example, that the apostle Paul expected every young Christian in Ephesus to live to be seventy or eighty years of age (Eph 6:2–3).

Still, the Bible never rationalizes the promises of blessing in this world. It certainly never says that they are to be spiritualized. It never teaches us in some reflection on the covenantal blessings promised to the faithful in Leviticus 26 and Deuteronomy 28 that they are but part of the story of even devout and faithful life in the world or that they apply in only some cases or at some times. The lack of such an explanation shrouds much of any Christian's experience in impenetrable mystery. Why this person; why that sorrow; why now; why so much here and so little there? The Bible gives us a few scattered clues but nothing resembling an explanation. All of that careful reflection on the biblical data, all of that consolidation of the Bible's teaching is left to us. And when all that can be learned has been learned, the mystery remains. We are never given a calculus by which we might understand why weal and woe alternate in believing life as they do or why one or the other is our lot at any particular

---

7. Wenham, *Leviticus*, 327–28; Kitchen, *Reliability of the Old Testament*, 292–93; Hillers, *Covenant*, 120–42.

8. Wright, *Deuteronomy*, 280. Alternations of blessings and curses are found in the Lord's teaching as well (Luke 6:20–26).

time. Nothing can eliminate the complex of opposites we are faced with in the Bible's description of devout life. We are taught repeatedly and emphatically that the faithful will ride on the heights of the land and feed on the inheritance of their father Jacob and that theirs will be lives of "peace and joy in the Holy Spirit" (Isa 58:13–14; Rom 14:17). We are taught that all of God's promises are "Yes" in Jesus Christ (2 Cor 1:20). But we are also taught that the holy life will be a life of tears (Ps 6:6–7; 42:3; Acts 20:19; Rev 7:17). That the tension cannot be removed is proved by the Bible's honest recognition that the godly have long struggled with confusion on this very point—whether Job, one of many psalmists, Jeremiah, the Lord Jesus himself (Mark 15:34), or, still more mysteriously, saints already in heaven (Rev 6:10). To the consistent witness of the Scripture must be added the saints' two-thousand-year-long experience of a similar confusion.

In other words, the complex of opposites in the Bible's anatomy of the believing life cannot be explained simply as a literary convention, as if we have nothing more here than typical Hebrew hyperbole at work, as if relativizing the absolute language would solve the problem. The original readers of the Bible were familiar with its characteristic manner of expression. That the collision between the promises of God and the experience of life produced punishing confusion for them is proof, if proof were needed, that there is paradox here, impenetrable mystery, a juxtaposition of the happy expectation and the keenest disappointment that no consolation and interpretation of the biblical data can satisfactorily explain.

The Holy and Happy Result

Elegant proof of both the reality of this dialectic and the capacity of the reborn heart to embrace it and experience it in all the wonderful power of this "contradiction" has been repeatedly provided in Christian experience and testimony throughout the ages. Think, for example, of Allen Gardiner, a former officer in the British Navy, an adult convert to the Christian faith, a man possessed of a deep longing for the salvation of the lost. He fixed his interest eventually on the inhabitants of the barren wastes of Tierra del Fuego at the bottom of South America.

> With six companions he started to work in 1850. The ship with provisions failed to arrive; and during the winter on that

inhospitable shore the whole party slowly died of starvation. But
Gardiner wrote in his diary:

"Poor and weak as we are, our boat is a very Bethel to our souls,
for we feel and know that God is here. Asleep or awake, I am,
beyond the power of expression, happy."[9]

However mysterious—and the mystery here is, as it is with so much
else in biblical teaching, the incomprehensibility of reality itself, the government of God, which far transcends our understanding—it remains the
deepest conviction of the Christian soul both that "no good thing does
he withhold from those who walk uprightly" (Ps 84:11) and that "many
are the afflictions of the righteous" (Ps 34:19).[10] The dialectic is found
not only in the teaching of Holy Scripture but in the daily experience of
the saints, who live, as Paul said the saints did in his day, "sorrowful, yet
always rejoicing" (2 Cor 6:10). It is precisely this equal confidence in both
the promise of blessing and of privation that is the obviously intended
result of both being laid side by side. The Bible's studied inattention to
the tension thus caused, its refusal to temper or qualify its absolute form
of words, is what has produced this double conviction in the believing
heart!

God his own doth tend and nourish, in his holy courts they flourish;
From all evil things he spares them, in his mighty arms he bears them.

Though he giveth *or he taketh*, God his children ne'er forsaketh;
His the loving purpose solely to preserve them pure and holy.

It is the confession not only of the apostle Paul but of all the faithful
followers of Jesus Christ that our Savior *"always* leads us in triumphal

---

9. Neill, *History of Christian Missions*, 320–21. Neill goes on to report that when
the bodies were found those words "echoed around the world. . . ." The sacrifice of
these men bore fruit later when the transformation of the inhabitants of that land was
so remarkable that even the most skeptical were deeply impressed. Charles Darwin,
no enthusiast for Christian missionary endeavor, wrote to the South American Missionary Society, "The success of the Tierra del Fuego Mission is most wonderful, and
charms me, as I always prophesied utter failure. It is a grand success. I shall feel proud
if your committee think fit to elect me an honorary member of your society."

10. "Disclosed to us in revelation is 'the mystery of our religion': the mystery of
God's grace [1 Tim. 3:16]. We see it; it comes out to meet us as a reality in history and
in our own life. But we do not fathom it. In that sense Christian theology always has to
do with mysteries that it knows and marvels at but does not comprehend and fathom."
Bavinck, *Reformed Dogmatics*, 1:619.

procession" (2 Cor 2:14–16) and that "we are afflicted in every way . . .
always carrying in the body the death of Jesus" (4:8–12).[11]

II. The Life of Prayer

The practice of prayer, indeed a life of prayer is an indispensable feature
of the Christian life. Together with the Bible, it is the instrument of communication and so of fellowship with God.[12] Prayer is both communion
with God and the means of preserving and deepening it. Children must
talk with their parents, husbands with their wives, subjects to their king,
friends with their friends, and vice versa if ever love, respect, familiarity, intimacy, and confidence are to mark their relationship. In the Bible
we are commanded to pray, we are repeatedly treated to the example of
the faithful at prayer, and we are provided a great many specimens of
their prayers. The Lord Jesus was not only himself a man of prayer, whose
conversations with his Heavenly Father required of him great sacrifices
of time and effort (Mark 1:35; Luke 22:44; Heb 5:7), but prayer was one
of the principal subjects of his teaching. In both example and instruction
he was followed in this by his apostles. Christian worship is so much the
practice of corporate *prayer* that it came to be identified simply as "the
prayer" (Acts 6:4).

Throughout the Bible both private and corporate prayer are a principal "means of grace": an instrument of gospel advance (Rom 15:30–31),
of the cultivation and practice of gratitude to God (Acts 4:24–31; Rom
1:8–9), of Christian solidarity and mutual support (Acts 12:12; 20:36;
21:5), and of personal sanctification (Eph 3:14–19; Phil 1:9).[13] As fundamental an activity as prayer is, no wonder it is described in many different ways: seeking the Lord, looking to him, speaking to him, calling
upon him, inquiring of him, praising him, giving thanks to him, making
promises to him, arguing with him, and even, as in the case of so many
prayers in the Psalms, complaining to him. Because *prayer is the practice
of the Christian life* at every turn, Christians are commanded to "pray
without ceasing" (1 Thess 5:17). Accordingly, every Christian learns that

11. I'm grateful to the Rev. Ian Hamilton for reminding me of this striking example
of Paul's paradoxicality.

12. "The one is the fountain of living water and the other the bucket with which we
are to draw." John Newton, cited in Aitken, *John Newton*, 199.

13. ". . . your prayers to God will make me perfect. . . ." Ignatius, *To the Philadephians*,
5:1, 109.

to be a Christian is to pray, to engage daily in what John Knox called "earnest and familiar talking with God." One cannot mistake the Bible's emphasis on prayer as "The Christian's vital breath, the Christian's native air," as James Montgomery has it in one of his hymns. It is today, as it has always been, one of the supreme consolations of the gospel that it liberates believers to "cast their burdens on the Lord" in the sure hope that "he will sustain them" (Ps 55:22). And it is the confession of every thoughtful and experienced Christian that "I call to God" and he "hears my voice" (55:16–17).

The Clash of Contraries

But if there is any biblical dialectic with which every Christian is personally and existentially familiar, it is the discordance between the promises made to prayer, especially petitionary prayer, in Holy Scripture and the reality—in both Scripture and experience—of unanswered prayer.[14] It is precisely because prayer looms so large in Christian practice, indeed in the very nature of the Christian life as a life in a relationship with God, that unanswered prayer creates the disappointment, the confusion, and often the existential crisis that it does. We have all heard stories of Christians who prayed in desperation for the life or the salvation of a loved one and whose faith was staggered if not destroyed by the silence of heaven. If prayer lies at the very heart of what it means to know God, to be loved by him and to love him in return, a silent heaven must strike at the vital center of a Christian's faith. Is there a question more often asked or that more often troubles the followers of Jesus Christ than "Why has God not answered my prayer?" It isn't only a skeptic like Alexander Pope who has reason to ask whether there is sufficient evidence to believe that prayer alters the course of events in this world.

> Think we, like some weak prince, the Eternal Cause
> Prone for his favourites to reverse his laws!
> Shall burning Etna, if a sage requires,
> Forget to thunder, and recall its fires?

14. William Cowper begins his poem on prayer, "What various hindrances we meet in coming to the mercy seat!" Surely first among those hindrances for many Christians is their doubt, raised by long experience, that their prayers will avail with God.

Prayer: The Power of God at the Disposal of Man

After all, in commending the life of prayer to us, Holy Scripture abounds in promises, unconditional and absolute, that God will hear and answer our prayers, hear and answer them *in the terms in which they are asked*. The Lord Jesus made such promises repeatedly. He told his disciples, "Ask, and it will be given to you; seek, and you will find; knock, and it will be opened to you. For everyone who asks receives, and the one who seeks finds, and to the one who knocks it will be opened." And, lest there be any doubt on that score, he hurried on to assure them, "If you then, who are evil, know how to give good gifts to your children, how much more will the Heavenly Father give the Holy Spirit to those who ask him" (Luke 11:9–13). He made that promise in a variety of forms, but always in an absolute form of words and all four of the Gospels contain these extravagant assurances. "Whatever you ask in my name, this I will do, that the Father may be glorified in the Son. If you ask me anything in my name, I will do it" (John 14:13–14). "If you abide in me, and my words abide in you, ask whatever you wish, and it will be done for you" (John 15:7, 16; 16:23–24). "Whatever you ask in prayer, you will receive, if you have faith" (Matt 21:22). "Therefore I tell you, whatever you ask in prayer, believe that you have received it and it will be yours" (Mark 11:24). ". . . if two of you agree on earth about anything they ask, it will be done for them by my Father in heaven. For where two or three are gathered in my name, there am I among them" (Matt 18:19–20).

Such promises, of course, are not unique to the teaching of the Lord Jesus; they are a biblical commonplace. Yahweh's words to Solomon hardly applied only to a king. "If you seek him, he will be found by you . . ." (1 Chr 28:9; 2 Chr 15:2). Indeed, the same promise is universalized in other texts (2 Chr 7:14; Prov 8:17; Jer 29:13). And the power of prayer is a regular feature of New Testament parenesis or exhortation. It is the teaching of the entire Bible that "whatever we ask we receive from him" (1 John 3:22; Jas 1:5; 5:15; Rev 3:20).

The Lord's answering the prayers of his people is a constant feature of the biblical historical narrative (Gen 20:17; Num 11:2; 1 Sam 1:10, 20; 2 Kgs 4:33; 20:2–6; 1 Chr 4:10; 5:20; Acts 4:31; 10:2, 4, 31; 16:25; Jas 5:16–18). Indeed, the whole Bible bears witness to the fact that the fortunes of both the individual believer and the kingdom of God depend upon the prayers of God's people (Mark 9:29). No wonder Alexander Whyte, the author of what, in my view, is the finest of the many fine books on prayer that have been written through the ages, should write, ". . . if prayer is anything at all it is everything. And that is exactly what the whole Word of God says about prayer; it is everything; absolutely everything."[15]

A Silent Heaven

But, if this is so; if we can have the ear of the Almighty whenever we want, for as long as we want; if we have personal access to unlimited power and to the source of everything truly good, why is it that, as Alexander Whyte also somewhere observed, "There is nothing we are so bad at all our days"? "Are we not as unwilling many times to begin, and as glad to make an end, as if God in saying, 'Call upon me,' had set us a very burdensome task?"[16] True enough, there is more than one reason why, as Thomas Shepard admitted of himself, there were times when he would rather die than pray. But certainly chief among those reasons is the fact that long experience has made it a struggle for us to believe that God will actually answer our prayers and give us what we ask. If, indeed, we could have whatever good and right thing we want by simply asking our Heavenly Father for it, would it not be much easier for all of us to pray? Indeed, wouldn't they have to drag us from our knees? It is not too much to say that, alongside the continuing sinfulness of Christians who hunger and thirst for righteousness, unanswered prayer is *the chief* existential threat to living and active faith. Who among us, after all, has not had occasion to wonder, "Will the Lord spurn forever, and never again be favorable" (Ps 77:7)?

But here too the Bible itself prepares us for disappointment. Side by side with those many promises that our prayers will be heard and answered is manifold evidence that prayer will not always be heard and answered, statements as absolute and unqualified as are the promises themselves. There is first a set of conditions laid down here and there that seem quite severely to compromise the promises God has made to us. Prayer must be offered *in the Lord's name*, which means not simply in a particular form of words but with a genuine interest in praying *on behalf of the Lord*, seeking his will for his sake. A single prayer is often not enough. Prayer must be *persevering*. Isaac married Rebekah when he

15. Whyte, *Thomas Shepard*, 64. The book referred to is the collection of his sermons on Luke 11:1, entitled *Lord Teach Us to Pray*.

16. Hooker, *Discourse of Justification*, 302.

was forty. When they could not conceive, he prayed that the Lord would give them children. The Lord answered that prayer, but not until Isaac was sixty. Twenty years is a long time to pray for something one wants desperately! We wonder how often Isaac's faith flagged as he waited in vain for his aging wife's pregnancy. The Lord's parable of the persistent widow was told in connection with the promise of his second coming, for which generations of Christians have prayed and are still praying. *Harboring sin* in one's life or praying with *sinful motives* will nullify a prayer's effect (Ps 66:18; Jas 4:3), a condition that must dishearten any believer spiritually minded enough to know how much sin he or she harbors in the heart and how mixed even the most godly believer's motives must be. Likewise, prayer must be offered with *sturdy faith* (Jas 1:6), a blow to all of us who struggle with doubts of one kind or another. Still more, our prayers must be agreeable with the Lord's will (1 John 5:14; Luke 22:42), a condition that multitudes of believers have had occasion to fear must nullify a great many of our petitions. We accept that God did not hand over to his people the government of the universe when he promised to answer their prayers; we also believe that the Judge of all the earth does right. We do not doubt that, no matter the requests we make to God, his will is far superior to our own.

> We, ignorant of ourselves,
> Beg often our own harms, which the wise powers
> Deny us for our good; so find we profit
> By losing our prayers.[17]

But why then did he say that he would give us what we ask for? If God knows what we need before we ask him and if all things come to pass according to the counsel of his will, it is hardly unlikely that even the most faithful believers will wonder from time to time if it actually is the case that we have not only because we ask not. C. S. Lewis spoke for multitudes when he admitted that, no matter his intellectual confidence, his experience with prayer led him sometimes to wonder if he were not posting letters to a non-existent address.[18]

17. Shakespeare, *Antony and Cleopatra*, 2.1.5–8.

18. "I think the trouble with me is *lack of faith*. I have no *rational* ground for going back on the arguments that convinced me of God's existence: but the irrational deadweight of my old skeptical habits, and the spirit of this age, and the cares of the day, steal away all my lively feeling of the truth, and often when I pray I wonder if I am not posting letters to a non-existent address." Lewis, *They Stand Together*, 398–99.

The fact is the Bible gives us a great many examples of prayers offered by genuine believers, devout and faithful men and women, whose prayers were not answered, prayers that seemed to meet the conditions of effectiveness. Among others, Moses, David, Jeremiah, the Lord Christ, and Paul pleaded with God for what they did not receive. In such cases the return of prayers was not simply delayed; it was refused. Again, in keeping with the Bible's typical presentation, the interrelation between the unqualified promises that God would answer our prayers and the many cases of unanswered prayer is never so much as acknowledged, much less examined and accounted for. Here, predictably, we have parataxis and parataxis only, seemingly contradictory statements, each absolute in form, set side by side without accompanying analysis.

The Mystery of Prayer

True enough, prayer in the Bible is a matter of personal interaction, not a mechanism of cause and effect. It is conversation between children and their Father. We accept that this must change things. C. S. Lewis was certainly right to say,

> Prayer is request. The essence of request, as distinct from compulsion, is that it may or may not be granted. And if an infinitely wise being listens to the requests of finite and foolish creatures, of course he will sometimes grant and sometimes refuse them.[19]

P.T. Forsyth goes deeper.

> To common sense the fact that God knows all we need, and wills us all good, the fact of his infinite Fatherhood, is a reason for not praying. Why tell him what He knows? Why ask what He is more than willing to give? But to Christian faith and spiritual reason it is just the other way. Asking is polar co-operation. Jesus turned the fact to a use exactly the contrary of its deistic sense. He made the all-knowing Fatherhood the ground of true prayer. We do not ask as beggars but as children. Petition is not mere receptivity, nor is it mere pressure; it is filial reciprocity. Love loves to be told what it knows already. Every lover knows that. It wants to be asked for what it longs to give. And that is the principle of prayer to the all-knowing love.[20]

19. Lewis, "Efficacy of Prayer," 4–5.
20. Forsyth, *Soul of Prayer*, 63.

It is the genius of the biblical pedagogy that it provokes this kind of deep, consoling, and stimulating reflection on the biblical antinomies. But it is perfectly obvious that the apparent contradiction has by no means been removed. It has been asserted in faith, but not resolved. We find solace and inspiration in the tension between promise and experience, but the tension remains, sufficient to trouble us repeatedly in the course of life.

Does prayer really change things? The Bible teaches us unequivocally that it does and does dramatically. According to the manifold witness of the Scriptures, much of the greatest importance hinges on the prayers of God's people. When Paul pleaded for the prayers of the saints for both his safety and the effectiveness of his ministry, he was as much as asking them to force out of heaven a blessing for him (Rom 15:30-32; 2 Cor 1:11). But the Bible is perfectly candid about the many times in which prayer does not change things, at least in the terms in which the petitions were made. For the Bible to assure us both that God will certainly answer and that he may not or will not answer is paradoxical, like so much else in the teaching of the Bible and so much else in the experience of the saints. No wonder that while Christians rejoice in the recollection of their answered prayers or bow in faith to the divine will when their prayers seem to produce nothing, unbelievers charge us with superstition precisely because so many prayers we pray do not seem to avail with God.[21] It is hardly difficult for them to believe that coincidence or wishful thinking is a more likely explanation for the prayers we believe to have been answered by our Heavenly Father. But for the Christian this confidence is precisely what it means to live by faith and not by sight.

What we *cannot* do is seek to resolve the paradox, as too many have done, by effectively denying the truth of one or the other of these

---

21. Dr. Buswell, in his little book *Problems in the Prayer Life*, 54, cites the then prominent Harvard biblical scholar Kirsopp Lake, who in the August 1924 issue of *The Atlantic Monthly* wrote, "... few educated men believe in [petitionary prayer's] efficacy. The laws of life—which is the will of God—are not changed by prayer, sacrifice, or fasting. ... I do not believe that the religion of tomorrow will have any more place for petition than for any other form of magic." His prophecy is certainly not yet fulfilled, but who can doubt that for a great many, even among those who consider themselves Christians, confidence that petitions made to God will be heard and answered is at a low ebb, at least in the Western world. Sportscasters may well promise their "prayers" for the grieving relatives of deceased former stars, but no one expects them to fall to their knees after the program is ended! The fact that prayer meetings have largely disappeared from evangelical church life is certainly some index of even modern believers' struggle to maintain confidence in the efficacy of prayer.

contrary assertions or by relativizing the dissonance between them. This is done when, for example, it is said, "The Lord answered the prayer; he said 'No,'" or when the answers to prayer for help in this world are assumed to be granted only in the world to come. There may be truth in both observations, but it is perfectly clear that the Word of God promises more than this. The Lord emphatically promises to hear our prayers and give us what we ask from him and much of what we are taught to ask for in the Bible can only be granted in this life. At the same time the Bible is forthright in acknowledging both a silent heaven and even the categorical refusal to answer prayers offered in faith.

The Fruit of This Paradox

Here as elsewhere Holy Scripture is severely paradoxical. This is obviously intentional. How both biblical assertions, each emphatically confirmed in both the teaching and the experience of the Lord Jesus, can be true remains the deepest mystery to us. How little we know of the workings of divine providence; how little we understand how our prayers are woven into the fabric of the divine plan for us and for the world. Indeed, who can explain how God returns the prayers of the saints to the earth as thunder and lightning (Rev 8:3–5)! But, by the working of the Holy Spirit, the truly remarkable thing is that Christians, although utterly unable to explain this "contradiction," have long believed both assertions to be true and have by faith retained both a robust confidence in the efficacy of prayer *and* a humble submission to God and willingness to say with their Savior, "Not my will, but yours be done." They are as likely to sing, "I love the Lord, for he has heard my voice and my pleas for mercy" (Ps 116:1) as they are to cry, "Though he slay me, I will hope in him; yet I will argue my ways to his face" (Job 13:15). This is the mystery of faith. Indeed, it appears to be a fact of Christian history that the stronger the faith and the deeper the devotion, the more confident a believer is in the power of prayer *and* the more ready to sit humbly and expectantly under a silent heaven. This is the ripe fruit of the biblical pedagogy in which contraries are asserted boldly, illustrated memorably, but left unanalyzed. In my view it is highly unlikely that anything other than this dialectic regarding prayer would or could produce that happy result.[22]

---

22. To put it another way, it is impossible for us mere creatures to put into words how these two biblical assertions are true at one and the same time. As Calvin said

apropos God's love for us and hostility to us at the same time on the cross, so it can be said that "in some ineffable way" [*ineffabili quodam modo*] God both hears and refuses our prayers, promises to give us what we ask and yet often does not. *Institutes*, II, xvii, 2.

8

Biblical Ethics

It is hardly surprising ... that the particular blessing which attaches to peace-makers is that 'they shall be called sons of God'. For they are seeking to do what their Father has done, loving people with his love. ... It is the Devil who is a troublemaker; it is God who loves reconciliation and who now through his children as formerly through his only begotten Son, is bent on making peace.

—JOHN STOTT

Do not think that I have come to bring peace to the earth. I have not come to bring peace, but a sword. For I have come to set a man against his father, and a daughter against her mother, and a daughter-in-law against her mother-in-law. And a person's enemies will be those of his own household.

—MATTHEW 10:34-36

WE ENCOUNTER THE DIALECTICAL pedagogy characteristic of biblical revelation in its ethical instruction as well. Not every ethical obligation is a complex of opposites, to be sure. For example, the first of the two great commandments, to love God, has no counter-position. It is not the case that we are taught in one place to love God and in another not to love him or to love someone or something else instead.[1] The revelation

1. It is, however, remarkable and something to ponder that while we are to love God with all our heart, soul, strength, and mind, God does not mind, indeed he even

of righteousness is not uniformly dialectical. But regarding many if not most of the obligations of believing life laid down in the Law, the obedience to which we are summoned is defined in polarities. Again characteristically, the relationship between the polarities is neither examined nor defined and we are left to form an ethic shaped by competing obligations.

A Number of Examples

We mentioned earlier the famous juxtaposition of contraries in the commandments laid side by side in Prov 26:4–5:

> Do not answer a fool according to his folly, or you will be like him yourself.
> Answer a fool according to his folly, or he will be wise in his own eyes.

Or consider Paul's similarly stark juxtaposition of obligations: "Bear one another's burdens" and "each will have to bear his own load" (Gal 6:2–5).[2] The Lord, in his condemnation of the scribes and Pharisees, ordered the apostles, in terms typically absolute and unqualified, not to allow themselves to be called "teacher" and to call any mere man their "father," honorific titles that fed the vanity of the religious leaders. The apostle Paul, however, reminded the Corinthians that he was their spiritual father (1 Cor 4:16), took to himself the title of "teacher" (1 Tim 2:7), and on more than one occasion laid great emphasis on the fact that he was an "apostle" of Jesus Christ. What the Bible never makes explicit is under what circumstances such titles may not be used and when they may. So it is that, predictably, the Bible has given comfort both to those who have made

requires his people take some of the devotion they owe to him and give it to others instead (1 Cor 7:32–36). The commandment to love our neighbor as ourselves has a more obviously dialectical form. While we are to love others, even our enemies, the Bible never explains how we may, at the same time, "hate those who hate you, O Lord" (Ps 139:21–22), refuse to "sit with the wicked" (Ps 26:5), "look at the faithless with disgust" (Ps 119:58), pray for their judgment (2 Chr 20:12; Rev 6:10), or love someone whose works or way of life we hate (Rev 2:6). The Lord himself loves everyone but hates some (Jer 12:8; Hos 9:15; Rom 9:13). God is love, that is, he has a "consuming passion for the well-being of others." Bruce, *Epistles of John*, 107. But there is no doubt that he acts against many human beings (Isa 13:11–13; Rev 2:16, 21–23).

2. Paul had a typically biblical penchant for absolute assertions that seem on their face the contradiction of one another. In one place he would never boast "except in the cross of our Lord Jesus Christ" (Gal 6:14), in others he boasted of a number of different things (1 Cor 9:15; 2 Cor 1:12, 14; 5:12; I Thess 2:19; 2 Thess 1:4; Phil 2:16).

a great deal of titles and those who think it right to eschew them altogether. For all the cautionary remarks regarding both the unimportance and positive danger of wealth (Prov 30:8–9; Matt 19:23–24; Luke 6:24; 16:14; 1 Tim 6:10), we certainly do not expect to read of the advantage the wealthy have in getting to heaven (Luke 16:9)![3] Surely there are not a few wealthy Christians who have availed themselves of that advantage and will receive a warm welcome in heaven for their pains.[4]

The Bible is pitiless in its condemnation of drunkenness and with equal emphasis celebrates the gift of wine, *even its physical effects* (Deut 7:12–13; Ps 104:15; Prov 20:1; 23:29–35; 31:6–7; Eccl 9:7; Song 1:2; Isa 5:11, 22; 25:6; 28:7; Zech 9:17; 1 Cor 11:21; Eph 5:18; 1 Tim 5:23). We learn in this way to receive God's gifts with thanksgiving but to use them properly. To drink wine can be a wicked act or a righteous one; everything depends upon how one drinks, to what end, and to what extent. It is the sad fact of Christian history that time and again Christians have embraced one biblical emphasis at the expense of the other and the equilibrium of truths has been lost. Teetotalers ignore the Bible's celebration of wine and description of its benefits as well as the Lord's own example. Epicures ignore its stern warnings against drunkenness and the careless indulgence of sensual pleasures.

In a typically stark juxtaposition of contraries the Lord commands us not to judge, lest we too be judged, but likewise not to throw our pearls before swine (Matt 7:1–6). How the latter is not an instance of the former is not explained. It becomes our task to answer that question. The finest explanation of the Lord's warning against passing judgment in Matt 7:1 is provided by Johann Albrecht Bengel in his justly famous *Gnomon Novi Testamenti* or *Notes on the New Testament*. In its original Latin, Bengel's commentary is a marvel of compression and his comment on Matt 7:1 requires but four words: *sine scientia, amore, necessitate*.[5] The judgment we are forbidden to practice is judgment that is "without knowledge,

---

3. "They" in the phrase "They may receive you into the eternal dwellings" is likely a circumlocution for God himself, in keeping with the Jewish custom of using the plural as a means of avoiding the use of the divine name. In that case, God himself will welcome the wealthy who have used their wealth to make friends for themselves. Strack and Billerbeck, *Kommentar zum Neuen Testament*, 2:221.

4. Clement of Alexandria's caution is certainly warranted, but hardly exhausts the ways in which a rich person might heed the exhortation of Luke 16:9. "The Lord did not say, give, or bring, or do good, or help, but make a friend. But a friend proves himself such not by one gift, but by long intimacy." *Who Is the Rich Man?*, XXXII, 600.

5. Bengel, *Gnomon Novi Testamenti*, 52.

love, or necessity." He reaches that conclusion precisely by reading verses 1 and 6 together and giving equal weight to each. *In other words, Bengel accurately reduces the biblical parataxis to a faithful hypotactical explanation or summary, which remains entirely true to the equilibrium of ethical obligations.* He adds, as Holy Scripture does not, a subordinate clause to clarify the meaning of the commandment. We come to true wisdom by respecting the contraries and living in the tension created by them, not by embracing one at the expense of the other. Not all judgment is forbidden, since the Bible commands us to render judgment in certain cases, imposes upon us the practice of church discipline, and calls us to exercise moral and spiritual discernment at every turn. Indeed, Christians are directly summoned in some cases to be judges of one another (1 Cor 6:1–8). But a great deal of the judgment we render is forbidden and the absoluteness of the prohibition forces us to face that fact.

Or consider the Lord's famous instruction for dealing with a known sinner among his followers (Matt 18:15–18). Given other relevant legal deliverances and illustrations of apostolic practice (Num 5:5–31; Deut 17:2–7; 22:13–30; 1 Cor 5:1–5; 6:9–11), the obligation on the discovery of sexual sin is to identify the culprits and either secure their repentance or discipline them accordingly. This is a settled principle of biblical polity. But the Bible never explains how we are to reconcile that emphasis on the maintenance of sexual purity in the church with the fact that Joseph, "being a just man and unwilling to put her to shame," despite the evidence that his betrothed had been promiscuous, "resolved to divorce her quietly" (Matt 1:19). How believers are obliged to honor both examples is never explained. We must consider cases and reach appropriate conclusions. Here the biblical pedagogy enforces a vital lesson. It is not possible to formulate a casuistry so exhaustive that every set of circumstances is provided for in the Law. As John Newton wisely concluded, "Love is the best casuist."[6] The decision of those elders who are most concerned to do the right thing, to be faithful to everything they read in Holy Scripture and so apply the Law to a set of circumstances in the most biblically responsible way, and who are most committed both to the glory of God and the welfare of God's people is most likely to be right.

More famously still, we are well aware of the emphasis placed on the Christian's obligation to obey the government, an obligation usually asserted absolutely and without qualification (Rom 13:1–5; 1 Pet 2:13–17),

6. Newton, *Works*, 1:544–545.

but we are equally aware of the heroic example of the apostles and early Christians who defied the government in order to fulfill the commission the Lord Christ had given them (Acts 4:19–20; 5:29). Unanalyzed, these "contradictions" have led Christians through the ages both to decidedly different conceptions of their duty and to profound and immensely helpful ethical reflection. The Bible obviously knows that human governments are often wicked, frequently requiring their citizens to live in open defiance of the Law of God and punishing them if they do not. But that makes only the more striking that it never lays down principles by which to determine at precisely what point the commandment to submit to the authorities may be regarded as null and void. The Lord paid his taxes fully aware that the Roman treasury funded many wicked things. Obadiah, whom the Bible describes as a godly man, was an important figure in the court of Ahab, but operated behind the wicked king's back to subvert his plans to eliminate the faithful ministry that remained in Israel and managed for some years to hide his true commitments (1 Kgs 18:3–6). But the apostles tempted fate by openly defying the orders of the government when told to cease their preaching. No wonder the long history of disagreement among the devout! The discernment required must be informed by the totality of the biblical revelation of the believer's duty to the state. And the polarities demand that each side of the equation be given equal weight.

The debate that has raged within American evangelicalism over the past half-century concerning the ordination of women and the headship of men in church and home perfectly illustrates the importance of respecting the Bible's penchant for polarities. Nothing is more predictable, nothing should be less surprising to readers of the Bible than that the Bible in many places lays tremendous emphasis on the equality of men and women in the kingdom of God. Indeed, almost everything the Bible teaches us about the Christian life is addressed to human beings irrespective of their sex. But in some places the Bible makes significant distinctions between men and women. We resist the temptation to imagine ourselves wiser than the Almighty but admit to being sorely tempted to wish he had thought it prudent to explain in greater detail precisely how the two emphases are to be related to one another and how both can be believed and practiced at one and the same time! Instead, we get the one emphasis here and the other there. What we are not permitted to do is to silence one assertion by reference to the other. Each must be given its due in constructing our ethic of the sexual economy.

In regard to matters only somewhat more mundane, consider, for example, the stress laid on the importance of a woman's inner beauty, her character, together with virtual denunciations of the physical adornment of her outward appearance (Prov 31:30; Isa 3:16–23; 1 Tim 2:9–10; 1 Pet 3:3–4). This is an emphasis, in OT and NT alike, of perhaps still greater importance for both men and women in the age of the camera. It is an emphasis both spiritually confirming and psychologically liberating in a society fixated on the superficial by the ubiquity of images of feminine allurement for the sake of either advertising or pornography. There has perhaps never been a time when this message is more urgently needed. But that is not all the Bible has to say about physical appearance. There are also texts in which a woman's physical attractiveness is explicitly noted and praised and other texts in which the adornment of female appearance is commended (Gen 24:16, 53; Esth 2:7; Song 4:1–7, 10–14; Jer 2:32; 4:30; Ezek 16:9–14). In a way altogether typical of the Bible, there are texts that, taken by themselves, would seem to rule out the use of cosmetics and the styling of hair, jewelry, and fashionable clothes, and other texts that celebrate the use of the same things.[7] We have texts that decry attention paid to the physical appearance of a woman and texts in which God himself calls attention to the fact that a particular woman was beautiful. In this way we are put on our mettle to incorporate both emphases in our understanding and practice.

Or consider the qualification for an elder in the church that he be "well thought of by outsiders" (1 Tim 3:7). It makes sense that a Christian man who is to be a representative Christian and an example for other believers should let his light shine. On the other hand, the Lord taught that if they hated the Master they would hate his servants, and Peter, Paul, and John all warn us "not to be surprised that the world hates us" (1 John 3:13), to expect to be slandered and persecuted, indeed that the greater the godliness the more the persecution (2 Tim 3:12). The martyrs, obviously, did not have the best reputation with outsiders but, far from being disqualified for church office for that reason, we rightly regard them as heroes of our faith. Again, the Bible sets these assertions side by side: it expects us to live such righteous lives as to provoke both the sneering disdain and the admiration of unbelievers. But never does it explain how this is possible, though that it is has been proved times without number.

---

7. It is certainly instructive that the same adornments of feminine attraction employed by the bride (Song 4:10–14) are found in the prostitute or adulteress' toolkit (Prov 7:16–17).

It is precisely the dialectical relation of these obligations that ensures that each is given its day in a true account of Christian living. Two further examples will serve both to illustrate this pedagogy and illustrate its virtue.

I. To Lie or Not To Lie

Tell the Truth!

The Bible is categorical in its denunciation of lying. Not only does the obligation of telling the truth find a place in the Ten Commandments, but over and again the Bible regards truth-telling as a defining characteristic of the godly character. The righteous "speak truth" in their hearts, and so much so that they are willing to speak it publicly, even to "swear," to their own hurt (Ps 15:2, 4). It is, contrarily, characteristic of the wicked that they are dishonest (Jer 5:1; Isa 59:14). The devil is the father of lies but God punishes liars (Ps 5:6; John 8:44; Rev 21:8). It is the nature of sin and unbelief to subvert the truth, to make liars of us all (Jer 9:5; John 8:44–45; Rom 3:13).[8] In the Bible, and emphatically, ". . . untruth is the hallmark of impiety."[9]

Divine grace, on the other hand, makes people to rejoice in the truth (1 Cor 13:6), speak truth to one another (Zech 8:16), and even love the truth (Zech 8:19). Since God is truth itself (Isa 65:16), the Son of God the truth and full of truth (John 1:14; 14:6), and the Holy Spirit the Spirit of truth (John 14:17), it is only to be expected that speaking the truth will be a principal feature of the conduct of those who are being remade in the image of the Triune God (Eph 4:22–25), since "no lie is of the truth" (1 John 2:21). "The Bible throughout requires veracity; we may never lie."[10]

It is only to be expected, therefore, that the *Westminster Shorter Catechism* should summarize the duties of the ninth commandment by saying that it requires "the maintaining and promoting of truth between man and man" and that it accordingly forbids "whatsoever is prejudicial to truth" (Qs 77–78). Indeed, the *Larger Catechism* elaborates the burden of the commandment by adding that the commandment forbids

8. "Man is then only disguise, falsehood, and hypocrisy, both in himself and in regard to others. He does not wish any one to tell him the truth; he avoids telling it to others, and all these dispositions, so removed from justice and reason, have a natural root in his heart." Pascal, *Pensées*, 100, 41.

9. Murray, *Principles of Conduct*, 128.

10. Murray, *Principles of Conduct*, 132.

"concealing the truth" and the use of "doubtful or equivocal expressions, to the prejudice of truth" (Q 145).

Add to this consistent witness to the obligation of truth-telling the undeniable fact that the Bible never relaxes our moral duty because of the troubles that may ensue on account of our obedience—indeed, what are the martyrs but men and women who died for speaking the truth and refusing to deny it?—we are left in no doubt that God expects his people to speak the truth—to speak it in love, to be sure, but to speak the truth. Christians learn over time how difficult an obedience that is. The godly soon discover with sadness the full extent of their unwillingness at many times and in many circumstances to speak the truth.[11] But that we should be people of the truth and scrupulous with the truth is a biblical commonplace. Hence the prayer of the righteous, "Deliver me, O Lord, from lying lips, from a deceitful tongue" (Ps 120:2).

This fact is further confirmed by the many instances in Holy Scripture of believers lying and being found out in their lies. In case after case we find, as it were, our noses being held in the stench of the moral failure of even the devout to tell the truth. The patriarchs told lies for a variety of reasons, from cowardice to greed (Gen 12:12–13; 18:15; 20:2–3; 26:7; 27:5–27), and suffered the consequences, though, by God's grace, not to the degree they might have. Peter's shameful lies are dutifully recorded and with them the bitter tears he shed when brought to his senses. In this way also we are taught the evil of dishonesty and the virtue of speaking the truth.

So Many Lies!

But this makes only the more noteworthy, if not actually stunning, the substantial evidence of biblical support for the *mendacium officiosum*, the dutiful lie. Not only once or twice, but with surprising frequency Holy Scripture bears witness to lies being told that seem very clearly to have its approval.[12] Joseph's elaborate deception by which he brought his brothers to repentance and new obedience seems clearly to receive the approval of the biblical narrator. Joseph, a God-figure in the history, orchestrated

11. "When a man really tells the truth, the first truth he tells is that he himself is a liar." Chesterton, *What's Wrong with the World*, part 4, xi.

12. John Frame supplies a list of some sixteen cases and that is not a complete list. *Doctrine of the Christian Life*, 836.

events behind the scenes by means of elaborate fictions, which in time brought spiritual healing to his family and turned the previously despicable Judah into a Christ-figure. Throughout the narrative Joseph played a part and, with consummate psychological skill and no doubt with the purest of intentions, rendered his brothers dupes.[13] The bold, certainly dangerous deceit perpetuated by the Hebrew midwives, according to the Exodus narrative, was motivated by their fear of the Lord and was rewarded by him accordingly (Exod 1:15–21). There is not so much as a hint in the narrative that Rahab's lie, by which the lives of the spies were preserved, was sinful (Josh 2:4–7; cf. 2 Sam 17:20); indeed, her duplicity was richly rewarded. After all, a spy, in the nature of the case, is a dissembler, but the spies were sent into Canaan in the first instance by the Lord himself (Num 13:1–3)[14] and later by faithful Joshua (Josh 2:1). Again, the burden of proof certainly rests heavily on the one who wishes to find fault with Moses for deceiving Pharaoh as to the true reason for Israel's request to travel into the desert (Exod 10:24–26); with Jonathan, that godly man, for lying to his father as part of his effort to protect David from Saul's bloodlust (1 Sam 20:28); with Elisha for telling Hazael to tell an outright lie to Ben-Hadad, which lie Hazael dutifully reported to the Syrian king (2 Kgs 8:9–15); or with Jeremiah for consenting to Zedekiah's plan to lie to the officials at court both for the prophet's sake and Zedekiah's own (Jer 38:24–27).

The morality of a lie is not as obvious in other cases where, again, the biblical narrator provides no indications of disapproval. Jehu's lie by which the prophets of Baal were collected in one place so that they might be executed is a case in point (2 Kgs 10:18–27). It is difficult to detect any disapproval of Jehu's actions and what evaluation of his actions is reported is entirely positive (10:30), but Jehu himself is acknowledged in the context to be a less-than-righteous man (v. 29). Some other deceptions, bold, elaborate, and perpetuated over time, though not explicitly condemned, do seem to have the features of culpable falsehood, including its unintended consequences. David's lies to Achish, the Philistine king, have been defended by some as the ethics of war, in which deceit is permissible—holy war, indeed, as the Amalekites were under divine

13. And among those deceptions were outright lies, e.g., Gen 42:14, 16; 44:15. Whatever Joseph did, it certainly amounted to "concealing the truth," which the Catechism condemns.

14. In a typically unresolved parataxis, we read in Deut 1:22–23 that the sending of the spies from Kadesh was the suggestion of the people to which Moses assented.

condemnation and David, by attacking them, was only doing what Saul had been commanded to do but had not done (1 Sam 27:1–12; 15:2–3). However, the narrator appears to discredit this justification when he reports that David's lies landed him in a desperate situation he never seemed to have contemplated and from which only providence could rescue him (1 Sam 29:1–11).

Given the Bible's stress on telling the truth, there has been, understandably, a tradition of regarding all such deceptions as culpable disobedience. However they may have served a purpose, even a holy purpose, they were lies, should not have been spoken, and had to be forgiven by the Lord. This was generally Augustine's view and has been held by many since. Christopher Love, the English Puritan, for example, in a beautiful passage in one of his sermons celebrates God's gracious judgment of his people's character, characteristically noting only their virtues when he might have drawn attention to their faults, and illustrates this by saying, "Mention is made of Rahab's entertainment of the spies [in Heb 11:31], but no mention is made that she told a lie, when she did so."[15]

But the fact remains that there are not only an impressive number of instances in which the devout tell an untruth and Holy Scripture, far from indicating disapproval, seems rather obviously to commend them for doing so, but in certain cases *the Lord himself is a partner to the deceit*. After all, it was Yahweh who instructed Moses to tell Pharaoh that the intention of the Israelites was only to take a three-day journey into the desert, there to offer sacrifices to Yahweh (Exod 3:18; cf. 3:16–17). In 1 Sam 16:1–5 the Lord tells Samuel to tell Saul that he has gone to Bethlehem to make a sacrifice, rather than disclose his true purpose, which was to anoint a son of Jesse as Saul's replacement as the king of Israel. While it may be argued, as John Murray did, that, while this was obviously an evasion, there was not an actual misstatement of fact since Samuel did offer

---

15. Love, *Preacher of God's Word*, 2:160. Similarly, James Durham, the seventeenth-century Scottish Presbyterian. "... denying of a thing to be, even when the granting of it would infer hurt and damage to another, is contrary to the truth, and we ought not to do evil that good may come of it. . . . And as no man can lie for himself for his own safety, so can he not for another's; thus to lie even for God is a fault. . . ." *Practical Expositions*, 389. Both Calvin and John Murray take the position that Rahab's lie was sinful and was, therefore, unjustified by the circumstances. Providence would have found some other way to protect the spies. Murray, *Principles of Conduct*, 138–39, 141–42. A better account of the history of debate on this question and the biblical evidence is found in Jones, *Biblical Christian Ethics*, 144–51; Frame, *Doctrine of the Christian Life*, 830–40; and Bonhoeffer, *Ethics*, 363–72.

a sacrifice, the fact remains that sacrifice was not the reason Samuel was sent to Bethlehem and the offering of sacrifice was a subterfuge designed to conceal that fact. Is it not pedantry to distinguish an outright lie from more subtle misrepresentations that are more effective precisely because of their subtlety? And is it not possible to betray *every* obligation of the Law as much by omission as by commission and as much by attitude as by action?[16] The narrative does not suggest that Samuel would have offered sacrifice in Bethlehem had he not needed to conceal the purpose of his visit. In any case, what Moses was instructed to tell Pharaoh regarding the intention of the Israelites was an untruth by any definition.

John Murray argued that there was justification neither for the Hebrew midwives to deceive Pharaoh nor for Rahab to lie to the king of Jericho. The fact is that Samuel had less reason to fear the consequences of truth-telling than either Rahab or the midwives, even perhaps than Peter the night of the Lord's arrest. But far more obviously problematic for those wishing to argue that any intentional misstatement of fact, no matter the circumstances, no matter the motivation, is a sin, is the account of Micaiah in 1 Kgs 22:19–23, in which Yahweh himself put a lying spirit in the mouth of Ahab's prophets precisely to ensure that they would deceive the king and so secure his death in battle. The God of truth arranged for and approved the lie to be spoken (1 Kgs 22:23).[17] Here again

16. What thoughtful Christian does not recognize the truth in William Blake's famous lines: "A truth that's told with bad intent/Beats all the lies you can invent." Certainly this particular case is an instance of "concealing the truth" and of a doubtful or equivocal expression to the prejudice of the truth, precisely what the *Larger Catechism* forbids as a violation of the Ninth Commandment.

17. John Murray argues, after an elaborate examination of some of the cases mentioned above, that "the upshot of our examination has been that no instance demonstrates the propriety of untruthfulness under any exigency" 146. Murray makes no mention of Exod 3:18 or 1 Kgs 22. Nor does he deal with Joseph's deception of his brothers. His argument regarding the Hebrew midwives and Rahab seems to me a failure to respect the manner of biblical communication, much better understood today than in Murray's day. We are nowadays more aware how commonly a biblical narrator *shows* rather than *tells* and indicates in more subtle ways his approval or disapproval of the actions of the *dramatis personae*. If a negative judgment is conveyed in the case of David's lies to Achish, his lies having landed him in a catch-22 that was no part of his plan (1 Sam 27:1–12; 15:2–3), no such judgment is found in those other cases; indeed, the narrative conveys approval, even praise, rather than disapproval. Another instance of a proper "deception" is likely found in the narrative of the Lord's behavior on the road to Emmaus (Luke 24:28). The Lord acted "as if" he were going further. Commentators argue whether the verb should be translated "pretend," but the primary meaning of the word is to act "as if" or "to pretend." Bock, *Luke*, 2:1918. The context certainly

we have stark polarities and undeniable paradox: the Lord putting a lying spirit within men or sending upon them a "strong delusion, so that they may believe what is false" (2 Thess 2:11–12) and the manifest testimony of Holy Scripture that "it is impossible for God to lie" (Heb 6:18).

Living the Paradox

It is just like the Bible to forbid lying in no uncertain terms, to lay heavy stress on the evil and the harm of it, and to illustrate at some length its danger and the full measure of divine disapproval, *and then to provide instances of falsehoods that are, in fact, not only permissible but necessary.* Again typically, the Bible leaves us with those sharply delineated polarities, provides no analysis by which to identify precisely which lies are forbidden and which are permitted, if not required, and leaves to us the hard work of fashioning an ethic of truth-telling based on all of this evidence. The result is, or ought to be, people who revere the truth and are perfectly willing to suffer on its behalf and, at the same time, have the wisdom to know when it is necessary to lie.

So it was that the Christians of Le Chambon, working at great risk to preserve the lives of Jews during the Second World War, spoke the truth to both Vichy and German officials to the extent that they could, even at great personal risk, but practiced deception when necessary to preserve the lives of the refugees who had sought their protection.[18] So it was that Dietrich Bonhoeffer, much to the surprise of his friend sitting with him at an outdoor cafe at the time, feigned wild enthusiasm at the loudspeaker's announcement of France's surrender, including the "Heil Hitler" salute. It was Bonhoeffer's way of ensuring that his deep and implacable opposition to Hitler and fascist military adventurism would not lead to immediate arrest but that he be able to continue his work against the wicked regime.[19] I will leave it to others to cast the first stone at C. S. Lewis. Here was a man who incurred the reproach of many, including many of his

---

seems to suggest that the Lord simulated an action he had no intention of performing in order to secure a certain result. If so this was certainly a form of deception, however mild, however well-intentioned. Otherwise, we must assume he actually intended to walk further away from Jerusalem, no matter the late hour, and his plan was interrupted by the request of the disciples. Another instance of a similar simulation may be found in John 7:8 (the better reading) and 7:10.

18. Philip Hallie, *Lest Innocent Blood Be Shed*, 125–28, 225–30.

19. Mataxis, *Bonhoeffer*, 361–62.

academic peers, for his fidelity to the truth,[20] yet upon encountering a bedraggled and exhausted fox enthusiastically deceived mounted hunters when they appeared by pointing them in the opposite direction to that taken by the animal, much as Rahab had done for the spies. "It went that-a-way!"[21] Two contradictory behaviors—telling the truth and telling a lie—without an explanation as to when we may lie and when we must be willing to suffer, and others with us, for telling the truth: this is the Bible's ethic of truth-telling.

II. To Preserve the Unity and the Purity of the Church

The loving unity of Christ's body was a matter of the greatest importance to him. It was the petition of his high priestly prayer that all his disciples, including those yet to become so, be one; that they share a unity that might be fairly compared to that enjoyed by the Lord Jesus with his Father (John 17:21). He regarded such unity as essential to the church's witness to the world. Indeed, he said that it would be this unity, this spiritual brotherhood expressed in their common life, that would be a potent demonstration of the love of God for the world (John 17:23). Moreover, the loving communion of his disciples with one another was the object of much else that he taught.

The Bond of Peace

The beatitude "Blessed are the peacemakers" is part of the Lord's commendation of the godly character and way of life. Since his kingdom is a kingdom of peace (Rom 14:17), its citizens are to live at peace with one another and make peace with everyone (Rom 12:18). Indeed, Christians are to live in peace even with their enemies, no matter the sacrifices that may be required to maintain a cordial fellowship (Matt 5:38–42; 1 Cor 7:13–16). And if they are to seek peace with their enemies, how much more so with their friends! From ages past it was always good and pleasant when brothers dwelled in unity and saw "eye to eye" (Ps 133:1; Isa 52:8). We are, after all, brothers and sisters of the same family (Matt 23:8). And so it was that the apostle Paul was anyone's doormat regarding matters on which it was possible for him to bend, even when his brothers

20. Marsden, *C.S. Lewis's Mere Christianity*, 58–65.
21. Sayer, *Jack*, 209.

were in error, because in this way he made and kept friends instead of multiplying enemies and so preserved the unity of the body of Christ (1 Cor 9:19–23; Rom 15:1–6). Indeed, the great apostle to the Gentiles invested considerable mental and spiritual resources in fostering brotherhood within individual congregations and across the landscape of Christendom in its first generation. No doubt his tongue was regularly sore from his biting it as often as it proved necessary for him to do! The calling of the Christian, so far as it depends on him or her, is to live at peace with all, "to seek peace and pursue it" (Ps 34:14; Rom 12:18; Eph 4:3; Heb 12:14; 1 Pet 3:11).

> It is hardly surprising . . . that the particular blessing which attaches to peacemakers is that 'they shall be called sons of God'. For they are seeking to do what their Father has done, loving people with his love. . . . It is the Devil who is a troublemaker; it is God who loves reconciliation and who now through his children as formerly through his only begotten Son, is bent on making peace.[22]

And so it has always been that when the Holy Spirit is mightily at work believers not only find themselves "of one heart and soul" but make many new friends for the gospel (Acts 4:32; 9:17). Divisions among the brethren are not only sinful but damaging to the church's witness and the influence of the gospel in the world (1 Cor 1:10; 6:1–8; 2 Cor 13:11; Phil 1:27).

The Sad Fact of Christian Disunity

But, in keeping with the dialectical pattern of Holy Scripture, it was the Lord himself who famously said,

> Do not think that I have come to bring peace to the earth. I have not come to bring peace, but a sword. For I have come to set a man against his father, and a daughter against her mother, and a daughter-in-law against her mother-in-law. And a person's enemies will be those of his own household (Matt 10:34–36).

Much as we might wish that others see our good works and glorify our Father in heaven, in many cases our loyalty to Christ and his kingdom will produce instead conflict and ill will. Indeed, the Lord went so far as

---

22. Stott, *Christian Counter-Culture*, 50.

to prophesy that "the hour is coming when whoever kills you will think he is offering service to God" (John 16:2). The history of the persecution of the church more than proves the truth of that forecast.

But it is the disunity that has so long marked the church's own life in the world that most betrays the peace, harmony, and family loyalty to which believers are summoned and that ought to separate the life of Christians from that of the world. Already in the apostolic age Christians were alienated from one another for various reasons: differences of class and socioeconomic status (Acts 6:1; 1 Cor 11:20–21; Jas 2:1–7), racial or ethnic identity (Gal 2:11–14), personalities (1 Cor 1:12–13), private disputes (Acts 15:36–41; 1 Cor 6:1–8; Phil 4:2–3), and convictions touching theology and ethics (Rom 14:1–12; Phil 3:2–3; Col 2:16; Jude 3–23; Rev 2:14–15).

The history of Christian disunity, infighting, and mutual hatred makes for dismal reading. Of how many different Christian sects through the ages might it be said what Augustine said of the Donatists of his day: "Yet these frogs croak from their swamp, 'There are no Christians but us'"?[23] It is terrifying to contemplate how great must be the damage done to the reputation of the Lord Jesus and to the influence of the gospel by squabbling Christians. Certainly the multiplication of Christian denominations has undermined the Christian claim that the Bible is reliably the source of truth. If believers themselves cannot agree as to what the Bible teaches and if their differing interpretations are sufficiently substantial as to require them to separate from one another, how can they claim that its teaching is even comprehensible, much less convincing? What good is the Bible if those who believe it to be the Word of God cannot find virtually universal agreement as to its teaching? More than that, Christian sectarianism, with all of its inevitable sins of temper, likewise vitiates the Christian claim that the gospel produces a new and supernatural kind of life. After all, unbelievers are well used to squabbling, alienation, and partisanship, so in this respect, embarrassingly public, Christians seem far more like them than different! So Voltaire's jibe:

> I know to be sure that the Church is infallible; but is it the Greek Church, or the Latin Church, or the Church of England, or that of Denmark and of Sweden, or that of the proud city of Neuchatel, or that of the primitives called Quakers, or that of the Anabaptists, or that of the Moravians? The Turkish Church has

---

23. Augustine, *Exposition on the Book of Psalms*, 473. The translation is that of Wills, *Font of Life*, 140.

its points, too, but they say that the Chinese Church is much more ancient.[24]

If unbelievers are to see our good works and glorify our Father in heaven, if the world is to be brought to an acknowledgment that God has come in the flesh to save sinners by the harmony of Christian believers—their love for one another surmounting all the barriers of culture, race, ethnicity, language, national identity, and difference of opinion that alienate human beings from one another—it must be admitted to our shame that the church has in this respect far too often been a miserable failure.

And it isn't only Christian witness that is crippled by our disunity. The damage done to the spiritual health of the church herself has been catastrophic. In what is rightly regarded as the classic work on the evil of Christian disunity, the seventeenth-century Scot James Durham's *Concerning Scandal*, the author supplies a long list of the spiritual and ecclesiastical harms done by infighting and the proud and unloving behavior that almost always accompanies it. He then summarizes the damage done in this way.

> Although sometimes the fault of division may be more on one side than another, yet seldom is any side free, at least, in the manner of prosecution. Therefore often it turns in the close to the hurt of both, and the one side becomes more schismatical and erroneous, at least, in many of their members. . . . The other side, again, has often become more cold and secure in the practice of holiness, carnal and formal in pursuing ceremonies and external things, with less affection and life in the main, because the edge of their zeal was bent toward these differences; and generally people have been stumbled and offended by them.[25]

In other words, fidelity to the gospel and purity of heart and behavior are diminished on both sides of such disputes, no matter that one side may have more of the right in the matter in dispute.

I grew up in separatist American Presbyterianism. I still believe that fidelity to the gospel was at stake in those twentieth-century divisions and that they were justified, if not inevitable.[26] But hardly anyone who

24. Cited from "The Questions of Zapata," in Hall, *Reading Scripture*, 22.

25. Durham, *Treatise Concerning Scandal*, 241–44.

26. John Brown, the eighteenth-century Scottish divine, acknowledged the "grievous disasters" that divisions in the Church may produce in the spiritual life of individuals and the Christian community and argued, therefore, that in all cases if at all

lived through those early- and mid-twentieth-century controversies and thought carefully about them in retrospect was unwilling to admit not only the sin committed on both sides, but the serious damage done to spiritual health and gospel witness.[27]

Living in Peace and Contending for the Faith

Of course, it is one thing to divide over lesser things, another altogether when fidelity to the gospel is the issue. Holy Scripture itself enjoins believers both "to contend for the faith that was once for all delivered to the saints" (Jude 3) and to have nothing to do with those who subvert the teaching of the Word of God (2 Cor 13:8–10; Gal 1:6–9; 1 Tim 1:18–20; 1 John 2:18–19). It is for this reason that some divisions are necessary (Acts 28:23–28; 2 Tim 3:5; 2 John 6–11), if not inevitable (1 Cor 11:19; 2 Cor 11:12–15; 1 Tim 1:20). Even if it were a separation imposed upon them and not of their own making, the apostles themselves presided over the original division in the church, that between Judaism and the followers of the Lord (Acts 28:25–28). It was the unavoidable result of the apostles'

---

possible they are to be avoided. But he went on to say, "Providence often points out 'the duty of separation by permitting some faithful ministers to be tyrannously thrust out of her communion.'" MacKenzie, *John Brown of Haddington*, 198–99. So it was in mid-twentieth-century Presbyterian history.

27. Francis Schaeffer defended the division between Presbyterians in the 1930s, in which division he was a participant, but later repented of the unloving spirit in which it had been too much conducted by his party. "I think we have to be involved in combat, but when we are fighting for the Lord it has to be according to his rules. . . ." Once again, such a conclusion is formed precisely by giving equal weight to the biblical contraries, in this case the obligation to maintain loving unity and to contend for the faith. Cited in Hankins, *Francis Schaeffer*, 45. Philip Melancthon, a Reformation figure possessed of an irenic spirit, referred to the differences that provoked many such disputes and divisions as the *rabies theologorum*, the fury or madness of the theologians! Surely Durham was only doing justice to the biblical stress on the vital importance of Christian unity when he wrote, "Never did men run to quench fire in a city; lest all should be destroyed, with more diligence, than men ought to bestir themselves to quench this in the church. Never did mariners use more speed to stop a leak in a ship, lest all should be drowned, than ministers especially, and all Christian men, should haste to stop this beginning of the breaking in of these waters of strife, lest thereby the whole church be overwhelmed." *Treatise Concerning Scandal*, 243, 260. An excellent exposition of the twin passions for unity and fidelity and the way in which they are simultaneously to undergird ecclesiology, an emphasis of the early Scottish Reformers, is found in MacPherson, *Doctrine of the Church*, 91–128. A vigorous protest against schism by those who were themselves, at least formally, schismatics, is the predictable "contradiction" that results from holding fast to biblical polarities.

determination to remain steadfast as ambassadors of the gospel of Jesus Christ. And so it is that once again we are left in a typical tension, being pulled in opposite directions at the same time. We are to make real sacrifices to preserve the unity of the body of Christ and to fight tooth and nail against any subversion of the faith. Holy Scripture never digresses on precisely how both things are to be done at one and the same time or where precisely the line between unity and compromise is to be found. It lays us under the obligation to do both, and in that twofold obedience the will of God is to be found.

Even the best-intentioned have struggled to find the balance. The famous maxim "In necessary things unity, in non-necessary things liberty, in all things charity"[28] does not define the difference between necessary and non-necessary things and the devil has raised terrible havoc in that detail! It is precisely in seeking to define the non-negotiable elements of Christian confession that believers have reached sharply different conclusions with dramatically different implications for conduct. Some have argued that the unity conferred by baptism renders every other consideration immaterial. And so it is that some churches include ministers and lay men and women who deny that Christ is God incarnate, that he rose from the dead, that the hope of heaven depends upon living faith in him, or that the Word of God alone remains our standard of belief and conduct. Others have been inclined to view virtually any deviation from their theological system as tantamount to heresy and so a reason for separation. And so it is that there exist churches whose members deny the most basic elements of Christian confession and Christians who agree with one another in virtually every detail of theological confession and polity but nevertheless have found reason to remain apart. There are churches that, having sprung from one division after another, find themselves at last a community of single-minded uniformity of outlook so complete that they fit into someone's living room.

The wonderfully wide-spirited John Duncan said of himself, "I'm first a Christian, next a catholic, then a Calvinist, fourth a paedobaptist, and fifth a Presbyterian. I cannot reverse this order."[29] But his being a

28. The adage is most reliably attributed to Rupert Meldenius, a seventeenth-century Lutheran theologian. Similar is the statement of Gregory I. "The holy church corrects certain things with fervor, she tolerates others with meekness, she closes her eyes on still others and bears them with reflective attention." The translation is Jill Raitt's in McGinn, *Christian Spirituality*, 485.

29. Duncan, *Colloquia Peripatetica*, 8.

Presbyterian, a Calvinist, and a paedobaptist inevitably separated him to a significant degree from others whom he cheerfully regarded as Christian brethren. Sad as the result may be in this respect, it is almost impossible to imagine how believers can live in faithfulness to the light they have and not suffer some formal parting from one another. The distinctive theological convictions of the various churches are not whims. They are the ripe fruit of centuries of devout and often brilliant theological reflection on the teaching of the Word of God. But their result is that the government of the church cannot be Episcopal, Presbyterian, and Congregationalist at the same time, and a pastor of Baptist conviction understandably and necessarily will not baptize the infant children of his congregation. The Roman Catholic Church requires allegiance to doctrines that many more serious Christians in the world than not believe to be contrary to Holy Scripture, some of which bear directly on the very nature of the gospel and the Christian life. What is to be done?

Biblical parataxis and absoluteness of statement require of us that we "dwell in unity" (Ps 133:1), eagerly seek to maintain the "unity of the Spirit in the bond of peace" (Eph 4:3), "striving side by side for the faith of the gospel" (Phil 1:27), and, at the same time, "[teach] what accords with sound doctrine" (Titus 2:1), handle the Word of Truth rightly (2 Tim 2:15), avoid "ignorant controversies" (2 Tim 2:23), look to the Spirit to guide us into the truth (John 16:13), and correct where possible and otherwise avoid altogether those who deny the truth (2 Thess 3:14; 2 Tim 2:25; 2 John 10–11).

What Can Be Done?

It is all very well to wish for a single mind. Within churches where a formal unity exists, there is often a crippling disunity of conviction and outlook. Some in this church or that believe in supernatural Christianity; others do not. This is unity in name only; hardly what the Lord prayed for and his apostles practiced. Fact is, the seeds of our present disunity are planted in Holy Scripture itself, where not only do we find the evidence of varying convictions among Christians, even in the apostolic age, but the right of biblical and theological judgment is, at least in part, invested in the individual believer and congregation of believers.

In the middle of the nineteenth century the Presbyterian Church USA was invited to send delegates to the First Vatican Council (1869–1870).

The reply to that invitation was entrusted to Charles Hodge, the Princeton theologian. He began by acknowledging the Presbyterian Church's cordial affirmation of the articles of the Apostles' Creed and, indeed, the doctrinal declarations of the first six so-called Ecumenical Councils. He then proceeded to deny that the Presbyterian Church was schismatic, insofar as it cordially recognized the membership in the body of Christ of all who profess the true faith together with their children, whatever their denominational affiliation. But there remained a reason why it could not participate in such a council. Then follows this noble passage.

> When we open the Scriptures, we find that they are addressed to the people. They speak to us. We are commanded to search them (John 5:39). To believe what they teach. We are held personally responsible for our faith. The Apostle commands us to pronounce accursed an apostle or an angel from heaven who should [teach] anything contrary to the divinely authenticated Word of God (Gal. 1:8). He made us the judges, and has placed the rule of judgment into our hands, and holds us responsible for our judgment. Moreover, we find that the teaching of the Holy Spirit was promised by Christ not to the clergy only, much less to any one order of the clergy exclusively, but to all believers. It is written, "Ye shall all be taught of God." The Apostle John says to believers: "Ye have an unction from the Holy One, and know all things . . . but the anointing which ye have received of him abideth in you; and ye need not that any man teach you; but as the same anointing teacheth you of all things and is truth, and is no lie, and even as it hath taught you, ye shall abide in him" (1 Jn 2:20, 27). This teaching of the Spirit authenticates itself, as this same apostle teaches us, when he says "He that believeth on the Son of God hath the witness in himself" (1 Jn 5:10). "I have not written unto you because ye know not the truth, but because ye know it, and that no lie is of the truth" (1 Jn 2:21). Private judgment, therefore, is not only a right, but a duty, from which no man can absolve himself, or be absolved by others.[30]

30. Hodge, "Letter to Pope Pius X," 16–20. See J. C. Ryle's defense of private judgment, its right, duty, and necessity in his tract *Prove All Things*, reprinted as "Private Judgment" in *Knots Untied*, 34–47. It is worth noting in passing the dialectical nature of the biblical teaching that all believers have an anointing from the Holy Spirit and know the truth. Undoubtedly the Bereans were "more noble" for their eager examination of the Scriptures to confirm the truth of what they had heard from the Apostle Paul. But, at the same time, the Bible not only acknowledges the false opinions sometimes entertained by believers but rings the changes on the essential role of teachers and sound teaching and the obligation of believers to submit to the teaching of faithful

For all of its abuses through the ages, the right and obligation of private judgment, exercised on the text of Holy Scripture, cannot be removed from the teaching of the Bible. And so it has come to this. Much Christian division is certainly sinful and should be repented of and, if at all possible, remedied. But much cannot be remedied, if remedy is understood in terms of formal ecclesiastical unity. With the best will in the world, faithful Christians do not agree about everything and some of their disagreements touch matters that have profound implications for practice.

Still, while standing firm in biblical convictions, by embracing at the same time the Bible's impressive emphasis on both the obligation of Christian unity and its vital importance for both the health and the witness of the Church, much has been done and can be done to vitalize Christian brotherhood. When Tertullian, in a celebrated passage in his *Apology*, compares the Christians' brotherly love with the social animosity typical of the Greco-Roman world of the time, he bears witness to the inevitable notice that true human unity and loving fellowship receives even in a hostile world. "See, they say, how [the Christians] love one another, for they themselves are animated by mutual hatred; how they are ready even to die for one another, for they themselves will sooner put to death."[31] Christians who are anxious to make that impression for Christ and the gospel will believe it must still be possible to make such an impression, find ways to make common cause with believers in other churches, make public the honor they pay to the members of other communions as fellow disciples of the Lord Jesus Christ, and take care to

---

men (Ps 105:12–15; Jer 2:8; Col 1:7; 1 Tim 4:11–16; 2 Tim 2:2; Heb 13:17). Still, not infrequently believers are directly rebuked for their inexcusable lack of knowledge! Indeed, lying beneath this dialectic is another still more fundamental: that between individual and corporate identity. If Paul says that the Lord "loved me and gave himself for me" (Gal 2:20), he also says that the Lord loved "the church and gave himself for her" (Eph 5:25). If living faith is the possession and the practice of the individual believer, as it surely is throughout Holy Scripture (1 Kgs 19:18; Rom 9:6), it is also everywhere the product and the possession of a community, necessarily given birth, nourished, shared, and preserved by others (e.g., Gen 18:19; 1 Tim 4:16). As Cyprian famously said, "He can no longer have God for his Father, who has not the Church for his mother." *Unity of the Church*, 6, 423. The apostles address themselves to congregations as if they were individuals, each with a Christian life marked by characteristic strengths and weaknesses and everywhere the life of the individual believer is part and parcel of the body of Christ with all its members. Still, each and every Christian is responsible for his or her faith and life before God.

31. Tertullian, *Apology*, XXXIX, 46.

ensure that for every comment made necessary by differing conviction there will be ten celebrating our common faith and our mutual love.

To part with what one believes to be a fundamental truth of God's Word in the interests of charity and unity is to betray the Lord with a kiss. But to violate the bonds of Christian brotherhood in the interests of sectarian theologizing is perhaps a greater betrayal for its indifference to the expressed desires of the Savior himself and the explicit command-ments found in his Word.[32] If there is anything the world should see when it looks at Christians and Christian churches, it is this equal passion for the truth as that truth has been revealed by God in his Word *and* the love with which we have been loved turned outward toward others. And, since even the pagans can love those who love them, it will be the dis-tinguishing mark of Christian love that it is cordially, even sacrificially extended to those with whom we disagree. Still further, since the most bitter controversy is often between those whose differences are magni-fied by their substantial areas of agreement, how much more impressive must be a spirit of love and unity between Christians who regrettably find it necessary to make their way in different churches! As C. S. Lewis observed in speaking to unbelievers,

> One thing I can promise you. In spite of all the unfortunate differences between Christians, what they agree on is still something pretty big and pretty solid: big enough to blow any of us sky-high if it happens to be true. And if it's true, it's quite ridiculous to put off doing anything about it simply because Christians don't fully agree among themselves. That's as if a man bleeding to death refused medical assistance because he'd heard that some doctors differed about the treatment of cancer.[33]

32. "I will not undertake to define what is so merely fundamental and absolutely necessary to salvation as that without it there is no hope. This much I am sure: First, the fundamentals are fewer than many of both sides make them. Secondly, that every lean-to and superstructure doth not raze the foundation." Robert Harris, the English Puritan, cited in Lloyd-Jones, *Puritans*, 233. J.C. Ryle was an outspoken Calvinist, but his definition of the evangelical faith in five particulars would satisfy virtually any Arminian. Rogers, *Tender Lion*, 21.

33. From Lewis's original introduction to the *Broadcast Talks* (later to be retitled *Mere Christianity*) but removed from the printed version. Hooper, *C.S. Lewis*, 307. "It would be well for Christendom if all the members of Christ's catholic church would endeavor to preserve the unity of the Spirit, and think oftener of the many and major points in which they agree than the few and minor ones in which they differ." Duncan, *Just a Talker*, 41.

As Lewis sought to defend, explain, and commend "mere Christianity" to his times, Christians by means of their loving unity should do the same, even while graciously defending their more distinctive understandings of biblical teaching. That would be the church at her best and that would be a witness to supernatural reality impossible to ignore![34] Such is the moral force of the biblical dialectic. It causes us to love and make common cause with all who have given us reason to believe they love the Lord Jesus Christ, on the one hand, and, on the other, to accept the force of Spurgeon's warning: "Trimming now, and debasing doctrine now, will affect children yet unborn, generation after generation."[35] And in the tension between those two convictions, and only there, will be found the proper balance between loving unity and fidelity to the truth.

34. A fine example of an effort to practice that unity amidst significant theological diversity has been furnished by the Christian Churches of Turkey who, under the auspices of the Turkish Bible Society, in 2017 published *Christianity: Fundamental Teachings*. This excellent work of Christian confession was produced by The Joint Commission of Churches in Turkey, which included three Orthodox bodies, the Catholic Church, and the Association of Protestant Churches.

35. Spurgeon, "Preacher's Power," 420.

9

Conclusion

THE ARGUMENT OF THIS book is that it is by the embrace of polarities, and so the expectation and acceptance of tension and paradox, that we come to believe and to practice the entirety of biblical teaching. Much of the Bible's theology and ethics, as its description of the faithful Christian life, is given to us as a complex of opposites that simply defies our efforts to resolve the discordant assertions into a simple harmony of truth. Perfect harmony exists in the mind of God, to be sure, but, even if our minds were capable of comprehending that harmony—and in a number of important cases it is clear they are not—Holy Scripture seems altogether uninterested in disclosing it to us. In other cases the dialectical tension created by seemingly contrary assertions, while not made necessary by the limitations of human intellect, serves either to impress upon our minds truths we would prefer to ignore or forces us to reckon with obligations we find less congenial. What is obvious is that the Bible consistently refuses to rationalize its "contradictions" or resolve the tension created by their equally emphatic assertion.

Holy Scripture's artless assertion of paradox leads us to conclude that the attempt to harmonize, explain, or resolve the contraries must always fall short of the full truth. Only in the tension created by the complex of opposites do we grasp the whole, however weakly, however imperfectly. Indeed, as the history of biblical interpretation demonstrates only too well, the tensions created across the entire field of biblical revelation can be relaxed only at the cost of a failure to take with full seriousness one or the other of the biblical polarities.

The result of this method of revelation is that we encounter paradox, tension, and mystery repeatedly. The limitations of the human intellect impose strict limits on our understanding of the ways of God and so of reality itself.[1] As we had occasion to observe, the assertions of Holy Scripture are, by and large, perfectly clear in and of themselves. We know what the words mean. But even the terminology and the sentences by themselves can mask deeps that we are unable to fathom and the inter-relation of those assertions—how two of them can be true at one and the same time—regularly lies beyond our comprehension. We cannot say what "Father," "Son," and "Holy Spirit," tell us about the persons of the Godhead; we do not know even what "person" means in reference to God; and we certainly cannot explain how the three are the one liv-ing and true God. So it must be for the creature before the Creator, the finite before the infinite. And where we may not encounter mystery to that degree, we nevertheless still encounter the Bible's studied refusal to satisfy our curiosity or harmonize its teaching. In either case we are left to confess two truths or to meet two obligations whose relation to one another, whose agreement with one another we cannot define or explain, at least in any fully satisfying way. With wonderful clarity the Bible says two things that can seem to us to be the virtual contradiction of one an-other and yet requires us to believe them both, or do them both, or expect them both in the experience of life. Holy Scripture thus presents us with its own *Sic et Non* but leaves us to confess with equal conviction both the "Yes" and the "No."[2] Surely this is one reason why the Bible is so much more interesting than a systematic theology!

1. Herman Bavinck begins his matchless exposition of the Christian faith with the sentence, "Mystery is the lifeblood of dogmatics." He goes on to say, "In truth, the knowledge that God has revealed of himself in nature and Scripture far surpasses human imagination and understanding. In that sense it is all mystery with which the science of dogmatics is concerned, for it does not deal with finite creatures, but from beginning to end looks past all creatures and focuses on the eternal and infinite One himself. From the very start of its labors, it faces the incomprehensible One." *Reformed Dogmatics*, 2:29.

2. *Sic et Non* ("Yes and No") is the title of Peter Abelard's twelfth-century work in which he set the contradictory opinions of the Church fathers over against one anoth-er. His interest, however, was in teaching how such contradictions could be resolved.

Submitting to the Bible's Paradoxicality

I have argued that among the advantages of this pedagogy are that it makes possible our understanding of reality, *so far as we are capable of understanding it*, and it adds powerful emphasis to truth we might otherwise resist and so either ignore or attempt to redefine. Indeed, as I have sought to show, the practical results of this pedagogy, at least when the polarities are equally embraced, are simply wonderful. It schooled the church to confess truths it is hard to imagine she would confess otherwise. It has made of Christians, and should have made of all Christians, a complex of opposites, which is to say the most well-rounded of human beings and the most useful. As G. K. Chesterton once observed in another context,

> Christianity, which is a very mystical religion, has nevertheless been the religion of the most practical section of mankind. It has far more paradoxes than the Eastern philosophies, but it also builds far better roads.[3]

However much this dialectical pedagogy may have originated in a characteristically Semitic and classical Hebrew intellectual and literary environment, what matters is that this is emphatically how the Bible teaches us the truth. This recognition, therefore, fixes the limits of our understanding, no matter if we think and express ourselves more systematically than the Bible does, as Christian theology has done from the beginning. Christian theologians, indeed Christian readers of the Bible, are not in the business of discovering, still less of establishing by research and contemplation the nature of God, the meaning of life, or the way of salvation. Our task is to understand and explain, to the extent it can be explained, the truth once and for all delivered to the saints (Jude 3).[4] That being so, the only faithful and useful Christian thinking and teaching is that which remains faithful to divine revelation, which, as a matter of simple fact, is undeniably dialectical in character. We cannot go where Holy Scripture does not take us. We cannot peer into God's secrets. It is presumption to suppose we could. We may apply reflection to the biblical data; we may consolidate and compare biblical assertions; we may even

---

3. Chesterton, *Why I Believe in Christianity*, 382.

4. Wilken, *Spirit of Early Christian Thought*, 3. ". . . let us remember . . . as in all religious doctrine, that we ought to hold to one rule of modesty and sobriety: not to speak, or guess, or even to seek to know, concerning obscure matters anything except what has been imparted to us by God's Word." Calvin, *Institutes*, I, xiv, 4.

sometimes qualify biblical assertions by relating one to another—Christian theology has always done so and often with valuable results—but we cannot transgress the limits imposed by the biblical polarities without inventing a theology which is not revealed in the Word of God. The temptation of theological reflection has always been to attempt a systemization of the biblical data that goes beyond anything taught in the Bible itself, even anything that may be safely inferred from the biblical materials. The result of that, I have argued, is invariably the denial or distortion of some biblical teaching or diminishment of some biblical emphasis.

There is analysis in the Bible. That is, we can find biblical authors relating one truth to another or qualifying one biblical assertion by another. We can certainly find in some cases the interrelation of ideas or commentary upon them. Even at least a partial resolution of some contraries can be found, such as we argued we find in Psalm 73.[5] But this is usually regarding surface inconsistencies or less severe discordance, not the deeper paradoxes. Written over the entirety of Holy Scripture is the caption: "Oh, the depths of the riches and wisdom and knowledge of God! How unsearchable are his judgments and how inscrutable his ways!" What Holy Scripture gives us as its fundamental teachings, its primary themes, is an equilibrium of truths rather than a single truth with its many parts presented to us in their systematic interrelation. We are given the truth in pieces, not in its whole. What we know, therefore, is what we are taught in the Bible, one theme after another, not how we might exhaust the meaning of those themes or how we might relate one to another in terms easily comprehended or explained.

---

5. The message of Habbakuk is a typical example. The prophet poses a question raised in his mind precisely by the apparent conflict between what he knows to be the character of God and the promises of God, on the one hand, and the outworking of divine providence in history on the other (1:13). This is the typical clash of polarities we encounter so often in the Psalter. The reply is admittedly partial, but it proves sufficient for the case. God will judge the wicked, even if he uses them first as an instrument of the judgment of his own people; he will be true to his character and his promises; he will preserve the faithful remnant; and at the last the kingdom of God will be absolutely and eternally triumphant (2:4, 12–14). It is hardly a complete relaxation of the tension, much mystery remains, but even in a time of severe judgment, even over the course of millennia while waiting for the return of the Lord, the fact that his people know the God of justice and mercy and can count on his faithfulness is itself reason for confidence and hope, even for "joy in the God of my salvation" (3:18). The Babylonians seem triumphant now, God's people's fortunes are at the lowest ebb, but all will be put right in the end!

To be sure, careful study of the genre of ancient Near Eastern and biblical wisdom may lead us to recognize that we are expected to realize that under certain circumstances we should answer a fool according to his folly and in other circumstances we should not. The consolidation of the biblical data may lead us to appreciate that the terminology of election is deployed throughout the Bible in different respects or that the divine reckoning of our lives at the Last Judgment is multidimensional. We are taught that the obedience of God's people is itself the fruit of the Spirit's working in our hearts and of the faith in Christ he has granted us, and thus the reward given to us for such obedience is itself the free gift of divine love. Further, careful reflection on biblical teaching will confirm, for example, Paul's "now, but not yet": that salvation proceeds in stages and that the realities of divine grace may be present in principle, in the seed, long before they arrive in full flower. The careful consideration of the commandments of God and the biblical record of the obedience and disobedience of God's people will lead us to conclude that forming within us a cheerful determination to meet competing obligations is precisely how the Lord expects the Christian life to come into its own, even if this is never said in so many words in the Bible. And we must, at all points, defend the analogy of faith, the fact that the Bible must remain its own interpreter. While these considerations do not dissolve the polarities, they enable us accurately to define them and to come to terms with and submit to Scripture's antinomies and paradoxes.

In such ways we may create a systematic account of the Bible's teaching. We may further work to develop precise definitions of biblical themes, taking care to relate one to another as far as possible, but always and only in keeping with the limitations imposed by the Bible's distinctive way of describing reality. We must remain always alert to the fact that we are no more able to explain the interrelationship between divine sovereignty and our accountability, or how it is that once the Lord has begun a work in us he will perform it to the end no matter that some who were once *in Christ* and who tasted of the powers of the age to come were then cut off and thrown into the fire, or how his promises to answer our prayers are fulfilled no matter the saints' experience of a silent heaven than we are able to explain how it is that God is not less in his parts than in his totality. What we must not do is seek to penetrate the empty spaces between and behind the biblical affirmations, the spaces that Holy Scripture does not fill. That we are tempted to do just that is one lesson of two thousand years of theological reflection. That it is invariably a mistake to do so is the other lesson.

The Summons of Biblical Paradox

Our summons is to believe everything we are taught in the Word of God. Many, if not all, heresies begin as partial truth and can claim some form of biblical support. The antidote to them is very often simply the insistence on a particular teaching's biblical counter-position. Even well-meant harmonizations by devout scholars seeking to be faithful to the fullness of revelation too often unwittingly suppress one biblical emphasis and so fall short of the entirety of the truth revealed in Holy Scripture. Again, the antidote is to give full attention to the complex of opposites and to insist on an equal submission to the polarities that lie at either end of any biblical continuum of truth.

As wise men have observed, only when we feel the tug of tension between the biblical assertions can we be sure we are giving proper attention to everything we are being taught. Suppressing the opposite pole on any biblical continuum does not leave us with even half the truth. The biblical emphasis we have embraced is misshapen by the lack of gravitational pull. Every biblical doctrine becomes less than itself if it is not embraced as part of an equilibrium of truths. Whether the nature of God, the identity of Jesus Christ, saving grace, the nature of believing life, the Last Judgment, heaven and hell, or any number of other biblical themes, what we have been given is truth in its polarities. The embrace of the truth, therefore, requires that we live with that intellectual and emotional experience of stress created by coordinate but seemingly contrary assertions. Indeed, this pedagogy should produce a restlessly thoughtful mind and way of life, as Christians swing from one truth to the other and back again, feel the force first of one emphasis and then of another. It must be so since we are incapable of holding both truths in mind at once as a single and integrated intuition. Only in this way can finite minds embrace a reality that is so much larger, so much more complex, and so much more mysterious than their active thoughts can master. And only in this way can they ensure that all the truth that God has taught them will leave its impression on their minds and hearts. As we saw with the Holy Trinity and the incarnation, so with much else in biblical teaching, our minds are capable of only one thought at a time. For this reason we must perpetually oscillate, moving backwards and forwards between the poles at opposite ends of any continuum of truth. It is in this way that the whole of biblical truth takes its rightful place in both our conviction and our conduct.

The Lessons of the Bible's Dialectical Pedagogy

Acceptance of our Limitations

The practical implications of the Bible's characteristically dialectical revelation of truth are obvious and significant. *The* first and most obvious of them is that we must learn to content ourselves with paradox and antinomy in our reading of Holy Scripture. Christians should expect and, indeed, welcome the complex of opposites by which God reveals his truth to his people. A humble conviction of the clarity of biblical assertions and the mystery of their interrelations, the ready acceptance of the uncharted depths that lie beneath even the Bible's straightforward assertions, is the foundation of a biblical mind! It should be part of our reverence for God that we cheerfully accept our intellectual limitations. We are creatures, not the Creator. We are finite, not infinite. We are temporal, not eternal. We see through a glass darkly and, to a significant extent, we will forever. Deeply grateful as we ought to be to know the truth that sets us free, all the more that the Holy Trinity should have revealed to us all that he has regarding himself and the way of salvation, we should never suppose that we know more than we do, miniscule as our knowledge must be compared to the omniscience of the Almighty. The more we contemplate the infinite personal God, the more outrageous it should seem to us that we could comprehend anything more than the periphery of reality. Such humility is a supreme virtue of the believing heart and, therefore, to face mystery after mystery as we do in Holy Scripture should be our satisfaction and our pleasure. That we know what we know should be only the more marvelous to us given how much we do not and cannot know. And our ignorance should make more wonderful the infinite knowledge of our God and Savior. We live in a time when many seem to imagine that, given enough time, they can know and will be able to explain almost everything. Christians should know better and cheerfully recite, with John Henry Newman,

I do not ask to see
The distant scene; one step enough for me.

Keeping Everything, Losing Nothing

Second, given the fact that the Bible regularly presents us with polarities, we must rest content with the "contraries" we encounter in Holy Scripture, alert to our temptation to subordinate one to the other or, worse, ignore or redefine one at the expense of the other. This is the biblically appointed means to restore to us the full set of biblical convictions, when we are all far too used to picking and choosing between them.

That Scripture teaches its truth in this way, scattering seemingly contradictory emphases throughout and studiously avoiding any effort to relax the tension thus created, should convince us that God wants us to receive the truth in this manner. He wants us to embrace both poles, believe both assertions, obey both commandments, no matter how seemingly incompatible. Had this not been the case, the Bible would not have been written as it was! Preachers should consider themselves duty bound to avoid picking and choosing among biblical themes, still less choosing to concentrate on more popular or pleasing themes at the expense of either those more stern and demanding or those more startling and mystifying. The appreciation of the Bible's pedagogy is a sure cure for the overly anodyne pulpit of the contemporary evangelical church.

Why, after all, does the Bible confront us, as it does repeatedly, with statements—so often absolute or unqualified in form—that are hard to reconcile with other things we read in the Word of God? Why does the Bible read as it does, with seeming contradictions confronting us at every turn? Is it not precisely so that we would not, as our hard and proud hearts tempt us to do, domesticate the truth of God and turn it into a platitude that sits only lightly on our minds and hearts, leaving us free to seek our lives here in this world, unencumbered with the weighty realities of eternity? No, again and again the Lord hits us between the eyes, unsettles us, confuses us, and forces us to take seriously something we would just as soon forget or ignore. In this way we today take our place alongside those early brethren who, supremely confident in their monotheism, nevertheless were forced to accept, impenetrable mystery that it was, that the otherwise ordinary-looking man standing before them was the Everlasting Father himself! Seemingly contrary assertions laid side by side, expressed in absolute terms, antinomy and paradox, the impression of all of which is deepened by an almost complete lack of analysis, generalization, abstraction, or explanation, are means by which the followers of Jesus Christ have been forced to accept truth for which they were not prepared or to which they were not inclined, have had their prejudices and their fantasies hunted down and put to death, and have been enabled and inspired to answer the challenge of living by faith, come wind, come weather, in the one who loved us and gave himself for us.

We are to be people who think and live paradoxically. *We are ourselves to be a complex of opposites!* Confidently resting our future on the immutable love of God and the triumph of Christ over sin and death, we work out our own salvation with fear lest, at last, we be disqualified for the prize. Rejoicing in our liberation from sin and the death of our flesh (Rom 6:6; 8:6–9; Col 3:3), we mourn our wretched captivity to that same flesh and take arms against it (Rom 7:14–20; Gal 3:16–24; Col 3:3–10). Feeling deeply the heartbreak of life and death in this broken world, we take comfort in the knowledge that nothing happens apart from the will of our Heavenly Father. Confident in that absolute divine sovereignty, we nevertheless live equally in the confidence that our every sin of thought, word, or deed occurs *by our own fault.* Consoled by the spiritual potency of baptism (John 3:5; Acts 2:38; 22:16; 1 Cor 6:11; Eph 5:26), we are ever alert to the fact that multitudes have been baptized who died in unbelief (Rom 4:11; 9:6; Phil 3:2–3; 1 Tim 1:19). Eagerly awaiting the return of the Lord, we daily reckon with the solemn fact that we must appear before the judgment seat of Christ. Comforted to know our guilt has been annihilated by Christ's death, we nevertheless remain on our mettle to extend ungrudging forgiveness to others lest our own sins not be forgiven. Loving our life in Christ, thrilling to the ways the Almighty has demonstrated the impossibly immense importance he attaches to us, we nevertheless loathe our sinful selves (Job 42:6; Rom 7:24). Sure of the prosperity the Lord has promised his faithful people, we accept as his will the deprivation, sorrow, and sometimes crippling pain that is often the believer's lot in this world. Praying in the conviction that the Lord will not fail to hear and answer, we persevere beneath a silent heaven. We are, at one and the same time, sticklers for truth, unbending in biblical conviction, and tolerant, flexible, and lenient for the sake of love and the gospel—indeed, controversially so in both respects! Cherishing life, so much so that we are willing to make great sacrifices to preserve and nourish our own and that of others, we welcome death, not merely submitting to it but greeting it with thrilling anticipation. This *is* the Christian life as it is taught in Holy Scripture and as it has always been lived by the faithful followers of Jesus Christ. Nothing so effectively lays the axe to the root of a vague or merely nominal faith than embracing in faith the paradoxes of Holy Scripture.

A Path to Greater Unity

Third, there is in this recognition of the dialectical pedagogy of Holy Scripture a powerful antidote to the disunity that so afflicts and weakens the body of Christ. Far too often our disputes take the form of competing assertions of only one pole or the other on a biblical continuum of truth, when the staunch defense of both would go at least a long way toward minimizing the offense each side finds in the position of the other. I made that point in particular in regard to the Arminian/Calvinist dispute regarding saving grace, but the same appeal would ameliorate the ferocity of other disagreements, if not, at least in some cases, dissolve them altogether. So often, in past and present, Calvinists and Arminians have found warm fellowship and common ground in ministry because it became obvious that they both believe that salvation is the gift of God and that every person is responsible to believe in Jesus Christ and obey his commandments, or else. However they might disagree, they have realized that they have more in common than they had thought. Alas, they will remain adversaries when Calvinists stubbornly resist the punishing emphasis Holy Scripture places on the contingency of life and when Arminians somehow cannot find in the Bible's plain speaking the absolute sovereignty of God.[6] But if we believe everything we are taught in Holy Scripture and forsake every effort to make its teaching conform to our cherished opinions, we will be drawn powerfully toward one another.

The recognition that advocates of other theological positions often strongly defend the very principles so precious to us must serve to foster unity. Obviously, if one chooses to assert one teaching at the expense of the other, finding ways, however desperate, to redefine the other polarity and so resolve the paradox, there is little that can be done. But for those determined to read Holy Scripture in its natural sense and to accept that

6. "Many authors have seen a conflict between this all-encompassing activity of God in grace and the self-agency of people maintained alongside of it. They have charged Scripture with self-contradiction and have for themselves sacrificed the one group of pronouncements to the other." Bavinck, *Reformed Dogmatics*, 4:254.

there are obvious reasons why their theological adversaries believe as they do, there is much to be gained by the admission that Scripture often seems to teach their side as firmly as it teaches ours, however little we may understand how to reconcile the two. The fact that it is in this way that the entire church has come to confess the Holy Trinity and the incarnation should give us pause. If the acceptance of paradox lies beneath our theological unity at the foundation of our faith, why not equally in every part of its superstructure?

Given the influential role he played through the years in bringing others to these convictions regarding the pedagogy of Holy Scripture, it is only right that I give Charles Simeon the last word!

> I love the simplicity of the Scriptures; and I wish to receive and inculcate every truth precisely in the way, and to the extent, that it is set forth in the inspired volume. Were this the habit of all divines, there would soon be an end of most of the controversies that have agitated and divided the Church of Christ.[7]

---

7. Cited in Moule, *Charles Simeon*, 77.

Bibliography

Aitken, Jonathan. *John Newton: From Disgrace to Amazing Grace.* Wheaton, IL: Crossway, 2007.

Alleine, Joseph. *An Alarm to the Unconverted.* Reprint, Edinburgh: Banner of Truth, 1964.

Alter, Robert. *Genesis.* New York: Norton, 1996.

Augustine. *The City of God.* Translated by Marcus Dods. Nicene and Post Nicene Fathers, 1st ser., vol. 2. Reprint, Grand Rapids: Eerdmans, 1979.

———. *Essential Sermons.* Translated by Edmund Hill. Edited by Boniface Ramsey. The Works of Saint Augustine: A Translation for the 21st Century. Hyde Park, NY: New City, 2007.

———. *Expositions on the Book of Psalms.* Translated by A. C. Coxe. Nicene and Post-Nicene Fathers, 1st ser., vol. 8. Reprint, Grand Rapids: Eerdmans, 1979.

———. *Letters 100–155.* Translated by R.J. Teske. Edited by Boniface Ramsay. The Works of Saint Augustine: A Translation for the 21st Century. Hyde Park, NY: New City, 2003.

———. *On Rebuke and Grace.* Translated by P. Holmes and R. E. Wallis. Nicene and Post-Nicene Fathers, 1st ser., vol. 5. Reprint, Grand Rapids: Eerdmans, 1971.

———. *On The Trinity.* Translated by A. W. Haddan. Nicene and Post-Nicene Fathers, 1st ser., vol. 3. Reprint, Grand Rapids: Eerdmans, 1978.

———. *Tractates on the Gospel of John.* Translated by J. Gibb. Nicene and Post-Nicene Fathers, 1st ser., vol. 7. Reprint, Grand Rapids: Eerdmans, 1978.

———. *The Trinity.* Translated by Edmund Hill. Edited by John E. Rotelle. The Works of Saint Augustine: A Translation for the 21st Century. 2nd ed. Hyde Park, NY: New City, 1991.

Barth, Karl. *Church Dogmatics.* Translated by G.W. Bromiley. Edited by G. W. Bromiley and T. F. Torrance. 4 vols. Edinburgh: T. & T. Clark, 1975–77.

Bavinck, Herman. *Reformed Dogmatics.* Translated by J. Vriend. 4 vols. Grand Rapids: Eerdmans, 2003–8.

———, ed. *Synopsis Purioris Theologiae.* 6th ed. Leiden: Donner, 1881.

Bengel, Johann Albrecht. *Gnomon Novi Testamenti.* Edited by M.E. Bengelium. 3rd ed. Tubingen: Ludov. Fues., 1855.

Berkhof, Hendrikson. *Christian Faith: An Introduction to the Study of the Faith.* Translated by S. Woudstra. Grand Rapids: Eerdmans, 1979.

Berkhof, Louis. *The Second Coming of Christ.* Grand Rapids: Eerdmans, 1953.

Berkouwer, Gerrit. *Man: The Image of God.* Translated by Dirk W. Jellema. Grand Rapids: Eerdmans, 1962.

Bettenson, H. *Documents of the Christian Church.* London: Oxford University Press, 1943.

Bickersteth, Edward H. *The Trinity.* Reprint, Grand Rapids: Kregel, 1957.

Block, Daniel I. *The Book of Ezekiel.* 2 vols. New International Commentary on the Old Testament. Grand Rapids: Eerdmans, 1997–98.

Bock, Darrell L. *Luke.* 2 vols. Baker Exegetical Commentary. Grand Rapids: Baker, 1994–96.

Bonar, Andrew. *Memoirs and Remains of the Rev. Robert Murray McCheyne.* Reprint, Edinburgh: Banner of Truth, 1960.

Bonhoeffer, Dietrich. *Ethics.* Translated by Neville Horton Smith. Edited by E. Bethge. New York: Macmillan, 1965.

Boston, Thomas. *The Complete Works of Thomas Boston.* 12 vols. Reprint, Wheaton, IL: Richard Owen Roberts, 1980.

Bradley, James, and Russell Howell. *Mathematics through the Eyes of Faith.* New York: HarperCollins, 2011.

Bragg, William. "Electrons and Ether Waves: The 23rd Robert Boyle Lecture." *Scientific Monthly* 14:2 (February 1922) 153–60.

Bratt, J. D. *Abraham Kuyper: Modern Calvinist, Christian Democrat.* Grand Rapids: Eerdmans, 2013.

Bray, Gerald. *Augustine on the Christian Life.* Wheaton, IL: Crossway, 2015.

Brentnall, John. *Just a Talker: Sayings of John (Rabbi) Duncan.* Edinburgh: Banner of Truth, 1997.

Bromiley, G. W. *Historical Theology.* Grand Rapids: Eerdmans, 1978.

Bruce, F. F. *The Epistles of John.* London: Pickering and Inglis, 1970.

Buswell, J. Oliver. *Problems in the Prayer Life.* Chicago: Bible Institute Colportage Association, 1928.

———. *What Is God?* Grand Rapids: Zondervan, 1937.

Caird, G. B. *The Language and Imagery of the Bible.* Philadelphia: Westminster, 1980.

Calvin, John. *The Acts of the Apostles, 1–13.* Translated by J. W. Fraser and W. J. G. McDonald. Grand Rapids: Eerdmans, 1965.

———. *Commentary on the Psalms.* Translated by J. Anderson. 5 vols. Reprint, Grand Rapids: Eerdmans, 1948-49.

———. *Commentaries on the Twelve Minor Prophets.* Translated by J. Owen. Vol. 1. Reprint, Grand Rapids: Eerdmans, n.d.

———. *Concerning the Eternal Predestination of God.* Translated by J. K. S. Reid. London: James Clarke, 1961.

———. *A Harmony of the Gospels Matthew, Mark, and Luke.* Translated by A. W. Morrison. 3 vols. Grand Rapids: Eerdmans, 1972.

———. *Institutes of the Christian Religion.* Translated by Ford Lewis Battles. Edited by John T. McNeil. 2 vols. Library of Christian Classics 21. Philadelphia: Westminster, 1960.

Carson, D. A. *Divine Sovereignty and Human Responsibility: Biblical Perspectives in Tension.* 2nd ed. Grand Rapids: Baker, 1994.

———. "Reflections on Christian Assurance." *Westminster Theological Journal* 54 (Spring 1992) 1–29.

Chesterton, G. K. *What's Wrong with the World*. London: Cassell, 1910. http://www.gutenberg.org/ebooks/1717.

———. *Why I Believe in Christianity*. Edited by David Dooley. G. K. Chesterton: Collected Works 1. San Francisco: Ignatius, 1986.

Clark, Gordon. *The Gospel According to John*. Grand Rapids: Eerdmans, 1991.

———. *Predestination*. Phillipsburg, NJ: Presbyterian and Reformed, 1987.

Clement of Alexandria. *Who Is the Rich Man That Shall Be Saved?* Translated by William Wilson. Ante-Nicene Fathers 2. Reprint, Grand Rapids: Eerdmans, 1979.

Collins, C. John. *Genesis 1–4: A Linguistic, Literary, and Theological Commentary*. Phillipsburg, NJ: Presbyterian and Reformed, 2006.

Coomes, David. *Dorothy Sayers: A Careless Rage for Life*. Oxford: Lion, 1992.

Conybeare, F. C. and St. George Stock. *A Grammar of Septuagint Greek*. Reprint, Grand Rapids, Zondervan, 1980.

Cranfield, C. E. B. *A Critical and Exegetical Commentary on the Epistle to the Romans*. 2 vols. International Critical Commentary. Edinburgh: T. & T. Clark, 1975–79.

Crawford, Thomas J. *The Mysteries of Christianity: Being the Baird Lecture for 1874*. Edinburgh: Blackwood and Sons, 1874.

Cyprian. *On the Unity of the Church*. Translated by E. Wallis. Ante-Nicene Fathers 5. Reprint, Grand Rapids, Eerdmans, 1978.

Dante Alighieri. *The Divine Comedy: The Inferno, Purgatorio, and Paradiso*. Translated by L. G. White. New York: Pantheon, 1948.

Davies, Paul. *God and the New Physics*. London: Dent, 1983.

De Jong, Alexander. *The Well-Meant Gospel Offer: The Views of H. Hoeksema and K. Schilder*. Franeker, NL: T. Wever, 1954.

Dibelius, Martin, and Hans Conzelmann. *The Pastoral Epistles*. Translated by Philip Buttolph and Adela Yarbro. Hermeneia. Philadelphia: Fortress, 1972.

Douma, Douglas J. *The Presbyterian Philosopher: The Authorized Biography of Gordon Clark*. Eugene, OR: Wipf & Stock, 2017.

Dowey, E. A., Jr. *The Knowledge of God in Calvin's Theology*. New York: Columbia University Press, 1952.

Dryden, J. de Waal. "Revisiting Romans 7: Law, Self, and Spirit." *Journal for the Study of Paul and his Letters* 5:1 (Summer 2015) 129–51.

Dudley-Smith, Timothy. *John Stott: A Biography*. 2 vols. Downers Grove, IL: InterVarsity, 1999–2001.

Duncan, John. *Colloquia Peripatetica*. Edited by William Knight. 4th ed. Edinburgh: Edmonston and Douglas, 1873.

Dunn, James D.G. *Romans 1–8*. Word Biblical Commentary 38A. Dallas: Word, 1988.

Durham, James. *A Treatise Concerning Scandal*. Edited by Christopher Coldwell. Reprint, Dallas: Naphtali, 1990.

———. *Practical Exposition of the Ten Commandments*. Edited by Christopher Coldwell. Reprint, Dallas: Naphtali, 2002.

Edwards, Jonathan. *The Works of Jonathan Edwards*. 2 vols. Reprint, Edinburgh: Banner of Truth, 1974.

Eichrodt, Walther. *Ezekiel*. Translated by Cosslett Quin. Old Testament Library. Philadelphia: Westminster, 1970.

Evans, C. Stephen. *Why Christian Faith Still Makes Sense*. Grand Rapids: Baker, 2015.

Flavel, John. *The Fountain of Life*. The Whole Works of the Rev. Mr. John Flavel 1. Reprint, London: W. Baynes and Son, 1820.

Frame, John. *The Doctrine of God*. Phillipsburg, NJ: Presbyterian and Reformed, 2002.

———. *The Doctrine of the Christian Life*. Phillipsburg, NJ: Presbyterian and Reformed, 2008.

———. *A History of Western Philosophy and Theology*. Phillipsburg, NJ: Presbyterian and Reformed, 2015.

Forsyth, P. T. *The Soul of Prayer*. London: Independent, 1916.

Gaffin, Richard B., Jr. *By Faith, Not by Sight: Paul and the Order of Salvation*. Bletchley, UK: Paternoster, 2006.

Gaither, C. C. *Physically Speaking: A Dictionary of Quotations on Physics and Astronomy*. Boca Raton, FL: CRC Press, 1997.

Gathercole, Simon J. *Where Is Boasting?: Early Jewish Soteriology and Paul's Response in Romans 1–5*. Grand Rapids: Eerdmans, 2002.

Genderen, J. van, and W. H. Velema. *Concise Reformed Dogmatics*. Translated by Gerrit Bilkes and Ed M. van der Maas. Phillipsburg, NJ: Presbyterian and Reformed, 2008.

Giles, Kevin. *The Eternal Generation of the Son*. Downers Grove, IL: InterVarsity, 2012.

Gill, John. *An Exposition of the New Testament: Both Doctrinal and Practical*. 5 vols. London: George Keith, 1776.

Goppelt, Leonhard. *Typos: The Typological Interpretation of the Old Testament in the New*. Translated by Donald H. Madvig. Grand Rapids: Eerdmans, 1982.

Gregory Nazianzus. *Fifth Theological Oration*. Translated by C. G. Browne and J. E. Swallow. Nicene and Post-Nicene Fathers, 2nd ser., vol. 7. Reprint, Grand Rapids: Eerdmans, 1978.

———. *The First Letter to Cledonius the Priest Against Apollinarius*. Translated by C. G. Browne and J. E. Swallow. Nicene and Post-Nicene Fathers, 2nd ser., vol. 7. Reprint, Grand Rapids: Eerdmans, 1978.

———. *Oration on Holy Baptism*. Translated by C. G. Browne and J. E. Swallow. Nicene and Post-Nicene Fathers, 2nd ser., vol. 7. Reprint, Grand Rapids, Eerdmans, 1978.

———. *Second Theological Oration*. Translated by C. G. Browne and J. E. Swallow. vol. 7. Reprint, Grand Rapids, Eerdmans, 1978.

———. *Third Theological Oration*. Translated by C. G. Browne and J. E. Swallow. Nicene and Post-Nicene Fathers, 2nd ser., vol. 7. Reprint, Grand Rapids: Eerdmans, 1978.

Grounds, Vernon. "The Postulate of Paradox." *Bulletin of the Evangelical Theological Society* 7:1 (1964) 3–21.

Gunton, Colin. *The One, the Three, and the Many: God, Creation, and the Culture of Modernity*. Cambridge: Cambridge University Press, 1993.

Hagner, Donald A. *Matthew 14–28*. Word Biblical Commentary 33b. Dallas: Word, 1995.

Hall, Christopher A. *Reading Scripture with the Church Fathers*. Downers Grove, IL: InterVarsity, 1998.

Hallie, Philip. *Lest Innocent Blood Be Shed*. Reprint, New York: HarperPerennial, 1994.

Halyburton, Thomas. *Memoirs of the Life of the Rev. Thomas Halyburton*. Edinburgh: John Johnstone, n.d.

Hankins, Barry. *Francis Schaeffer and the Shaping of Evangelical America*. Grand Rapids: Eerdmans, 2008.

Helm, Paul. "Are They Few That Be Saved?" *Universalism and the Doctrine of Hell*, edited by N. M. de S. Cameron, 255–81. Carlisle: Paternoster.

———. *Faith with Reason*. Oxford: Oxford University Press, 2000.

Heppe, Heinrich. *Reformed Dogmatics: Set Out and Illustrated from the Sources.* Translated by G. T. Thomson. London: Allen and Unwin, 1950.

Hilary. *On the Trinity.* Translated by E.W. Watson and L. Pullan. Nicene and Post-Nicene Fathers, 2nd ser., vol. 9. Reprint, Grand Rapids: Eerdmans, 1979.

Hildebrand, Franz, and Oliver A. Beckerlegge, eds. *A Collection of Hymns for the Use of the People Called Methodists.* The Works of John Wesley 7. Oxford: Oxford University Press, 1983.

Hillers, Delbert R. *Covenant: The History of a Biblical Idea.* Baltimore: Johns Hopkins University Press, 1969.

Hodge, Charles. "A Letter to Pope Pius X." *Banner of Truth* 580 (January 2012) 16–20.

Hodgson, Leonard. *The Doctrine of the Trinity: Croall Lectures, 1942–1943.* London: Nisbet, 1943.

Hoekema, Anthony. *The Bible and the Future.* Grand Rapids: Eerdmans, 1979.

———. *Saved by Grace.* Grand Rapids: Eerdmans, 1989.

Hooker, Richard. *A Learned Discourse of Justification, Works, and How the Foundation of Faith Is Overthrown.* 2 vols. The Works of Mr. Richard Hooker 2. 3rd American ed. New York: Appleton, 1863.

Hooper, Walter. *C.S. Lewis: The Companion and Guide.* London: HarperCollins, 1996.

Hurd, Ryan M. "Dei via Regia: The Westminster Divine Anthony Tuckney on the Necessity of Works for Salvation." *Westminster Theological Journal* 81 (Spring 2019) 1–17.

Ignatius. *To the Philadelphians.* Edited and translated by Cyril C. Richardson. Early Christian Fathers. New York: Macmillan, 1970.

Irenaeus. *Against Heresies.* Ante-Nicene Fathers 1. Reprint, Grand Rapids: Eerdmans, 1979.

John of Damascus. *Of the Orthodox Faith.* Translated by S. D. F. Salmond. Nicene and Post-Nicene Fathers, 2nd ser., vol. 9. Reprint, Grand Rapids: Eerdmans, 1979.

Jones, David Clyde. *Biblical Christian Ethics.* Grand Rapids: Baker, 1994.

Kelly, Douglas F. *Systematic Theology.* Vol. 1, *The God Who Is: The Holy Trinity.* Fearn, Scotland: Christian Focus, 2008.

Kempis, Thomas [GRAVE>]à. *Of the Imitation of Christ.* Translated by G. Stanhope. London: J. J. and P. Knapton, 1733.

Kitchen, Kenneth. *On the Reliability of the Old Testament.* Grand Rapids: Eerdmans, 2003.

Kuyper, Abraham, Jr. *Johannes Maccovius.* Leiden: D. Donner, 1899.

Lane, Anthony N. S. *Justification by Faith in Catholic-Protestant Dialogue: An Evangelical Assessment.* Edinburgh: T. & T. Clark, 2002.

Leo the Great. *Letter XXVIII to Flavian, Commonly Called "The Tome".* Translated by C. L. Feltoe. Nicene and Post-Nicene Fathers, 2nd ser., vol. 12. Reprint, Grand Rapids: Eerdmans, 1979.

Letham, Robert. *The Holy Trinity: In Scripture, History, Theology, and Worship.* Phillipsburg, NJ: Presbyterian and Reformed, 2004.

Lewis, C. S. *The Discarded Image: An Introduction to Medieval and Renaissance Literature.* Cambridge: Cambridge University Press, 1964.

———. "The Efficacy of Prayer." In *The World's Last Night and Other Essays*, 3–11. New York: Harcourt, Brace, and World, 1960.

———. *Mere Christianity.* New York: Macmillan, 1960.

———. *They Stand Together: The Letters of C.S. Lewis to Arthur Greeves (1914–1963)*. Edited by Walter Hooper. New York: Macmillan, 1979.

Loder, James E., and W. Jim Neidhardt. *The Knight's Move: The Relational Logic of the Spirit in Theology and Science*. Colorado Springs, CO: Helmers and Howard, 1992.

Lloyd-Jones, Martyn. *The Puritans: Their Origins and Successors*. Edinburgh: Banner of Truth, 1987.

Love, Christopher. *Preacher of God's Word: Sermons by Christopher Love*. Morgan, PA: Soli Deo Gloria, 2000.

———. *The Works of that Faithful Servant of Christ Christopher Love*. 2 vols. Dalry, UK: J. Gemmill, 1805.

Luther, Martin. *The Bondage of the Will*. Translated by J. I. Packer and O. R. Johnston. Grand Rapids: Baker, 2012.

———. *Dr. Martin Luther's Vermischte Deutsche Schriften*. Vol. 63. Translated by Robert E. Smith. Erlangen: Heyder and Zimmer, 1854. https://www.ligonier.org/learn/articles/martin-luthers-definition-faith/.

MacGregor, Geddes. *Corpus Christi: The Nature of the Church according to the Reformed Tradition*. London: Macmillan, 1959.

MacKenzie, Robert. *John Brown of Haddington*. Reprint, Edinburgh: Banner of Truth, 1964.

Macleod, Donald. *The Person of Christ*. Downers Grove, IL: InterVarsity, 1998.

MacPherson, John. *The Doctrine of the Church in Scottish Theology*. Edinburgh: MacNiven and Wallace, 1903.

McGinn, Bernard. *Thomas Aquinas' Summa Theologiae: A Biography*. Princeton, NJ: Princeton University Press, 2014.

McGinn, Bernard, and John Meyendorff, eds. *Christian Spirituality: Origins to the Twelfth Century*. World Spirituality: An Encyclopedic History of the Religious Quest 16. New York: Crossroad, 1988.

Marck, Johannes à. *Christianae Theologiae Medulla Didactico-Elenctica: Ex Majori Opere, Secundum eius Capita, et Paragraphos, Expressa*. 1st American ed. Philadelphia: J. Anderson, 1824.

Marsden, George M. *C.S. Lewis's Mere Christianity: A Biography*. Princeton, NJ: Princeton University Press, 2016.

———. *Jonathan Edwards: A Life*. New Haven, CT: Yale University Press, 2003.

Mataxis, Eric. *Bonhoeffer: Pastor, Martyr, Prophet, Spy*. Nashville: Thomas Nelson, 2010.

Melanchthon, Philip. *Loci Communes*. Translated by L. J. Satre. Library of Christian Classics: Ichthus Edition. Philadelphia: Westminster, 1969.

Michel, J. P. *Surprised by Paradox: The Promise of And in an Either-Or World*. Downers Grove, IL: InterVarsity, 2019.

Moltmann, Jurgen. *The Trinity and the Kingdom*. Translated by Margaret Kohl. San Francisco: Harper & Row, 1981.

Moody Stuart, Alexander. *The Life of John Duncan*. Reprint, Edinburgh: Banner of Truth, 1991.

Moody Stuart, Kenneth. *Alexander Moody Stuart: A Memoir, Partly Autobiographical. By His Son Kenneth Moody Stuart*. London: Hodder and Stoughton, 1899.

Moon, Joshua N. *Hosea*. Apollos Old Testament Commentary 21. London: IVP Academic, 2018.

Motyer, J. Alec. *Isaiah: An Introduction and Commentary*. Downers Grove, IL: InterVarsity, 1993.

Moule, Handley C. G. *Charles Simeon*. Reprint, London: InterVarsity Fellowship, 1948.

Mueller, John T. *Christian Dogmatics: A Handbook of Doctrinal Theology for Pastors, Teachers, and Laymen*. St. Louis: Concordia, 1955.

Muller, Richard A. *Dictionary of Latin and Greek Theological Terms*. Grand Rapids: Baker, 1985.

———. *Divine Will and Human Choice: Freedom, Contingency, and Necessity in Early Modern Reformed Thought*. Grand Rapids: Baker, 2017.

Murray, Iain. *Evangelicalism Divided: A Record of Crucial Change in the Years 1950–2000*. Edinburgh: Banner of Truth, 2000.

———. *The Forgotten Spurgeon*. Edinburgh: Banner of Truth, 1966.

———. *J.C. Ryle: Prepared to Stand Alone*. Edinburgh: Banner of Truth, 2016.

———. *Spurgeon v. Hyper-Calvinism: The Battle for Gospel Preaching*. Edinburgh: Banner of Truth, 1995.

Murray, John. *Principles of Conduct*. Grand Rapids: Eerdmans, 1957.

Neill, Stephen. *A History of Christian Missions*. Hammondsworth, UK: Penguin, 1964.

Newton, John. *The Works of John Newton*. 6 vols. Reprint, Edinburgh: Banner of Truth, 1985.

Noll, Mark. *Jesus Christ and the Life of the Mind*. Grand Rapids: Eerdmans, 2011.

Oden, Thomas, *The Living God: Systematic Theology, Volume One*. Reprint, Peabody, MA: Hendrickson, 1998.

———. *The Word of Life: Systematic Theology, Volume Two*. Reprint, Peabody, MA: Hendrickson, 1998.

Olinger, Danny E. *Geerhardus Vos: Reformed Biblical Theologian, Confessional Presbyterian*. Philadelphia: Reformed Forum, 2018.

Owen, John. *A Dissertation on Divine Justice*. Works of John Owen 10. Reprint, Edinburgh: Banner of Truth, 1967.

Packer, J. I. *Evangelism and the Sovereignty of God*. London: InterVarsity Fellowship, 1961.

———. *Keep in Step with the Spirit*. Old Tappan, NJ: Revell, 1984.

———. *Knowing God*. Downers Grove, IL: InterVarsity, 1973.

———. *A Quest for Godliness*. Wheaton, IL: Crossway, 1990.

———. "What Did the Cross Achieve?: The Tyndale Biblical Theology Lecture, 1973." *Tyndale Bulletin* 25 (1974) 3–45.

Pascal, Blaise. *Pensées*. Translated by W. F. Trotter. New York: Random House, 1941.

Pelikan, Jaroslav. *Bach among the Theologians*. Philadelphia: Fortress, 1986.

———. *The Christian Tradition: A History of the Development of Doctrine*. 5 vols. Chicago: University of Chicago Press, 1971.

Pieper, Francis. *Christian Dogmatics*. Translated by T. Engelder. 4 vols. St. Louis: Concordia, 1950–57.

Raven, C. *Apollinarianism*. Cambridge: Cambridge University Press, 1923.

Rayburn, Robert G., II. *Yesterday, Today, and Forever: The Narrative World of Psalm 95 as a Hermeneutical Key to Hebrews*. Berlin: Peter Lang, 2019.

Ridderbos, Herman. *Paul: An Outline of His Theology*. Translated by John Richard deWitt. Grand Rapids: Eerdmans, 1975.

Robertson, A. T. *A Grammar of the Greek New Testament in the Light of Historical Research*. Nashville: Broadman, 1934.

Rogers, Bennett W. *A Tender Lion: The Life, Ministry, and Message of J.C. Ryle*. Grand Rapids: Reformation Heritage, 2019.

Ryken, Leland. *J.I. Packer: An Evangelical Life*. Wheaton, IL: Crossway, 2015.

Ryle, J. C. *Knots Untied: Being Plain Statements on Disputed Points in Religion from the Standpoint of an Evangelical Clergyman*. Reprint, Cambridge: James Clarke, 1977.

———. *Old Paths: Being Plain Statements on Some of the Weightier Matters of Christianity*. Reprint, Cambridge: James Clarke, 1972.

Sayer, George. *Jack: C.S. Lewis and His Times*. New York: Harper & Row, 1988.

Sayers, Dorothy. "The Greatest Drama Ever Staged Is the Official Creed of Christendom." In *The Whimsical Christian: 18 Essays by Dorothy Sayers*, 11–16. New York: Macmillan, 1978.

Schmid, Heinrich. *The Doctrinal Theology of the Evangelical Lutheran Church*. Translated by Charles A. Hay and Henry E. Jacobs. 3rd ed. Reprint, Minneapolis: Augsburg, 1961.

Silva, Moisés. *Biblical Words and Their Meaning: An Introduction to Lexical Semantics*. Grand Rapids: Zondervan, 1983.

Simeon, Charles. *Horae Homileticae*, 21 vols. Harrington DE: Delmarva, 2014. Kindle ed.

Spurgeon, Charles H. *Autobiography*. 2 vols. Rev. ed. Edinburgh: Banner of Truth, 1973.

———. *New Park Street Pulpit*. 6 vols. Reprint, Pasadena, TX: Pilgrim, 1975.

———. "The Preacher's Power, and the Conditions of Obtaining It." *The Sword and the Trowel* (August 1889) 413–21.

Stott, John. *Between Two Worlds: The Art of Preaching in the Twentieth Century*. Grand Rapids: Eerdmans, 1982.

———. *Christian Counter-Culture: The Message of the Sermon on the Mount*. Downers Grove, IL: InterVarsity, 1978.

Strack, Herman L., and Paul Billerbeck. *Kommentar zum Neuen Testament aus Talmud und Midrasch*. 6 vols. Munich: C. H. Beck, 1924–61.

Tertullian. *Apology*. Translated by S. Thelwall. Ante-Nicene Fathers 3. Reprint, Grand Rapids: Eerdmans, 1978.

Thiselton, Anthony C. *A Concise Encyclopedia of the Philosophy of Religion*. Grand Rapids: Baker, 2002.

Trench, Richard Chenevix. *Notes on the Parables of Our Lord*. London: Macmillan, 1866.

Trueman, Carl. *Luther on the Christian Life*. Wheaton, IL: Crossway, 2015.

Turretin, Francis. *Institutes of Elenctic Theology*. Translated by G. M. Giger. 3 vols. Phillipsburg, NJ: Presbyterian and Reformed, 1992–97.

Waltke, Bruce. "Interaction with Peter Enns." *Westminster Journal of Theology* 71 (Spring 2009), 115–28.

Warfield, Benjamin B. "Are They Few That Be Saved?" In *Biblical and Theological Studies*, 334–50. Philadelphia: Presbyterian and Reformed, 1952.

———. "The Biblical Doctrine of the Trinity." In *Biblical and Theological Studies*, 22–59. Philadelphia: Presbyterian and Reformed, 1952.

———. "Predestination." In *Biblical and Theological Studies*, 270–333. Philadelphia: Presbyterian and Reformed, 1952.

———. *Selected Shorter Writings of Benjamin B. Warfield*. Edited by John E. Meeter. 2 vols. Nutley, NJ: Presbyterian and Reformed, 1970–73.

———. "The Spirit of God in the Old Testament." In *Biblical and Theological Studies*, 127–56. Philadelphia: Presbyterian and Reformed, 1952.

————. "The 'Two Natures' and Recent Christological Speculation." In *The Person and Work of Christ*, 211–62. Philadelphia: Presbyterian and Reformed, 1950.

Weil, Simone. *Waiting for God*, Translated by E. Craufurd. New York: Putnam, 1951.

Wells, David. *The Person of Christ: A Biblical and Historical Analysis of the Incarnation*. London: Marshall Morgan and Scott, 1984.

Wenham, Gordon J. *The Book of Leviticus*. New International Commentary on the Old Testament. Grand Rapids: Eerdmans, 1979.

Whyte, Alexander. *Biblical Characters: Our Lord's Characters*. 4th ed. Edinburgh: Oliphant, Anderson, and Ferrier, n.d.

————. *Bunyan Characters*. 3rd ser. Edinburgh: Oliphant, Anderson, and Ferrier, 1902.

————. *A Commentary on the Shorter Catechism*. Edinburgh: T. & T. Clark, 1910.

————. *Thomas Shepard: Pilgrim Father and Founder of Harvard*. Edinburgh: Oliphant, Anderson, and Ferrier, n.d.

Wilken, Robert. *The Spirit of Early Christian Thought*. New Haven, CT: Yale University Press, 2003.

Wills, Garry. *Font of Life: Ambrose, Augustine, and the Mystery of Baptism*. Oxford: Oxford University Press, 2012.

Wright, Christopher J. H. *Deuteronomy*. New International Biblical Commentary. Peabody, MA: Hendrickson, 1996.

Yarbrough, Robert W. *1–3 John*. Baker Exegetical Commentary on the New Testament. Grand Rapids, Baker, 2008.

Made in United States
Orlando, FL
06 May 2022